Before the Ghetto

BLACKS IN THE NEW WORLD
August Meier, Series Editor

Before the Ghetto

BLACK DETROIT IN THE
NINETEENTH CENTURY

David M. Katzman

University of Illinois Press
Urbana, Chicago, London

© 1973 by The Board of Trustees
of the University of Illinois

Manufactured in the United States of America

Library of Congress Catalog Card No. 72–76861

ISBN 0–252–00279–2

TO MY PARENTS
B.M.K. and H.M.K.

Contents

Tables

Figures

Maps

Preface

IN THE NINETEENTH CENTURY, before the rise of the racial ghetto, Detroit's black population lived and worked among whites; yet, at the same time, they were separate and apart. This study is a social and economic history of the experiences of Detroit's black people in the nineteenth century, their successes and their failures, their cohesiveness and their divisions, and the development and structure of their community and its institutions. This account focuses primarily on black-white relations, residential patterns, the black economy, and the community's class structure.

It is my hope that other historians will examine the framework of other Negro communities as well as the quality of black life. And it is my belief that similar studies of ethnic communities in nineteenth-century cities are needed if we are to understand the uniqueness or prevalence of black experiences. A variety of studies of small communities would enable us to make broader generalizations about American life in the nineteenth and twentieth centuries. This study is meant as a first step.

I am grateful to Robert Warner, director of the Michigan Historical Collections, and Ida Brown, Janice Earle, Charles Jones, and Ken Sheffel of his staff for responding so efficiently to my demands for books, newspapers, and manuscripts housed in the Collections. Geneva Keebler of the Michigan Historical Commission was generous in imparting her knowledge of the state archives, and James Babcock, former director of the Burton Historical Collection, helped me by-pass various bureaucratic entanglements. Mary E. Rollman of the General Library of the University of Michigan saved me time and travel by locating and expediting the delivery of a large number of newspapers, journals, and books, which I obtained through inter-library loan.

I am grateful to Stephen Serlin, who gave me his records of the 1880 manuscript census, and who broke new ground in studying the Negro in Detroit, and Arthur LaBrew, who shared with me his extensive knowledge of black Detroit. Also I am thankful to Larry Engelmann and Robert Rockaway for their noting of items relating to Negroes in Michigan which they uncovered in their own research.

I am grateful also to Reynolds Farley, Shaw Livermore, Jr., Bradford Perkins, Robert Warner, and Sam B. Warner, Jr., for reading sections of the manuscript and offering incisive comments.

I also wish to acknowledge the endurance of my wife, Sharyn, and my daughter, Andrea Rachel, and Sidney and Ruth Brooks, Steven and Eve Fisher, Marty and Helen Katz, Louise Katzman, and Michael and Karyl Katzman, all of whom have lived too close to this study, and who, for four years, have helped lighten the burden while sharing in little of the joy. My greatest debt is to Sidney Fine, who has served as teacher and critic at every stage of the work. This study represents but a small return on my obligation to him. Whatever errors remain are a testament to my own stubbornness.

Grants from the Horace Rackham School of Graduate Studies, University of Michigan, from the Graduate School of the University of Kansas, and from the Henry Rowe Schoolcraft Research Fund of the Historical Society of Michigan helped defray travel, microfilm, Xeroxing, and typing expenses.

D. M. K.
Lawrence, Kansas

Part I

Before the Fifteenth Amendment

CHAPTER I

Beginnings

I

ALL THE BLACKS in Detroit turned out early in the morning on April 7, 1870, to celebrate the ratification of the Fifteenth Amendment. Clothes dealer William Lambert, black and thin with a whisk of a beard, was chairman of the day. Visitors from the interior of the state and from across the Canadian border joined the good-humored Detroiters, and they all joked about the struggles of the previous decades. George DeBaptiste, one-time servant, barber, caterer, and "capitalist" and occasionally given to braggery, warmed the crowd with a sign attached to his building at Jefferson and Beaubien:

NOTICE TO STOCKHOLDERS,

OFFICE OF THE

UNDERGROUND RAILWAY

This office is permanently closed. Hereafter Stockholders will receive dividends according to their desserts. For further information apply to Senator Revels, Washington.[1]

A cannon fired at ten o'clock and the parade began. The chief marshal was followed by a white band and a contingent of metro-

[1] This paragraph and the following ones on the Fifteenth Amendment celebration are drawn from the *Detroit Tribune*, Apr. 8, 1870, p. 1, and the *New National Era and Citizen* (Washington), Apr. 28, 1870, p. 3.

3

politan policemen. One hundred and fifty Union League members carried a banner commemorating Crispus Attucks; fifty members of the Youths' Mental Improvement Club carried a portrait of William Lloyd Garrison. Colored Masons followed with a portrait of Charles Sumner; on the obverse side was the slogan: "Equal privileges to all." Spotted in the procession were pictures of Thaddeus Stevens and Frederick Douglass—"The Pioneer." Nearly one hundred black school boys marched with a banner representing a ballot box. Portraits of Presidents Grant and Lincoln, Senator Hiram Revels, and John Brown swept by.

Four hundred Negro citizens followed on foot. And then came the pride of the black citizenry: fifty members of the 102nd United States Colored Infantry. Fully armed and equipped, they were reunited under their old regiment flag. The citizens of Detroit, in carriages, brought up the rear. Overall there were 1,500 people in the procession.

After winding its way through the city's streets, the pageant arrived, on schedule, at the Opera House. One-third of the crowd jamming into the theater were white. Chairman Lambert called the assembled throng to order and, in his characteristically religious manner, gave thanks to God for such a blessing. Toussaint L'Ouverture Lambert, William Lambert's eldest son, read President Grant's proclamation and special message on the ratification of the Fifteenth Amendment.

After the warmly greeted appearance of Michigan Governor Henry Baldwin, and some humorous remarks by George DeBaptiste, James Madison Bell turned the occasion to more serious thoughts. Bell, the black "bard of the Maumee," and occasional plasterer and former abolitionist, delivered a long poem written specifically for the Detroit celebration.[2] White Republican leaders William A. Howard, William Jennison, and D. Bethune Duffield, long associated with abolitionism, addressed the assemblage. The recently appointed customs inspector and leading black politician, John D. Richards, gave the address of the day. Richards defended congressional reconstruction and affirmed his faith in the United States as a country shared by all of its component classes and parts. The afternoon meeting ad-

[2] A sketch of James Madison Bell by Bishop B. W. Arnett can be found in the *Poetical Works of James Madison Bell* (Lansing, 1901), pp. 3–14.

journed after the singing of William Lambert's "The Martyr's Triumph." The song celebrated the day—"Freedom reigns to-day!"—and the Republican party—"The ballot-box has come, now let us all prepare to vote/ With the party that made us free. . . . Hallelujah."

Detroit in 1870 differed greatly from the frontier city that William Lambert had first encountered in 1838. The good will and spirit of fellowship that reigned on April 7, 1870, was a product of the North's victory in the Civil War and of the Republicanism of one of the most solidly Republican states in the nation in the nineteenth century. In Michigan in 1838 slavery had been dead officially but one year, blacks were second-class citizens at best, and black codes, disfranchisement, and a race riot had marred the frontier democracy being created in the Old Northwest.

Slavery in Michigan had persisted into the nineteenth century, and it had left its mark on the laws of the territory and state. Slavery had been preserved in the Old Northwest as control of the colonial frontier land passed from the French to the English and then, in 1796, to the Americans. Although the Northwest Ordinance of 1787 had prohibited the extension of slavery into the triangle bordered by the Ohio and Mississippi Rivers, the ban was interpreted only as a bar against bringing additional slaves into the region; existing bondsmen had remained enslaved. This principle that property in Negro slaves remained inviolate had been established in the 1760s when the territory northwest of the Alleghenies was ceded by the French to the British. The 1760 Articles of Capitulation, providing for the surrender of Montreal to General Amherst; the Treaty of Paris of 1783, ending the American Revolution; and Jay's Treaty of 1794, ceding the Northwest posts, including Detroit, to the United States, all protected slavery. The result was that slavery east of the Detroit River (Canada) continued until the 1833 Imperial Act abolished slavery in the British Empire, and slavery west of the Detroit River (Michigan) continued until it was forbidden by the state's first constitution, which became the basic law of the state in 1837.[3]

Although slavery was abolished in 1837, racial distinctions remained in the law. During territorial days suffrage had been limited to free

[3] David M. Katzman, "Black Slavery in Michigan," *Midcontinent American Studies Journal*, XI (Fall, 1970), 56–66.

white male residents over twenty-one years of age, and the state constitution continued this restriction. Disfranchisement meant jury exclusion since jury duty was a privilege only of electors. Similarly, militia service was open only to whites under various territorial acts, affirmed by the 1835 constitution. Another statute forbade black and white to marry in the state. The most serious legal restriction was the 1827 law, "An Act to regulate Blacks and Mulattoes, and to punish the Kidnapping of Such Persons."[4]

Ostensibly an act to protect free Negroes, the 1827 Michigan black code was really an attempt to exclude blacks from the growing territory. Significantly, the act was passed as the Erie Canal was transporting waves of eastern migrants, including some blacks, into the sparsely settled state. Originally introduced to prevent runaway slaves from coming into the territory, the bill's author was motivated by fears that the black migrants were thieves. John McDonell of Wayne, sponsor of the measure during the 1826 territorial legislative session, argued that he intended to regulate, not exclude, both fugitive slaves and slave hunters. The line between exclusion and regulation drawn by the measure, passed on April 13, 1827, seemed narrow indeed. The statute required all Negroes in the territory to have a valid court-attested certificate of freedom and to register with the clerk of the county court. The stiffest provision of the act required Negroes emigrating into the territory to file a bond of $500 guaranteeing good behavior. In return the Negroes were given additional legal defenses against slave hunters; the act established an extradition process and

<hr />

4 Mary Joice Adams, *The History of Suffrage in Michigan*, Publications of the Michigan Political Science Association, III (March, 1898), 10–11; *Laws of the Territory of Michigan* (4 vols.; Lansing, 1874), III, 1242–1248, II, 48–53, 137, 255, III, 1217; *The Compiled Laws of the State of Michigan* (2 vols.; Detroit, 1857), II, 950, 953, 959; *Laws of the Territory of Michigan*, II, 634–636. Occasionally these restrictive laws were loosened, but only in the interests of the territorial government, not for the benefit of the blacks. During the Anglo-American conflict in the years preceding the War of 1812, for example, a company of Negroes under the command of Peter Denison and two other blacks was commissioned to help defend United States territory at Detroit. Governor William to James Madison, December 22, 1808, in Clarence Edwin Carter, *The Territorial Papers of the United States*, X, *The Territory of Michigan 1805–1820* (Washington, 1942), 252–253.

ensured legal protection against the kidnapping of accused fugitives.[5]

Since the statute does not appear to have been obeyed,[6] the legislature, in June 1828, passed an amendment to ensure enforcement. The new act not only empowered sheriffs and constables as well as overseers of the poor to evict noncomplying Negroes from the state but also required "that the presiding judge, when holding the circuit or county court in any of the counties in this Territory, shall constantly give this act in charge to the grand jury . . . who shall diligently inquire if the said act is duly executed, and to present any violation of the same that may come to their knowledge." Sheriff Thomas Sheldon of Wayne County, Detroit's county, responded by inserting in the territory's newspapers a "Notice to Blacks & Mulattoes," setting forth the requirements of the law. In spite of this, Negroes continued to enter the state without filing bonds.[7]

Blacks were coming into Detroit, but in small numbers. The 1820 census recorded 1,355 whites and 67 blacks in the small frontier town; in 1830 there were 2,096 whites and 126 blacks; and an 1834 census enumerated nearly 5,000 people in all, including 138 blacks. Detroit

[5] *Detroit Gazette*, Nov. 21, 1826, p. 2, May 1, 1827, p. 1; *Laws of the Territory of Michigan*, II, 634–636.

[6] The only known enforcement of the act was in Washtenaw County in October 1837. A black man in the town of Scio was banished when he was unable to post bond. Arthur Raymond Kooker, "The Antislavery Movement in Michigan, 1796–1840," Ph.D. dissertation, University of Michigan, 1941, p. 263.

[7] *Laws of the Territory of Michigan*, II, p. 676; *Detroit Gazette*, Sept. 11, 1828, p. 2. The sheriff's notices ran in the weekly *Gazette* until October 23. Twenty-two years later, with the state no less Negrophobic but moving toward a solidly abolitionist consensus, the United States Marshal's Office in Detroit released a public notice which sharply contrasted with Sheldon's 1828 advertisements:

> It has come to the knowledge of this office that individuals have been actively engaged in representing to the colored population of this city, that a *large number* of writs (one hundred or upwards,) for the arrest of "fugitive slaves," have been issued and are now in the hands of the officers of the law. It is done with a view to induce them to abandon their homes and property, at sacrificing prices, and for speculation.
>
> I take this method of pronouncing said representation without the slightest foundation.
>
> Henry R. Minzer, Deputy.

Detroit Free Press, Oct. 11, 1850, p. 2.

and Michigan did not experience a population explosion until state-
hood came in 1837, and Detroit did not become a magnet for blacks
until the southern black codes were tightened in the 1830s and 1840s.[8]

The first Negro settlements in Michigan were in rural areas; small
black communities could be found in the region surrounding Detroit
and in the county to the west, Washtenaw. Many of these Negro
settlers had followed the Erie Canal westward in the 1820s and 1830s.
A majority were Yankees and Yorkers and, like their fellow white
pioneers, they shunned the towns and mechanic trades. These settlements later formed a black hinterland for Detroit's Negro
community.

That Negro migrants avoided Detroit until the late 1830s was in
no small part a result of the 1833 Blackburn riot, an event that turned
black against white and brought a call for the enforcement of the
1827 and 1828 black laws. During June and July 1833, slave hunters
visited Detroit, and Negroes rioted and threatened to burn the city.
In the course of the conflict, federal troops were mustered in the city,
volunteer wardens guarded against fire, and a citizen's committee
issued an account of the riot—probably the first race-riot commission
report.[9]

Few blacks felt secure when slave hunters invaded the state. An
aborted attempt by slave hunters to capture runaways a few years
earlier had left bitter feelings among the Negroes in Detroit. As a

[8] In 1810 there were 96 nonwhites, including Indians and 17 slaves. *Third
Census 1810*, p. 88; *Fourth Census 1820*, p. 41; *Fifth Census 1830*, p. 153; for 1834,
Clarence M. Burton, *History of Detroit 1780 to 1850: Financial and Commercial*
(Detroit, 1917), p. 95.

[9] The story of the 1833 Blackburn riot is pieced together from the following:
Detroit Courier, June 19, 26, July 24, 31, 1833; M. Chapin to Lewis Cass, July 25,
1833; Lewis Cass to M. Chapin, July 26, 1833, Marshall Chapin Papers, Burton
Historical Collection, Detroit Public Library; Eliza B. Mason to Catharine A.
Mason, June 22, 1833, Eliza B. Mason to Catharine A. Mason, July 20, 1833, Eliza
B. Mason to Catharine A. Mason, July 27, 1833, John Mason Papers, Burton
Historical Collection; and Charles M. Bull, Jr., July 23, 1833, in Sidney Glazer
(ed.), "In Old Detroit, 1831–1836," *Michigan History Magazine*, XXVI (Spring,
1942), 206–207; *Journal of the Proceedings of the Common Council of the City
of Detroit, 1824–1843* (n.p., n.d.), pp. 243–247. The report of the committee of
ten citizens who investigated the riot can be found in the *Detroit Courier*, July
24, 1833.

precaution, many freeborn Negroes carried certificates attesting to their freedom.[10] When a group of slave hunters from Kentucky came to Michigan in June 1833, the black community became alarmed. The slavers were looking for Thornton and Ruth Blackburn, fugitives from Kentucky, who had been in Detroit since July 1831, and were well known in the community. The *Detroit Courier*, a reform weekly favoring gradual emancipation, praised Thornton Blackburn as "a respectable, honest and industrious man and considerably superior to the common class of Negroes." From the first rumors of the presence of slave hunters in the city, Detroit blacks prepared to protect the Blackburns.[11]

Tension heightened when the Blackburns were delivered to the city jail. At their hearing on June 15 they offered no evidence in defense of their freedom, and the court upheld the Kentuckians' claim to the two fugitives under the provisions of the 1793 fugitive slave act. The large number of blacks who attended the hearing threatened, however, to prevent the white man's justice from being carried out. Word quickly spread through the Negro community that the Blackburns had been denied a fair hearing. Alarmed by the rumor, Sheriff John M. Wilson retained custody of the Blackburns rather than turning them over to the Kentuckians. He had hoped that the situation would ease, but his troubles had only begun. The next day, Sunday, June 16, the city's blacks assembled on the commons near the jail which held the Blackburns. The Negroes armed themselves with clubs, "exhibiting a determination to attempt a rescue, and continued there until the departure of the steamboat in the evening, when they were dismissed for the night by their leader."[12] The newspapers later reported the presence of Negroes from Malden and other Canadian towns, along with blacks from areas near Detroit.

Sometime that day, unknown to her jailors, Mrs. Blackburn escaped.

[10] A certificate of freedom, registered with the county clerk, can be found in the John J. Bagley Papers, Box II, Michigan Historical Collections, University of Michigan. Larry Engelmann brought this document to my attention.

[11] *Detroit Courier*, June 19, 1833, p. 2; Carter, *The Territorial Papers of the United States, XI, The Territory of Michigan 1820–1829* (Washington, 1943), 1123–1242.

[12] Report, *Detroit Courier*, July 24, 1833, p. 3.

During the afternoon a number of visitors had been permitted to spend time with the Blackburns. Mrs. George French remained after dark and exchanged clothes with Ruth Blackburn, and the ruse proved successful when the "visitor" left.[13] Mrs. Blackburn stole across the river that night and the stratagem was revealed the following morning, to the frustration of the slave hunters.

Monday was the day of confrontation. All day long blacks, armed with clubs, stones, and pistols, loitered around the jail and near the wharf where the steamboat *Ohio* was docked. The Negroes made no attempt to conceal their plans, but most citizens dismissed their behavior as "impulse or braggadocio threat."[14] When a cart appeared at the jail to carry the prisoner to the wharf, a scuffle ensued, and the insurgent blacks gained possession of the horse and cart. The sheriff went to the front steps to disperse the crowd, and bedlam resulted. The report later charged that Blackburn had drawn a pistol, but it seems improbable that the prisoner would have had such a weapon. In any event, the crowd of blacks rushed the sheriff, and Blackburn drove off to freedom in the cart that had been hired to send him back to slavery. Stoned and clubbed by the balance of the group, the sheriff remained in critical condition for several days, his skull fractured and teeth knocked out, and he would die within a year from his injuries. Meanwhile, Thornton Blackburn and his rescuers appeared to have escaped by way of the pike, but a posse overtook them some miles in the woods. The pursuers, however, found the cart empty; Blackburn had joined his wife in Canada.

That night a guard patrolled the river to thwart any Negroes attempting to cross. The city authorities arrested nearly thirty blacks, some involved in the conspiracy, some not. Canadian officials also arrested blacks across the river. Although the Blackburns had been freed, they were quickly arrested and held by the Canadian authorities. The Blackburns were later freed again, and remained in Canada. In 1852 Thornton Blackburn appeared as a vice president of the Canadian Mill & Mercantile Company, Buxton, Canada West, and

[13] Mrs. French was released after a writ of habeas corpus was obtained. She then fled to Canada. Clipping [*Detroit Post*, February, 1870], in Friend Palmer's Scrapbook, III, 120, Burton Historical Collection.

[14] *Detroit Courier*, June 19, 1833, p. 2.

an 1870 newspaper article reported that in 1867 Blackburn was a wealthy citizen of Toronto.[15]

Overall the riot served to intensify the fear of and hostility toward blacks in general. In June 1833, the citizens of the city, at a public meeting, resolved that the territorial black codes be enforced, and Mayor Marshall Chapin thereafter issued a proclamation ordering "all Negroes out of town who could not give a certificate of freedom and bond of good conduct,"[16] although there is no evidence that the Negroes complied. The citizens also appointed a committee of prominent whites to investigate the riot, and to make recommendations for ensuring tranquility and the rule of law. The committee of ten blamed the affair on the local black community:

> Neither their habits, nor their morals, with a few exceptions, make them a safe or desirable addition to our population. Indeed—but a small number of the colored people seen in our street, can be considered as residents of the city. The greater portion are vagrant and transient persons, who are continually shifting their quarters from one side of the river to the other, as they find employment, or it is to be feared, for the greater convenience of carrying on their depredations against the property of our citizens.

The committee gave warning to fugitive slaves: "Composed as the Negroes who resort to this frontier, for the most part are of the most worthless of the slave population; we can have no adequate motive to encourage their emigration hither." The report called for the enforcement of the 1827 black code, a nine o'clock curfew on Negroes, and a prohibition on blacks' landing boats on the Detroit shore.[17]

The threat of black retaliation further heightened white fears. According to the riot committee report, the blacks had threatened to burn down the city. On July 11 the jail was set afire but damage was slight, and four days later a stable attached to the jail burned to the ground. Memories of the 1805 Detroit fire that had completely leveled the frontier town intensified the whites' anxieties, and Mayor

[15] *Voice of the Fugitive*, May 6, 1852, p. 4; clipping [*Detroit Post*, February, 1870], in Friend Palmer's Scrapbook, III, 119.

[16] Eliza B. Mason to Catharine A. Mason, July 27, 1833.

[17] Report, *Detroit Courier*, July 24, 1833, p. 3.

Chapin requested that United States troops be dispatched to the city to restore tranquility. The company of soldiers remained in Detroit two weeks, but the restoration of order left the whites' attitudes unchanged; Eliza Mason, a Detroit housewife, confessed in a letter: "I never did like Negroes and this has given me a more horrible idea of them—the children on going from school are as much afraid of them as we used to be of Indians." [18]

While the wake of the riot left blacks generally unwelcome in Detroit, it did not deter whites from coming to the city on the straits. Capital of the new state of Michigan, which was admitted to the Union in 1837, Detroit commercially served a large area whose hinterland stretched northward to Mackinac, westward to Lake Michigan, southward to Toledo, and eastward into the Canadian countryside. The docks were the lifeblood of the new expanding agricultural economy. Dwellings clustered around Jefferson Avenue, paralleling the river, and up Woodward Avenue, the major thoroughfare. By 1838 there were two daily newspapers and four hotels in the city; the first common school was less than one year old; and the commercial district was rapidly growing. The streets were primitive but a fairly extensive sewage system made them passable. With the statehouse in the city, as well as eight churches, four banks, a United States land office, and three city markets, Detroit was an urban community in 1838.[19]

The black community in Detroit in 1838 was small. The city directory of the preceding year, the first one in Detroit, had listed only eleven blacks. They were all of the "better sort," for the greater number of Negro day laborers, dockworkers, and boatmen were not included in the directory. Five were listed as hairdressers or barbers, three as boatmen, and the remaining three as a teamster, a cook, and a laborer. Some of the barbers owned their own shops and they lived near the river, at the foot and to the east of Woodward Avenue. In the next hundred years the black community would expand slightly to the east and considerably to the north—but never to the west.

[18] Eliza B. Mason to Catharine A. Mason, July 27, 1833.
[19] Almon Ernest Parkins, *The Historical Geography of Detroit* (Lansing, 1918), pp. 182–183.

Woodward Avenue remained almost as impenetrable a barrier as the river to the south.[20]

The first relatively large black migration into Michigan began about 1840. From 193 Negroes in Detroit and 707 Negroes in Michigan in 1840, the number grew to 587 in Detroit and 2,583 in Michigan in 1850. Border and southern state blacks looked to the old North-west as a haven from slavery and Negrophobia, and a group of free blacks and ex-slaves formed a rural colony in Cass County, Michigan, in the southwestern sector of the state. The urban Negroes of Detroit, however, comprised the single largest group of blacks, nearly one-quarter of the state's black population in 1850. The bulk of Detroit's black families were descended from free Negro migrants from the urban Virginia centers of Richmond, Fredericksburg, and Petersburg. Mechanics and tradesmen, they had migrated to Michigan in the late 1830s and 1840s in order to escape the tightening enforce-ment of the black codes in Virginia.[21]

Detroit's blacks began to organize as a community in the 1830s and 1840s. Though never a completely homogeneous group, Detroit's Negroes were more united at this time than they would be again in the nineteenth century. Social and economic differentiation was at a minimum, and the associational spirit that swept America at the time, combined with the growing militancy of the blacks in their struggle for human rights, served to tie the community together. Men such as William Lambert from New Jersey, clothier Robert Banks from the West Indies via New York, barber shop owner Obadiah C. Wood from New York, Rev. William C. Monroe from Indiana, carpenter Madison J. Lightfoot from Virginia, the renowned ex-slave, abolitionist and editor Henry Bibb from Kentucky, and other recent arrivals gave leadership to the community. Resentful of second-class citizenship, they worked unceasingly to remove the social and political stigmas placed upon Michigan's blacks.

Those who migrated to Detroit came from varied backgrounds

[20] *Directory of the City of Detroit 1837* (Detroit, 1837).

[21] W. B. Hartgrove, "The Story of Maria Louise Moore and Fannie M. Rich-ards," *Journal of Negro History*, I (January, 1916), 23–33; enumerated schedules, U.S. Census, 1850.

and followed diverse paths. George DeBaptiste, for instance, one of the wealthiest and most active race leaders in antebellum Detroit, had been born of free parents in 1814 in Fredericksburg, Virginia, where he had learned barbering but had worked as a personal servant. In 1838 he and his bride migrated to Madison, Indiana. There, because of DeBaptiste's active aid to fugitive slaves, a justice of the peace ordered DeBaptiste to comply with the 1831 Indiana black code requiring the payment of a bond. DeBaptiste chose to fight rather than comply, and Stephen C. Stevens, a former justice of the state supreme court, took the case on appeal. Although they lost their contention that the act was unconstitutional, the Indiana Supreme Court did rule that DeBaptiste's expulsion was defective, and that he could remain in the state. He then became a servant to William Henry Harrison, and when the general was inaugurated president, DeBaptiste became a White House steward. After the president's death, DeBaptiste returned to Madison where he opened a barber shop. By 1846 DeBaptiste found the atmosphere in Indiana so hostile that he moved to Detroit, bringing with him experience both in business and black affairs.[22]

In Detroit, DeBaptiste became an important race figure. He purchased an interest in Thomas Johnson's barber shop, and worked as chief clerk and salesman for Robert Banks's clothing store on Jefferson Avenue. At the same time he became an active leader of the black community and in 1848 he was elected, along with Banks, Henry Bibb, Johnson, William Lambert, and George Tucker, as a delegate to the Cleveland National Convention of Colored Citizens. After

---

[22] *Detroit Advertiser & Tribune*, Feb. 23, 1875, p. 4; Emma Lou Thornbrough, *The Negro in Indiana: A Study of a Minority* [Indianapolis, 1957], pp. 60–61. In 1870, in a series of articles celebrating the enfranchisement of blacks, the *Detroit Post* printed DeBaptiste's certificate of freedom:

City of Richmond to wit:

Registered in the office of Hustings for the said city, the twenty second day of January, 1835, No. 606, George Baptiste, a mulatto boy, about five feet seven and a half inches high, and about twenty years old, who was born free, as appears by the oath of Jacob Golz. There is a dark spot on the white of the left eye, on the left side of the pupil; and no other mark or scar apparent on his head, face or hands.

Clipping, *Detroit Post*, May 15, 1870, supplement, in Friend Palmer's Scrapbook, III, 111.

Banks's shop burned down in 1850, DeBaptiste bought out William Lee's Jefferson Avenue bakery and ran it for several years. Then he sold the bakery and purchased the *T. Whitney*, a steamship running between Detroit and Sandusky, Ohio. Since a black man could not hold a license to run a steamboat, DeBaptiste employed a white captain. After a few seasons he sold the boat and began what was to become a successful catering business.[23]

In the 1850s DeBaptiste was among the leaders in aiding fugitive slaves, and during the Civil War he was instrumental in raising the Michigan colored regiment. With John D. Richards, he toured the state recruiting blacks, and he and Richards served as sutlers of the regiment, spending six months' duty in South Carolina. On his return he reentered the catering business, with headquarters at Jefferson and Beaubien, and he catered at important public dinners. In 1867 his realty holdings in Detroit were valued at $10,000. He also continued his race activities, and in 1868 DeBaptiste served as a temporary agent for the Freedmen's Aid Commission, collecting supplies for freedmen's schools in Louisiana. In 1870 he served on the first Detroit jury composed of colored citizens. Two years later he expanded his business by purchasing a four-story building at 7 Fort Street. The restaurant and ice cream parlors there were outfitted with marble tables, chandeliers, and carpeting, but the new outlet failed to turn a profit. This business failure, however, did not diminish his generosity; in 1873, for instance, he treated the boys of St. Anthony's Orphan Asylum to ice cream and sweets at his Fort Street parlors. In 1874 he leased a fine residence in Hamtramck to add to his restaurant on Michigan Grand Avenue near the city market, and he turned the country place into a restaurant with dancing floors, and set up tents on the grounds for picnics. Failing health forced him to close the place, and a few months later the former abolitionist died of cancer.[24]

In contrast to George DeBaptiste, Henry Bibb was a fugitive slave who spent only eight years in Detroit. Born a slave in Kentucky in

[23] *Detroit Advertiser & Tribune*, Feb. 23, 1875, p. 4; *Daily Free Press*, Aug. 25, 1848, p. 2; *Detroit Daily Advertiser*, May 19, 1849, p. 2.

[24] *Detroit Advertiser & Tribune*, Feb. 23, 1875, p. 4; Apr. 16, 1867, p. 3; May 14, 1868, p. 3; Apr. 6, 1870, p. 1; July 1, 1872, p. 4; Aug. 16, 1873, p. 4; Sept. 11, 1873, p. 4; June 29, 1874, p. 4.

1815, Bibb first escaped in 1837 but was reenslaved when he returned to free his wife. Later he made his way free again, and in January 1842 he came to Detroit. His total formal education consisted of two weeks under the tutelage of William Monroe, but he wrote an auto-biographical antislavery tract, *Narrative of the Life and Adventures of Henry Bibb, an American Slave*, and published an emigrationist organ in Canada, the *Voice of the Fugitive*. Bibb's primary work was abolitionism and race interests, and employment took a secondary place; "my occupation varied according to circumstances...," he confessed in 1850. He was a frequent antislavery speaker in Michigan, and in 1844 he campaigned in the state for the Liberty party. Active in many of the reforms of the day, he served as an agent for Raisin Institute, Laura Haviland's southeastern Michigan manual labor school for colored youth. Bibb was influential in unifying black abolitionist efforts in Michigan, and was sufficiently successful to be a thorn in the side of the Democrats; in 1850 the *Detroit Free Press* charged that the whigs "have employed a hypocrite by the name of Bibb, a colored man and a rascal... a scamp, unworthy of belief." The 1850 fugitive slave act forced Bibb to emigrate and he moved across the Detroit River to Windsor. Since Bibb's major contribution had been made as a public speaker, his inability to visit Detroit and Michigan served to cut him off from the black community there. Radicalized by his forced migration to Canada in 1850, Bibb became a strong voice for emigration and colonization, and he tried, with only limited success, to interest the Detroit community in these efforts in the early 1850s.[25]

Not all black men were either migrants or deeply involved in community interests. Peter Copper, born in Detroit in 1795 of a black father and an Indian mother, was probably the most successful Detroit-born black in the pre–Civil War period, yet there is no record of his participation in any race issues. An orphan, he married another orphan, Angelique Smith, a servant in a Detroit French family. His

[25] Fred Landon, "Henry Bibb, the Colonizer," *Journal of Negro History*, V (October, 1920), 437–447; Henry Bibb, *Narrative of the Life and Adventures of Henry Bibb, an American Slave* (New York, 1850), pp. 174, 176, 178, 180; *Signal of Liberty*, May 20, 1844, p. 15; *Detroit Daily Advertiser*, Jan. 30, 1845, p. 2; *Detroit Free Press*, Oct. 18, 1850, p. 2. For Bibb's later career in Canada see William and Jane Pease, *Black Utopia: Negro Communal Experiments in America* (Madison, Wis., 1963).

first permanent job was as a porter in a Detroit hotel, and in the 1830s he worked as a teamster. Intelligent but uneducated, a strongly built dark-skinned black man, Copper was well known for his humor and had a reputation as "an honest man." In 1851, six years after a syndicate of blacks brought the first two-wheeled cabs into Detroit, Copper bought a cab in Windsor and brought it to Detroit. In 1860 he bought a hack, and was a familiar sight at the train station and docks. Later he added another hack and his business prospered, but his "liberal disposition" kept him poor.[26]

Of those blacks who came to Detroit, many were neither businessmen nor spirited reformers nor race leaders. An unknown number were transients, drifting here and there in search of freedom or work. Isaac Riley, a fugitive from Missouri who at first lived near Windsor, bore witness to the motivations of those who stayed but briefly: "I crossed over and got work and better pay in Michigan," he recalled. "They would have liked to have me remain...but I did not feel free in Michigan, and did not remain." Others were less fortunate than Riley in obtaining respectable work, and a number of blacks formed a criminal element. Most of the whites in the community would have argued that the criminal element comprised the largest sector of the black community; the 1833 riot report had implied as much, and the *Detroit Free Press*, Democratic and Negrophobic, made a point of reporting black crime. Negroes gravitated toward occupations open to them, and the wall of prejudice and discrimination took its toll. From the earliest days in Detroit some blacks engaged in gambling and other illegal and "immoral" activities, possibly as a reaction to their exclusion "from the usual privileges of society." The underworld was integrated, and if churchgoers and reformers looked askance at the illegal activities, it is apparent that most men welcomed the illicit traffic in an age when public morality seemed high and leisure time and recreational space were scarce. General public indifference and possibly secret delight can be seen in the city's attempt to do battle with the ten-year-old firm, Slaughter, Peg Welch & Company.[27]

[26] Clipping, in Friend Palmer's Scrapbook, III, 168.

[27] Riley quoted in Benjamin Drew, *The Refugee or the Narratives of Fugitive Slaves in Canada* (Boston, 1856), p. 298; *Detroit Gazette*, Dec. 17, 1819, p. 2, Jan. 7, 1820, p. 2.

Slaughter, Peg Welch & Company operated a house of ill fame. James Slaughter, black, and Elizabeth Welch, white, were partners. Their dwelling, at the corner of Randolph Street and Michigan Avenue, delighted some but annoyed others. Despite an 1836 city ordinance prohibiting such public nuisances, the house remained in business. At a city council meeting in October 1841, Alderman Bagg moved that the house be razed, and when his motion failed, he moved that the following sign be erected, with appropriate dues paid to the community's sensitivity to color:

> House of Ill-Fame; for the Commission of Fornication and Adultery by Permission of the Common Council; Price According to Age, Sex, Color and Standing in Society.

The motion to erect a sign failed, as did one to buy out Slaughter, Peg Welch & Company. Finally, a month later, a resolution passed ordering the city marshal to tear down the house. The council's orders were carried out, only to embroil the city in the courts. The outcome was disastrous for the reformers; both Elizabeth Welch and James Slaughter won their cases.[28]

Detroit's black criminal element were few in number, however, and the pre–Civil War black community, contrary to the contention of Negrophobes, was characterized by the active and energetic building of community institutions. The first permanent Negro institutions in Detroit, and the cornerstone of nearly all black activities, were the churches. By 1846 the small Detroit black community had three churches, the Second Baptist Church, with roots back to 1836; the Bethel African Methodist Episcopal Church, organized in 1839; and St. Matthew's Church, a Protestant Episcopal mission founded in 1846. While each of the churches served the community at large and supported functions that tended to unite the entire population, they also served their own congregations in ways that tended to divide the community.

The basements of the black churches were used as colored public schools, their chapels as political halls. Female benevolent societies

[28] *Journal of the Proceedings of the Common Council of the City of Detroit 1824–1843*, pp. 722–726, 728, 730, 732, 736, 753; *Slaughter* v. *the People*, 2 Douglass 334 (1842); *Welch* v. *Stowell*, 2 Douglass 322 (1846).

involved the women, while Sunday schools gathered in the children. With recreational space in the home at a minimum, social activity centered either around the saloon or the church, and nearly all the black families in the city, out of necessity, chose the church. Generally the ministers of the churches provided the community with leadership, and their names appeared repetitiously at every meeting of black associations. The ministers served the interests of black unity by initiating protest movements against legal and social injustices, by sponsoring benevolent and charitable organizations to aid the infirm and the unemployed, and by preaching the fellowship of black brotherhood. But at the same time, the churches served as the loci of competing groups of blacks and as the basis for increasing differentiation in the community.

The first black church in Detroit, the Second Baptist, arose because the white First Baptist Church had failed to adequately and fairly serve the needs and interests of its black brethren. In 1832, less than five years after its organization, the First Baptist Church accepted its first black member, William Butler. Although the "hand of fellowship" toward Butler was withdrawn within two years because of his failure to attend services, his intemperance, and his indifference to the church's appeals, other blacks entered the congregation, and by 1836 there were at least eleven blacks among the one hundred or so members. On April 7, 1837, George French reported to the First Baptist that black Baptists "wished to hold meetings on Sunday and Thursday evenings." The church responded by requesting "the coloured brethren to report to the Church in writing at the next meeting whether they wish to continue their standing with the Church, and attend the meetings of the Church—or whether they wish to separate from Church." Two months later the blacks requested that the church end its segregated gallery, permitting blacks "to take their seats below with the whites."[29]

The major issue seemed to be the question of segregation; as long as blacks were confined to the gallery they felt excluded from the

[29] See "Records of the Clerk, 1827–1838" of the First Baptist Church in the Burton Historical Collection, Detroit Public Library. I am grateful to Arthur R. LaBrew for loaning me his notes on "Records of the Clerk," and his unpublished manuscript, "Early History of the Second Baptist Church" (1969).

fellowship of the church. The black demands were strengthened by the construction and use, the previous year, of the church-school on Fort Street. The white members of the First Baptist attempted to prevent a white-black split by voting "to permit the Brethren to hold meetings as they wish," while requesting "coloured people one and all to remain in the Gallery as before." The compromise was unacceptable, and three colored congregants—Madison J. Lightfoot, Cornelius Mitchell, and William Scott—withdrew from the church in July 1837. In October the church voted "to notify the col^d brethren and Sisters that it is expected they will sit below when we hold conference meetings and Ch[urch] meetings." The issue appeared repeatedly in the pages of the clerk's journal, and it is apparent that the offer came too late; within one year all of the remaining blacks would leave the church to join the existing religious society then meeting in the Fort Street building, which would become a Baptist affiliate after the influx of new members. The First Baptist, in a final gesture of concern for the black brethren, voted to recognize the new Baptist church by dismissing the Negroes "with the privilege of uniting with a sister Ch[urch] of the same faith or uniting in the constitution of a Ch[urch] of the same faith." The Second Baptist Church, also known as the Colored American Baptist Church, flourished, remaining on Fort Street until 1857 when a new building on Croghan Street replaced the old one destroyed by fire three years earlier. In 1840 Rev. William Monroe became the first regular pastor of the church.[30]

The Bethel Church, the second black church in the city, became an AME church in 1841. It had originally been founded in 1839 as the Colored Methodist Society. In July 1839 the society successfully petitioned the common council of the city for the use of the old Military Hall, since the city, a number of times, had donated unused public halls to churches. The hall was moved first to Congress Street near Woodward, then to Croghan and Hastings, and finally to East Fort Street in 1841. The second church hall, on East Lafayette Street, was dedicated in 1847. In the early 1840s the AME church was

[30] First Baptist Church, "Records of the Clerk, 1827–1838," Burton Historical Collection; *Detroit Advertiser & Tribune*, Apr. 18, 1867, p. 4, Apr. 19, 1867, p. 3; *Michigan Christian Herald*, Nov. 16, 1846, p. 2.

the most influential black church in the city. Travelers to Detroit, like Martin R. Delany, noticed that the "best" black citizens in the city had been Methodists in the early 1840s, as they were in other midwestern cities. The Bethel AME was the largest black church in Detroit throughout the century.[31]

When St. Matthew's Protestant Episcopal Mission was organized in 1846 it replaced the AME church as the most influential black church in the city. It is likely that Rev. William Monroe's conversion to Episcopalianism and his ordination as a priest in 1846, and William Lambert's service as St. Matthew's warden, had a great effect on the black community's leaders, all of whom had been at one time or another associated with Monroe and Lambert in the community's social and political institutions. Another factor that weighed heavily with the black leadership was the personality of Pastor Gardiner, the AME minister in the mid-forties. Gardiner was attacked as an "illiberal person, speaking against every manner of moral improvement," and was accused of being dictatorial. In the light of these factors and the generally high prestige of black Episcopalian churches in Philadelphia and New York, the newly organized mission found little difficulty in joining together nearly all of the small community's economic, political, and social leaders.[32]

St. Matthew's acquired its own building in 1847, and built a small chapel on the southeast corner of St. Antoine and Congress in 1851. Many of the parishioners left the city during the 1850s, fearful of the effects of the Fugitive Slave Law of 1850. After William Monroe emigrated to Liberia in 1859 the rectors left no mark on the community, and the Civil War further depleted the congregation. In 1864 the mission suspended activities, selling the building to the Hebrew congregation Shaarey Zadek, and the adult members joined other Episcopalian churches, while the children continued as a Sunday school at Christ Protestant Episcopal Church.[33]

---

[31] Michigan Historical Records Survey, *Inventory of the Church Archives: African Methodist Episcopal Church, Michigan Conference* (Detroit, 1940), p. 8; *Journal of the Proceedings of the Common Council of the City of Detroit 1824–1843*, pp. 565, 501–502, 513; *Detroit Daily Advertiser*, Sept. 18, 1847, p. 2; *North Star*, Aug. 4, 1848, p. 2.

[32] *North Star*, Aug. 4, 1848, pp. 2–3.

[33] Typewritten history of St. Matthew's, Historical Records Survey; "Chro-

When St. Matthew's was reestablished in the 1880s it would be one of the important links in the chain of upper-class black life, but even before the Civil War, when residential differentiation by class was not yet apparent, when classes were not yet bound together by family ties, and when the accumulation of real estate and wealth in the black community was just beginning, religious affiliation was already an indicator of political, social, and economic standing in the community.

The black institutions generated by the churches and those using the church halls as meeting places were many and varied. The churches and their ministers were in the forefront of the reform movements that had swept the United States in the decades before the Civil War, and the church-oriented societies reflected this situation. When the Colored Vigilant Committee of Detroit inventoried the Negro community in 1843 it found a young men's society, a debating club, a reading room, a library, and a temperance society, all of them meeting in the churches. Both of the churches as of that date also had a Sunday school and a female benevolent association. Overall, there were about twenty known benevolent and improvement societies in black Detroit of the 1840s—about one for every ten black adults. Additional cultural and benevolent societies were organized in the 1850s, including the Afric-American Philharmonic Association and its juvenile affiliate.[34]

The city's black churches worked as closely with the colored schools as they did with the other black institutions, and they competed for control of the schools just as they competed for control of the social and political institutions. The development of public education for Detroit's black children lagged behind that of white children, and black parents had to bear the double burden of paying the general school tax while supporting separate private schools. When the city opened its school rooms to black children in the 1840s,

---

nology and Outlines of the Episcopal Church," Papers of the Protestant Episcopal Church of Michigan, Michigan Historical Collections, University of Michigan; *Joint Celebration of the 75th Anniversary of St. Matthew's Church* ... [Detroit, 1924], p. 3.

[34] *Detroit Democratic Free Press*, Jan. 25, 1843, p. 2; Michigan, Senate, *Documents*, No. 15 (1845), p. 8; Earl E. Nelson, "Sketches of Our Music History," *Michigan Challenge*, VIII (June, 1968), p. 34.

it provided inferior segregated facilities. Negroes had received brief educational attention from the Sunday School Association of Detroit in 1819 and 1820, but not until 1836, long after schools for white children had been established, was any effort made to provide for the systematic education of black children. In that year the Fort Street school hall and church was built under the auspices of white church leaders and some blacks; the colored schools would remain united with the churches until 1855.[35]

Denied access to the tax-supported white schools, Detroit's blacks had to assume, involuntarily, the double cost of paying school taxes and funding their own private colored school. The first black school met in the Fort Street East building, with James Field, a black, as the teacher. After 1838, two white men succeeded Field until 1841, when the school was placed in Rev. William Monroe's hands. Financing the school must have been a great burden for the small black community as the depression of 1837 led at least some white benefactors to respond to "the pressure of the times" by withdrawing their financial aid. In 1839 the legislature chartered St. Philip's College as a colored school, but it failed to open. Instead, District School Eight was established as a colored school under the general organization of public schools in the state; but the continuing depression forced fiscal retrenchment, and the legislature repealed the school act. When in 1842 the state reestablished free public schools and authorized a separate tax-supported colored school for Detroit, the newly formed board of education assumed control of the existing school, and fired Monroe. The board organized its own colored school, replacing Monroe with a white teacher. Black parents, led by William Lambert and M. J. Lightfoot, met to organize a day school. Praising Monroe for improving their "children and youth in morals and intellect," they resolved that "we have the utmost confidence in his ability and integrity and are anxious to secure his services for another year," and fifteen persons pledged financial support. The new school taught by Monroe took over the old school's rooms in the Second Baptist Church while the public school occupied the basement of the AME

[35] *Detroit Gazette*, Jan. 7, 1820, p. 2; *Detroit Advertiser & Tribune*, Apr. 19, 1867, p. 3.

Church. The fate of the private school at the Second Baptist is unclear, but Monroe left the school when he joined St. Matthew's in 1846. It lasted only one more year, under a white man. When the AME no longer offered its hall free of charge in 1851, the public school was shifted to St. Matthew's, and once again Monroe became the teacher. In 1855 the school moved to the Fourth Ward School building which had been vacated by a white school. Illness forced Monroe to abandon teaching in 1856, and incompetent white teachers and inadequate shelter almost ended the school. Finally, in 1860, the classes moved back to Fort Street, near St. Antoine, and grew strong again under the leadership of an experienced white principal, John Whitbeck.[36]

Although in 1852 the Detroit Board of Education declared that "it has been our policy to allow to the colored population equal advantages in this respect with the whites," blacks contended that colored schools maintained by the board were inferior to white schools and of poor quality. The State Colored Convention of 1843 had charged that Negroes were allowed "but a scanty and inadequate participation in the privileges of education," and blacks would agitate and litigate against segregated schools in Detroit for over a quarter of a

[36] Benjamin Willoughby school tax receipt, August 10, 1839, Lambert Papers, in file "Negro," Historical Records Survey of Michigan, Michigan Historical Collections (hereafter cited as NHRSM); *Detroit Advertiser & Tribune*, Apr. 19, 1867, p. 3; Jane Stewart to Mrs. Marshall Chapin, August 3, 1837, Marshall Chapin Papers, Burton Historical Collection; Arthur B. Moehlman, *Public Education in Detroit* (Bloomington, Ill., 1925), p. 68; Caroline W. Thrun, "School Segregation in Michigan," *Michigan History*, XXXVIII (March, 1954), 6, 8; *Introductory Report of the Board of Education of the City of Detroit* (Detroit, 1842); *Detroit Daily Advertiser*, July 13, 1842, p. 2, Dec. 19, 1842, p. 2; "Annual Report of the Board of Education of Detroit," in *Annual Report of the Superintendent of Public Instruction 1852* (Lansing, 1853), p. 152; "Annual Report of the Board of Education, 1857," clipping, *Detroit Daily Advertiser*, Jan. 26, 1857, in Burton Historical Collection. The history of Detroit colored schools which appeared April 19, 1867, in the *Detroit Advertiser & Tribune* must be used cautiously. It inaccurately represents and confuses the history of the two colored schools from 1842 to 1846. It alleged that the board of education continued Monroe as teacher after 1842, and that the public school remained in the Baptist church. It also offers no explanation for the founding of the second school which disappeared after 1847. Contemporary records—the board of education minutes in the July *Detroit Daily Advertiser*, supra, and the 1852 "Annual Report," supra—clearly contradict these assertions.

century. Finally, after the Civil War, the school board would recognize the validity of their complaints; in 1869, the board of education would admit that the black schools were "poorly calculated for school purposes."[37]

Detroit's acknowledged residential clustering of blacks enabled the board of education to hope to satisfy the educational needs of black children with only one school. If black families had been scattered throughout the city, no one school could have been centrally convenient, nor, alternatively, would a black school in each ward have been economically feasible. Throughout the nineteenth century nearly all of Detroit's black families clustered within the city's near east side amid an overwhelmingly white population. Thus segregation in Detroit, as in other Michigan cities, restricted blacks to a small area of the city which was nonetheless racially mixed. Housing discrimination, job discrimination, and the desire of blacks to be near their friends and black institutions in an ethnically organized city were important factors in determining where Negroes lived.

From the earliest days blacks had clustered in one area of the city, generally marked by its poor housing. As population expanded northward from Jefferson Avenue, the first commercial street in the city, and outward from Woodward Avenue, Detroit's black population moved northward within a relatively narrow zone. Thus in the 1830s and 1840s Detroit's black population resided primarily in the third and fourth wards. Two barbers and hairdressers lived west of Woodward on Jefferson, but they lived in the rear of their shops. The area of Negro residence was convenient to the docks and the commercial quarter of the city, but it was away from the industrial area. The three black churches in the city were clustered together. From 1838 to 1854 the Second Baptist Church was located on Fort Street, between Beaubien and St. Antoine. From 1841 to 1847 the Bethel AME Church was on Fort Street East, moving a block northwest of the Second Baptist in 1847 to Lafayette Street, between Brush and Beau-

[37] "Annual Report of the Board of Education of Detroit," in *Annual Report of the Superintendent of Public Instruction, 1852,* p. 152; *Minutes of the State Convention of the Colored Citizens of the State of Michigan* (Detroit, 1843), pp. 10–11; *Twenty-sixth Annual Report of the Board of Education* (Detroit, 1869), p. 33.

bien. St. Matthew's was located a block to the southwest of the Second Baptist, on the southeast corner of East Congress and St. Antoine.

As Detroit expanded northward from the river in the 1830s and 1840s, the Negro population remained clustered together on the city's near east side. By the 1850s a permanent pattern had emerged. In 1854, 83 percent of Detroit's blacks lived in wards four, six, and seven—three irregularly shaped adjacent wards (see table 1). The

T A B L E 1 *Distribution of Negro and Total Population, Detroit 1854*

Ward	Negro Population	Total Population
1	13	5,212
2	32	2,411
3	56	3,435
4	340	5,098
5	22	5,352
6	206	8,076
7	196	5,468
8	25	6,211

Source: Michigan Census 1854.

Negro population actually clustered within these wards at the points of convergence. Ward eight, a distance from the heart of the city, was mostly residential and rural. Wards one and two, near the river and west of Woodward, were the industrial part of the city; more than two-thirds of the workers in manufacturing, nearly all of them white, worked in these wards. The small number of blacks scattered in wards one, two, five, and eight represent Negroes engaged in service occupations.

In 1860, 80 percent of the black population of Detroit clustered into a small contiguous area. Some streets and alleys were referred to as the Negro area, but actually no street in the city was even 50 percent black occupied.[38] The intermixed population tended to be working class, native, and foreign-born, but only rarely Irish.

---

[38] Although precise statistics are unavailable, because the manuscript census did not record street addresses, this generalization is based on the sequential

TABLE 2 *Distribution of Negro and Total Population, Detroit 1860*

Ward	Negro Population	Total Population
1	61	3,778
2	15	1,460
3	326	3,703
4	373	5,063
5	52	5,493
6	191	7,003
7	267	6,512
8	17	5,610
9	68	3,521
10	32	3,476
Total	1,402	45,619

SOURCE: U.S. Census 1870.

NOTE: The increased black population in ward three from 56 in 1854 to 326 in 1860 and the decline in the sixth ward's black population during the same period represent a shift in the ward boundaries. In 1857 the area bounded by St. Antoine, Randolph, Croghan, and Gratiot streets, a heavily black area, was assigned to the third ward; previously it had been part of the sixth ward. Wards nine and ten were created in the same year. Farmer, *History of Detroit and Michigan*, pp. 147–148.

The contiguous geographical area in which the small black population lived in 1860 permitted some differentiation in residential patterns. Dr. Joseph Ferguson in the fourth ward lived near a white physician. Other black community leaders tended to live near one another. In all wards, black owners of real estate clustered together, apart from the renters. Some wealthy blacks like William Lambert lived apart from the community, dwelling in the tenth ward.

The quality of black neighborhoods and housing differed sharply. A majority of blacks lived in the city's older houses. These rented dwelling units, many in alleys, were in poor condition. Many blacks lived in small, frame tenement units occupied by two or three families. Housing was so bad that a white woman sympathetic to the blacks was able to find some benefit in the 1863 riot. "*Abstractly* considered," she stated, "the burning of those houses was something to be thankful for. They must build better ones if they build any."

listing of houses in the census, combined with addresses and information drawn from the city directories.

Other houses were quite substantial, reflecting the working-class level of many artisans.[39]

The black population rose sharply during the 1860s, reaching 2,235 in 1870, an increase of more than 50 percent since 1860. The wartime state census of 1864 recorded 1,444 blacks in the city, and an 1868 police census estimated Detroit's black population at 1,754. As the result of emancipation and the end of the war, the black population of Detroit grew more rapidly in the latter part of the 1860s than it had during the war years. The sharp rise in the black population forced many Negroes to settle north of Gratiot Avenue. Since the churches, schools, and other black social institutions were located in the Fort Street and St. Antoine Street area, Negro families found it a hardship to move into the new area at the northern extension of St. Antoine, Beaubien, and Hastings streets. As part of the transient population shifted northward and as the white population began to leave the core of the city, the vice area of the city, which had been located in the integrated quarter south of Jefferson along Brush, Beaubien, and St. Antoine, moved to the "Kentucky" area—north of Gratiot.[40]

The Kentucky area, around Kentucky Street, was filled with saloons, dance halls, houses of prostitution, and thieves' alleys. Proprietors and customers were of both races. The old Potomac Quarter near the river became a warehouse and light-industry district by the 1870s, with only prostitutes remaining as residents. Unfortunately for the many blacks who could find no other housing than that available north of Gratiot in the Kentucky district, the police tolerated the illegal activity as long as it remained nonviolent and confined to the region. In addition, social services were slow in coming to the area. When the centrally located churches of the black community rebuilt and expanded their church buildings after the war, they remained in their old localities. In the late 1860s parents in the northern district complained that the colored school was too far away, and the board of education responded by opening a school to service the area and to avoid integrating the schools. Finally, in 1870, residents of the area

[39] Elizabeth Douglass to Samuel Douglass, March 11, 1863, Samuel T. Douglass Papers, Burton Historical Collection.

[40] 1868 census: *Detroit Tribune*, May 6, 1868, p. 1.

founded the Independent Methodist Church to serve the quarter, and
the Grace AME and Ebenezer Church soon followed. Though crime
continued to flourish in the area, the once open neighborhood was
giving way to more stable community institutions.[41]

Although the pre–Civil War Detroit black community was not yet
large enough nor sufficiently sophisticated to reflect the distinct social, political, and economic divisions that would split the community
in the late nineteenth century, occupational as well as residential differentiation was becoming apparent. The 1850 census, the first to
provide data about individuals in Michigan, recorded 140 Detroit
blacks working in twenty-six different occupations:

Laborer	31	Shoemaker	5
Sailor	24	Waiter	4
Barber	20	Blacksmith	4
Cook	9	Tailor	3
Carpenter	9	Clerk	2
Mason	8	Minister	2
Servant	5	Butcher	2

One each: merchant, farmer, physician, grocer, coachman, musician,
cooper, harnessmaker, hatter, painter, hackman, drayman.

These occupations can be broadly reclassified as follows:

Professional and proprietary	6
Skilled	35
Semiskilled	29
Laborer	31
Service	39

The narrow occupational range, skewed toward the lower-paying,
less-skilled occupations, reflects both the relatively unspecialized occupational distribution of a nonindustrial city and the relatively low
position of the blacks on the city's social and economic ladder.[42]

[41] *Detroit Post & Tribune*, Feb. 16, 1880, p. 4; *Detroit Advertiser & Tribune*,
Aug. 26, 1866, p. 1; *Detroit Tribune*, Jan. 4, 1870, p. 1, Oct. 24, 1870, p. 3; Silas
Farmer, *History of Detroit and Michigan* (Detroit, 1884), p. 577.

[42] The data in this and the following paragraphs were collected from the
manuscript census returns. The groupings used are arbitrary designations based
on my own understanding of status, prestige, and economic reward. *Professional
and proprietary*: physician, minister, merchant, grocer, farmer. *Skilled*: carpenter,
mason, shoemaker, blacksmith, tailor, musician, harnessmaker, butcher, hatter,
cooper. *Semiskilled*: sailor, clerk, painter, hackman, drayman. *Service*: barber,

By 1860 the social and economic differences among Detroit's blacks were sufficiently marked to be revealed in the ward statistics. Twenty-four percent of Detroit's blacks had been born in Michigan, 20 percent in Virginia, 18 percent in Kentucky (mostly recent arrivals), and 6 percent in New England, New York, New Jersey, and Pennsylvania.[43] They were distributed among the wards as shown in table 3.

TABLE 3   *Birthplace and Distribution of Black Population, Detroit 1860*

Ward	Born in Virginia, %	Born in Kentucky, %	Born in Northeast, %	Born in Michigan, %	Born elsewhere, %
4	15	23	6	26	30
3	17	21	3	22	37
7	45	5	5	22	23
6	18	13	11	24	34
9	9	13	6	19	53
1	10	41	5	13	31
5	13	19	8	17	43
10	23	6	9	34	28

As indicated in table 4, the occupations varied in each ward.[44] The ward occupational variations reflect a number of factors. In 1850

---

cook, waiter, coachman, servant. A few barbers and some skilled artisans owned their own shops, but I have retained the original census designation. The number of blacks who were in the professional and proprietary class was actually greater than that listed, as the census recorded some proprietors merely as workers (e.g., barber shop owners as barbers), but it is impossible to determine the exact number of proprietors at any one point during this period.

[43] Ten percent of Detroit's blacks had been born in Canada. In reality, these blacks were similar to the small-town and rural Michigan blacks who migrated to the large city. Their migration to Detroit was merely a shift from the hinterland to the metropolitan city.

[44] *Professional*: farmer, fruit dealer, clothier, musician, minister, physician. *Skilled*: plasterer, tobacconist, tailor, blacksmith, shoemaker, carpenter, cooper, baker, butcher, mason, tanner, cigar maker, clothes cleaner, music teacher. *Semiskilled*: sailor, paperhanger, ragpicker, deck hand, whitewasher, drayman, city scavenger, gardener, repairer of old clothes, hackman, peddler, hustler, teamster, painter, steam fireman. *Service*: servant, cook, waiter, porter, bellboy, washing and laundry, errand boy, saloonkeeper, barkeeper.

TABLE 4 *Occupation and Distribution of Black Population, Detroit 1860*

Ward	Profes-sional	Skilled	Semi-skilled	Laborer	Service
4	6	8	16	26	22
3	3	23	15	13	26
7	2	17	15	3	20
6	1	9	27	7	10
9	1		1	9	1
1			2		23
5			2	2	3
10		2	3	2	2

Virginians comprised approximately one-third of the entire Detroit black work force, and 28 percent of those in service occupations. Less than 30 percent of the laborers, and fewer than one-quarter of the semiskilled were Virginians, but, by contrast, they constituted over 50 percent of the skilled workmen. Kentuckians, on the other hand, made up nearly one-quarter of the work force, yet only four of forty-one Kentucky-born blacks were above the semiskilled level. Overall, Negroes born in Virginia and the East and their children born in Michigan tended to be better educated and more familiar with urban living than other Negroes in the city. The Virginians had been skilled artisans in their home state's cities where many had been landholders, and had come to Michigan with some capital. Kentuckians in Detroit, who were more often illiterate and without skills, tended to be laborers, sailors, and servants. Whereas the Virginians came in family groups, the Kentuckians drifted to Detroit in small numbers, many alone. They comprised much of the poorer class of blacks, and as a group they tended to remain at the bottom of the social order. Although the children of many Virginians moved up into higher economic positions, mobility among the Kentuckians was restricted. The Kentuckians who were servants and laborers were not all young men nor recent arrivals. The three Kentucky-born blacks among the first-ward Negroes in 1860—two servants and a porter—were all above forty-five years of age. Thus the urban Virginians, relatively well educated by Michigan standards, black or white, and aggressive practitioners of the work ethic, clearly were outstripping their brethren from Kentucky and from elsewhere in the South.[45]

Many of the black Virginians had brought their skills and businesses to Detroit, where they joined the earlier group of black businessmen who had turned services or skills into small businesses with white clienteles. The *Detroit City Directory 1837* listed eleven Negroes, six of whom were independent businessmen. Five owned barber shops and one was a teamster. In the 1840s, Robert Banks, graduate of Gerrit Smith's New York manual training institute and agent for Frederick Douglass's *North Star*, sold ready-made clothes and imported assorted cottons and woolens. William Lambert had learned his trade in Banks's shop and then opened his own store, and later he ran a tailor shop and a clothes-cleaning store. Benjamin Willoughby, William Lambert's father-in-law, owned a wood lot in the 1840s and regularly loaned out his growing capital at interest. In the 1840s and 1850s Virginians James D. Carter and R. E. Wortham opened carpentry shops, while Richard Gordon, the Richards brothers, and Lomax B. Cook established barber shops. Another arrival to the city opened a grocery store, while entrepreneur George DeBaptiste engaged in a variety of enterprises. Black musicians played for whites at the city's balls and cotillions and on the Lake Erie excursion steamships.[46]

Nearly all of the prominent leaders of the Detroit black community were drawn from the group of shop keepers and skilled tradesmen, and they, like other Americans, were caught up in the reform mood of the day. The spirit of benevolence and reform led to a multitude of interests in the decades before the Civil War; utopianism and temperance, Sunday schools and revivalism, women's suffrage and prison reform, and free public schools and industrial education were the concerns of an entire generation. Above all else in significance, the issues of slavery and Negro suffrage attracted the interest of reformers. But if abolitionism was the most visible of the issues of

[45] Hartgrove, "Maria Louise Moore," pp. 23–33. Enumerated schedules, U.S. Census, 1850, 1860, 1870.

[46] *Detroit City Directory 1837; Signal of Liberty*, Apr. 3, 1843, p. 4, July 22, 1844, p. 5; Hartgrove, "Maria Louise Moore," pp. 29–32; Nelson, "Sketches of Our Music History," p. 34. See the promissory notes of Benjamin Willoughby in the Lambert Papers, NHRSM.

the era, nevertheless it had to share the stage with the other reform movements.

Many leading blacks such as William Lambert and William Monroe participated not only in the state abolitionist societies but also in the Liberty party convention and temperance groups. Even at meetings and conventions primarily concerned with gaining suffrage or equal rights, blacks tended to stress reform issues of the day. When blacks reorganized the Colored Vigilant Committee in 1842, the elected committee solicited black support for the city's colored school, and sought to induce Detroit blacks to sign a temperance pledge. The committee also boasted of the black cultural institutions existing in the city. A year later, at the state colored convention, the delegates endorsed general education, both civil and religious, supported temperance, and called for the organization of moral reform societies; and in the rhetoric of the age of Jackson, they resolved to "wage war against tyranny in every form, whether emanating from a crowned head abroad, or an overbearing aristocracy at home." The convention also adopted resolutions supporting agriculture and the mechanical arts and proclaimed "that indolence is the parent of vice."[47]

Michigan's Negroes exerted their greatest militancy in the political sphere. The central issue for them in Michigan was the denial of suffrage to the black man, and they fought this restriction in every way possible—by petition, convention, referendum, and court test. Occasionally Negroes balloted by fraudulently swearing that they were eligible electors. In the 1844 presidential election, Negroes had openly voted, "neither party having the hardihood to offer a challenge on the ground of color." Aside from the "open" election of 1844, Negroes were reported to have voted in Cass County in the late 1840s, and in 1846 a Detroit Negro vainly sued an election inspector who had refused him a ballot.[48]

Michigan abolitionists were active in fighting for Negro suffrage, one of the few causes that led the majority of abolitionists in the state

[47] *Signal of Liberty*, Apr. 28, 1841, p. 1, Feb. 20, 1843, p. 1; *Detroit Daily Advertiser*, Apr. 27, 1842, p. 1; *Minutes of the State Convention of the Colored Citizens of the State of Michigan*, pp. 11, 13, 14, 15, 16–23.

[48] Michigan, Senate, *Documents*, No. 15 (1845), p. 11; *North Star*, July 6, 1849, p. 2; *Gordon v. Farrar*, 2 Douglass 411 (1847).

to concern themselves with the black residents of Michigan.[49] A number of petition campaigns were mounted, most successfully in 1846 but also in 1843, 1844, 1847, 1855, and 1859. The *Signal of Liberty*, the state abolitionist weekly from 1841–1848, printed petitions favoring Negro suffrage that could be ripped out and circulated for signatures. Other abolitionist newspapers gave voice to the black efforts; the *Michigan Liberty Press* (1848–49) succeeded the *Signal of Liberty* and the *Michigan Freeman* (1840–41) in representing the interests of Michigan blacks, and the *Western Excelsior*, a Negro newspaper, appeared briefly in 1848. The Michigan Liberty party and the Michigan State Antislavery Society also supported Negro suffrage. The society's and the party's actions were no doubt influenced by the presence at their annual conventions of men like William Monroe, M. J. Lightfoot, Robert Banks, and William Lambert, along with blacks from Washtenaw County. From time to time a legislative committee recommended submitting the issue to the people of the state, but equally as often a committee endorsed the existing disfranchisement. Dialogue on the issue proved impossible; the opponents of black enfranchisement drew upon the ideal of perpetuating European civilization, while the proponents appealed to humanitarian concerns. In 1842, for instance, a senate committee reported that "our government is formed by, for the benefit of, and to be controlled by the descendants of European nations," and that Negro suffrage would be "inexpedient and impolitic." Four years later a house committee headed by future Republican Governor Austin Blair supported enfranchisement, arguing that "we have by the scorn of the community and its oppressive laws driven the colored man in most instances into the most menial employments (none other being left open to him) and thus has he become a blacker of white man's boots, and a sweeper of white man's chimneys."[50]

[49] The benevolent activities of the Quaker abolitionists in Lenawee County constituted an exception to the generalization concerning the disinterest of Michigan abolitionists in Michigan's Negroes. See Merton L. Dillon, "Elizabeth Chandler and the Spread of Antislavery Sentiment to Michigan," *Michigan History*, XXXIX (December, 1955), 481–494, and Laura S. Haviland, *A Woman's Life-Work* (Cincinnati, 1882).

[50] The journals of the senate and house of representatives of the state of Michigan annually recorded the large number of petitions that the legislators

White leaders who opposed Negro suffrage made few attempts to mask their antagonism toward blacks. Delegates at the Michigan Constitutional Convention of 1850 had crudely and aggressively asserted their belief in black inferiority. John Bagg of Detroit acknowledged that blacks were socially separated from whites and argued that they should remain "in their present sphere." Many agreed with Bagg's view that blacks were "dark bipeds—a species not equal to ourselves [whites]." The inevitable apparition of miscegenation haunted some delegates: "Why not give our daughters to their sons...?" asked delegate Nathan Pierce. The convention submitted the question of Negro suffrage to the people as a separate proposition and, although the constitution was approved in Detroit, Negro enfranchisement was turned down in the city by a seven-to-one margin. In Michigan the electorate defeated the proposition by a vote of 32,026 to 12,840.[51]

Before the passage of the Fifteenth Amendment, Michigan blacks achieved two small victories in their battle for enfranchisement. The 1855 Michigan legislature enfranchised blacks in school district elections, an action necessitated by the organization of schools in the overwhelmingly black rural township of Calvin in Cass County. Because the Detroit Board of Education was appointed and not elected, Detroit blacks remained totally disfranchised. In 1866, in *People* v. *Dean*, the Michigan Supreme Court ruled that William Dean, a mulatto from Nankin Township, near Detroit, was to be registered as a

received. Committee reports favoring passage of Negro suffrage were issued in 1843–47, 1855, 1857, and 1859. Reports against enfranchisement of blacks were issued in 1842–46, 1857, and 1861. Michigan, House, *Documents*, Nos. 3, 14 (1843); No. 24 (1844); No. 12 (1846); No. 25 (1859); Michigan, Senate, *Documents*, No. 15 (1845); No. 28 (1861); Michigan, Senate, *Journals*, 1855, pp. 112–113; 1857, p. 319; 1859, p. 544; Emil Olbrich, *The Development of Sentiment on Negro Suffrage to 1860*, Bulletin of the University of Wisconsin, History Series, III (1912), 93; *Signal of Liberty*, Jan. 16, 1843, p. 2; Apr. 28, 1841, p. 1; Feb. 20, 1843, p. 1. For a sample of a printed petition see *Signal of Liberty*, Dec. 9, 1844, p. 130. I am grateful to Professor Ronald P. Formisano of the University of Rochester for allowing me to read his unpublished manuscript, "Attitudes to Colored Suffrage, Michigan, 1835–1861."

[51] Ronald P. Formisano, "Attitudes to Colored Suffrage, Michigan, 1835–1861"; *Report of the Proceedings and Debates in the Convention to Revise the Constitution of the State of Michigan 1850*, pp. 62, 289, 290; *Detroit Free Press*, Nov. 13, 1850, p. 2.

lawful elector. The court had to decide who could be considered a white man, and thus a lawful elector, under the state constitution. Splitting hairs, the court ruled that a man who had less than one-quarter African "blood" was white, thereby overruling the lower court's judgment that one-sixteenth was the dividing line. Chief Justice Martin dissented, arguing that a preponderance of blood either way should determine a man's color. Local boards of registration, however, including those in Detroit, refused to enroll anyone they arbitrarily considered to be a Negro. Six Nankin Township blacks who fell within the court's definition of a white man, including William Dean's son, were thus turned away by the registrars and had to obtain court writs to vote. In Detroit, barber shop owners John Bailey and Obadiah C. Wood similarly found their applications to vote rejected by Detroit's fourth-ward board of registration; they were finally registered under supreme court order.[52]

In 1867 Michigan convened a constitutional convention, the first since 1850, and with the Radical Republicans dominating the proceedings, the chances for black enfranchisement seemed high. As nearly all of the delegates declared for Negro suffrage, the debate focused on whether or not the proposition should be included within the constitution's article on elections. Although one delegate, S. Titus Parsons of Shiawasse County, warned the convention that if Negro suffrage were included within the constitution, the whole document might be defeated by the electorate solely because of this provision, the convention did not submit a separate referendum on the issue to the voters.[53]

The campaign over the constitution proved a bitter one for Michigan's blacks. "Negro suffrage," declared the Democratic convention, is "contrary to the true interests of our people, and will be opposed by the Democratic party." The Democratic newspapers in the state predicted an invasion of Michigan by hordes of Africans. The Republican press, on the other hand, praised the convention for not

[52] *Acts of the Legislature of the State of Michigan 1855* (Lansing, 1855), pp. 44–45, 413–416; *People* v. *Dean*, 14 Michigan 406 (1866); *Detroit Advertiser & Tribune*, Nov. 9, 1866, p. 1; *Detroit Tribune*, Oct. 21, 1868, p. 3, Oct. 27, 1868, p. 3.

[53] *Debates and Proceedings of the Constitutional Convention of the State of Michigan 1867*, II, 712, 713, 715.

submitting Negro suffrage as a proposition apart from the constitution and thought that this would ensure its passage. The Republican state convention endorsed the constitution, and black enfranchisement specifically. Since the Republicans dominated the state—Michigan had a Republican administration and a legislature of ninety-nine Republicans to thirty-three Democrats—the Radicals and blacks expected the passage of the constitution. But in the referendum, prejudice proved stronger than reason; the voters defeated the constitution by a three-to-two margin. Throughout the state only five of Michigan's fifty-nine counties returned majorities in favor of the constitution, and it was defeated, 110,582 to 71,733. In Wayne County, 63.6 percent of the voters opposed the constitution.[54]

Two and one-half years later, in November 1870, the Michigan electorate narrowly approved an amendment to the state constitution striking out the limitation of suffrage to whites by a vote of 54,105 to 50,598. Only fifteen counties in the state returned negative pluralities, and Wayne County reversed its previous votes by endorsing black suffrage by a four-to-one margin, providing a 1,550-vote plurality. This shift on Negro enfranchisement in Wayne County, from opposition in 1868 to approval in 1870, is difficult to explain. Primarily the electorate was apathetic toward the issue. This time the question had elicited little comment in the Detroit newspapers, and the Democratic opposition did not initiate the usual Negrophobic campaign. Furthermore, many voters probably believed black enfranchisement to be a moot question because of the recent enactment of the Fifteenth Amendment. Few voters bothered to cast a vote on the issue, and it is probable that mostly the supporters of the issue balloted; in Wayne, the combined vote for and against the impartial suffrage amendment equaled only one-eighth of the total county vote cast for governor at the same election. The closeness of the vote in the state, nevertheless, reveals the white prejudice against Negroes, and a good part of the narrow winning margin was almost certainly provided by blacks themselves who had voted in the election.[55]

[54] *Appleton's American Cyclopaedia 1868* (New York, 1869), pp. 493, 495; *Detroit Advertiser & Tribune*, Aug. 15, 1867, p. 2; *Detroit Tribune*, Feb. 20, 1868, p. 2, Mar. 19, 1868, p. 1, Apr. 6, 1868, p. 1, Apr. 25, 1868, p. 1.

[55] *Detroit Tribune*, Nov. 18, 1870, p. 3, Dec. 15, 1870, p. 1; Harriette M. Dilla, *The Politics of Michigan 1865–1878* (New York, 1912), p. 107.

Blacks themselves were the most important force in the battle for Negro suffrage and equal rights. As early as April 1841 they campaigned to convince the legislature and the citizens of the state of the justice of their cause. Robert Banks addressed a protest meeting in Detroit and recalled the still-fresh slogan, "no taxation without representation." Banks also reviewed the service of Negroes in the Revolutionary War, and sought to appease the large majority of Negrophobes in the state by assuring them that blacks sought political, not social, equality.[56]

During 1842 Detroit's blacks reorganized the two-year-old Colored Vigilant Committee. The reorganization was partly a result of the international controversy initiated by the celebrated Nelson Hackett case of early 1842, in which Hackett, a fugitive slave who had managed to find his way to Canada, was returned to United States authorities in Detroit. The incident strengthened the feelings of Detroit blacks that "the long lost rights and liberties of our people in this community, or in any other, could only be regained by our own exertions . . . ." The 1842 meeting voted to elect a nine-man committee, three men to be elected each year for three-year terms. The first representatives included William Lambert, Madison Lightfoot, Robert Banks, and Benjamin Willoughby.[57]

In 1843 the call of the National Negro Convention in Buffalo provided a catalyst for the holding of Negro meetings and state conventions. In response to the circular issued by the Central Corresponding Committee of the State of New York, the leaders of the Vigilant Committee organized a mass meeting of the colored citizens of Detroit which assembled in the basement of the Second Baptist Church on June 27, 1843. The meeting elected William C. Monroe, Robert Banks, barber shop owner Richard Gordon, and William Lambert as delegates to the Buffalo convention, and in their resolutions reiterated the rationale of the Vigilant Committee and foreshadowed the calling of the state convention: "Resolved, That all history shows, and our

[56] *Signal of Liberty*, May 5, 1841, p. 2.
[57] *Detroit Daily Advertiser*, Apr. 27, 1842, p. 2; *Detroit Democratic Free Press*, Jan. 23, 1843, p. 2; *Signal of Liberty*, Mar. 9, 1842, p. 3, June 27, 1842, p. 2. By the late 1840s the Colored Vigilant Committee had ceased functioning, but in 1851 it reappeared as the Committee of Vigilance. *Voice of the Fugitive*, Dec. 3, 1851.

experience proves, that the Rights and Liberties of a people must be obtained by their own exertions, and it is high time we put our shoulders to the wheel." One month after the Buffalo convention, the Michigan delegates issued a call for a state convention of colored citizens.[58]

The convention met in Detroit on October 26, 1843, at the Second Baptist Church. There were twelve delegates from Detroit and eleven from outstate black communities. They elected William Lambert as chairman pro tem., and William Monroe as president of the convention. The convention resolutions and its "An Address to the Citizens of the State of Michigan" condemned the Negroes' loss of rights, endorsed the principles of the Declaration of Independence, and called for "equal civil and political privileges." Suffrage was the major issue, the delegates expressing their belief that "the elective franchise [is] a right which invigorates the soul, and expands the mental power, and is the safeguard of the liberty and prosperity of a free and independent people." The convention also called for "the immediate abolition of American slavery" and approved a resolution, introduced by the future advocate of emigration, Henry Bibb, pledging the delegates "never to consent to emigrate or be colonized from this, our native soil, while there exists one drop of African blood in bondage in these United States."[59]

Throughout the 1840s black leaders William Lambert, William Monroe, and Robert Banks were unceasing in their efforts to destroy the rigid caste system. Henry Bibb spent much time out of Detroit, attacking slavery and raising his voice for equal justice while traversing the state. A state convention of colored citizens convened in Marshall on March 6, 1850, and sent Bibb to appear before the state constitutional convention, where he spoke for equal rights and enfranchisement.[60]

[58] Howard H. Bell, "A Survey of the Negro Convention Movement, 1830–1861," Ph.D. dissertation, Northwestern University, 1953, pp. 80–81; *Signal of Liberty*, July 24, 1843, p. 2, Oct. 9, 1843, p. 1.

[59] *Minutes of the State Convention of the Colored Citizens of the State of Michigan*, pp. 11, 13, 14, 15, 16–23.

[60] *Detroit Free Press*, June 10, 1850, p. 2; *Report of the Proceedings and Debates in the Convention to Revise the Constitution of the State of Michigan: 1850* (Lansing, 1850), p. 94.

Despite the protests and organized efforts of the blacks in Detroit, the caste system seemed to tighten rather than loosen. Aside from a benevolent 1855 Michigan legislature which enfranchised blacks in school-district elections and passed the personal liberty laws, there were few bright days for Michigan's blacks in the decades preceding the Civil War. The inauguration of public schools in Detroit in the 1840s meant segregated education, and separate and unequal proved to be the rule. Although the 1850 constitutional convention debated the question of Negro suffrage and a few delegates favored enfranchisement, the majority opposed it. John Bagg of Detroit summed up much of the white feeling in the state when he declared: "I would not let them [Negroes] come into our civil, political, social, conjugal or connubial relations." The *Detroit Free Press* led the campaign against the referendum on black suffrage authorized by the convention, and Negro enfranchisement was overwhelmingly defeated. When Wilbur F. Storey assumed the editorship of the *Free Press* in 1853, it became even more Negrophobic. Most discouraging was the 1858 supreme court decision that gave legal recognition to the custom that Negroes were "excluded from ordinary social and familiar intercourse with white persons." In response, many of Michigan's black leaders looked beyond legal remedies for relief. Increasingly black leaders in Detroit challenged their own status as second-class citizens, and the presence of slavery in the United States. They turned away from remonstrances to more direct, sometimes extra-legal, action—actively aiding fugitive slaves, supporting emigration, and involvement in John Brown's liberation schemes.[61]

Some of Michigan's blacks illegally aided fugitive slaves. An unknown number of escaped slaves made their own way to or through Detroit, and the black community, as in the Blackburn or Hackett cases, could be depended upon to guarantee their well-being, and safe passage to Canada if they were threatened by slave hunters. Wil-

[61] *Acts of the Legislature of the State of Michigan 1855* (Lansing, 1855), pp. 44–45, 413–416; *The Introductory Report of the Board of Education of the City of Detroit* (Detroit, 1842); Annual Report of the Detroit Public Schools, 1857, clipping, *Detroit Daily Advertiser*, Jan. 26, 1857, Burton Historical Collection; *Debates, Constitutional Convention, 1850*, p. 61; *Detroit Free Press*, Aug. 24, 1850, p. 2; Formisano, "Attitudes to Colored Suffrage," MS, p. 31; *Day v. Owens*, 5 Michigan 520 (1858).

liam Lambert, George DeBaptiste, and Henry Bibb became associated with the Underground Railroad and are credited with membership in a Negro secret society devoted to antislavery activities, known variously as the African-American Mysteries, the "Order of the Men of Oppression," or the "Order of Emigration." No doubt they aided many fugitives, but the exact nature of their activities is impossible to determine. What is important, however, is that these black men were willing to involve themselves in such illegal operations.[62]

Of more importance was the increasing Negro interest in colonization and emigration. Increasingly in Detroit, as in other black communities, the frustrations of the 1840s and 1850s led moderate black leaders to share in the "Negro Nationalism" of those years—"a zealous advocacy of all things Negro, to the exclusion, insofar as possible, of planning, supervision, or meddling by whites." In 1851 a group of Michigan black leaders reversed their traditional opposition to emigration by attending the emigrationist North American Convention of Colored People at Toronto. Robert Banks, William Lambert, tailor Alfred Derrick of Detroit (born in the District of Columbia), and Methodist minister and farmer John W. Brooks and barber shop owner Thomas Freeman, both of Ann Arbor, joined Samuel Ringgold Ward, Martin R. Delany, William Still, and Henry H. Garnet at the 1851 convention sponsored by Henry Bibb. Significantly, of the Michigan Negroes involved, all except Banks had attended the 1843 antiemigrationist Michigan convention, and though absent from that convention, Banks had declared himself against colonization a

[62] *Signal of Liberty*, Mar. 9, 1842, p. 3; May 8, 1847, p. 10. For the traditional interpretation of the Underground Railroad in Michigan, see Wilbur H. Siebert, *The Underground Railroad from Slavery to Freedom* (New York, 1898), pp. 70, 88; Farmer, *The History of Detroit and Michigan*, pp. 346–347; and Katherine DuPre Lumpkin, " 'The General Plan Was Freedom': A Negro Secret Order on the Underground Railroad," *Phylon*, XXVIII (Spring, 1967), 63–77. On the other hand, most of the evidence confirms Larry Gara's conclusions in his *The Liberty Line: The Legend of the Underground Railroad* (Lexington, Ky., 1961). The leading conductor of the Underground Railroad in Michigan saw only four fugitives in the decade of the 1850s and probably no more than 100 during the 1840s. Few of these refugees settled in Michigan, almost all continuing on to Canada. See Nathan Thomas MSS, especially Nathan Macy Thomas, "History of Antislavery Movement," Box I, and Ella Thomas, "The Underground Railroad," Box II, Nathan Macy Thomas Papers, Michigan Historical Collections.

few years earlier. As conditions worsened, a few Negroes emigrated to Canada and Africa, others flirted with colonization schemes, and some just drifted away from Detroit.[63]

Henry Bibb and William Monroe were the leading emigrationists in Detroit and both eventually left the United States, Bibb going to Canada and Monroe moving to Africa. Both men died outside their native land. Fear of retribution under the Fugitive Slave Law of 1850 no doubt motivated Bibb to seek refuge in Canada, but his autobiography and the *Voice of the Fugitive* clearly reveal that concern for his own personal safety was secondary in importance to his loss of faith in the United States. On January 1, 1851, Bibb began publication of the bi-weekly *Voice of the Fugitive*, an organ advocating "the immediate and unconditional abolition of chattel-slavery everywhere." The paper was also dedicated to persuading "every oppressed person of color in the United States to settle in Canada." To this end Bibb repeatedly broadcast the prosperity of the black Canadian settlements and promoted the establishment of the Refugee Home Society, a Detroit and Windsor-based benevolent society dedicated to encouraging migration to Canada, and supporting the Negro communities there. His activities brought many of Michigan's black leaders into the emigrationist sphere: Madison Lightfoot was an agent of the *Voice*; Richard Gordon supported the Refugee Home Society; and Banks, Lambert, and Derrick attended the 1851 emigrationist convention in Toronto.[64]

William C. Monroe, spiritual leader of the small but influential group of black Episcopalians in Detroit, also lost faith in domestic solutions to the race problem. Monroe had joined Mrs. Henry Bibb at the 1854 emigrationist National Negro Convention in Cleveland; in 1859, after promoting African colonization for several years, he

[63] Howard H. Bell, "Negro Nationalism in the 1850's," *Journal of Negro Education*, XXXV (Winter, 1966), 100. For a broader view see Hollis R. Lynch, "Pan-Negro Nationalism in the New World, before 1862," in Jeffrey Butler (ed.), *Boston University Papers on Africa*, II, 147–179; *Voice of the Fugitive*, May 7, 1851, p. 2, June 4, 1851, p. 1, Aug. 13, 1851, p. 2, Sept. 24, 1851, pp. 2–3; Robert Banks, *An Oration Delivered at a Celebration in Detroit, of the Abolition of Slavery in the West Indies* (Detroit, 1839), p. 14.

[64] *Voice of the Fugitive*, Jan. 1, 1851, p. 2.

left his pulpit and went to Liberia as a missionary.[65] Others close to him also despaired; Lewis Hayden left for the larger and more militant Boston black community, while Robert Banks traveled to California. Most significantly, William Lambert's faith in American society was shaken sufficiently during the decade to lead him into taking an active part in the John Brown Chatham conventions of 1858.

In May 1858, John Brown invited William Lambert and William Monroe and some Canadian blacks, including James Madison Bell and Martin R. Delany, to attend a "quiet convention" at Chatham in which Brown intended to establish a provisional government and lay plans for an armed excursion into the South in order to incite an uprising of the slave population. The forty-five delegates present elected Monroe convention president. Brown planned to mount a military excursion into the South, but when someone in his group leaked word of the planned invasion, the Massachusetts reformers financing Brown's antislavery activities cut off funds. Brown postponed his planned attack until the following year, when he and his band raided Harper's Ferry.[66]

Throughout his life William Lambert was noted for his wisdom, the reflective quality of his mind, and his generally conservative outlook. His commitment to John Brown's scheme and his signature on the provisional constitution should therefore not be viewed as a rash decision. The cumulative frustrations of the 1840s and 1850s, combined with the growing involvement of his close friends in emigrationism and colonization, probably led to his avowal of John Brown's methods. Lambert and Monroe, for instance, had been delegates to the 1854 Cleveland emigrationist National Convention of Colored Men. By 1858 it must have seemed to men like William Lambert that

[65] "Chronology and Outlines of the Episcopal Church," Papers of the Protestant Episcopal Church of Michigan, Michigan Historical Collections; George F. Bragg, *History of the Afro-American Group of the Episcopal Church* (Baltimore, 1922), pp. 118, 191.

[66] James Redpath, *The Public Life of Captain John Brown* (Boston, 1860), pp. 230–233; Frank A. Rollin, *Life and Public Services of Martin R. Delany . . .* (Boston, 1883), pp. 86–89; Oswald Garrison Villard, *John Brown 1800–1859* (Boston, 1910), pp. 331, 335. A reproduction of George B. Gill's commission as secretary of the treasury, signed by Monroe, can be found in Richard J. Hinton, *John Brown and His Men* (New York, 1894), p. 468.

only resort to arms could destroy the evil that slavery had spread in both the South and the North.[67]

II

With the coming of the Civil War, black interest in emigration and colonization and in movements such as that of John Brown diminished, although racism and conditions for Michigan's Negroes did not change. Many blacks felt that emancipation was now inevitable and that the end of the struggle for equal rights was within sight. To Negroes the beneficial effects of the ascendancy of the Republican party in state and national politics were of greater consequence than the malevolence of the rhetoric of the Copperheads and the actions of the Irish. With war on the horizon in early 1861, Michigan's Negroes held a state convention to secure equal rights and sent an address to the state legislature petitioning for suffrage. Emancipation appeared as a threat to many whites, however, and its imminence rekindled the fear of waves of blacks invading the state. Some whites, therefore, mounted a petition campaign directed at the repeal of the state's personal liberty laws. Blacks might have taken some comfort from the failure of the petition campaign, but the 1863 riot in Detroit, like those that swept other cities of the North, was a disheartening if temporary setback to the goals of the black community.[68]

Although race riots occurred in St. Paul, Cincinnati, and Toledo during the Civil War, the Detroit race riot of March 6, 1863, was the only major riot in the Midwest. Exploding racial conflict between immigrants—mostly Irish—and the blacks underlay the midwestern riots, as well as their counterparts in New York, Boston, and the smaller New York cities of Brooklyn, Buffalo, and Troy. As recent immigrants, the Irish manifested relatively little interest in the war to

---

[67] Joseph H. Johnson, *In Memoriam: William Lambert, Sermon Preached at St. Matthew's Church* (reprinted from *Michigan Church Life*, July, 1890).

[68] See V. Jacques Voegeli, *Free But Not Equal: The Midwest and the Negro During the Civil War* (Chicago, 1967), for white attitudes; Michigan, House of Representatives, *Journals*, 1861, pp. 258, 437, 462, 485, 629, 805, 845.

preserve the Union; the sons of Eire were more concerned about the competition of black laborers for unskilled and service jobs. The Democratic newspapers never tired of playing on the fears of the Irish; the *Detroit Free Press*, for example, often used "vulgar and bigoted language" in attacking blacks. James William Massie, an English traveler in the United States, visited Detroit and other northern cities in 1863 and concluded that the Irish "habitually dread the freedom of the Negro, lest he should become a competitor in the labour market." Massie found that in the states thoroughly loyal to the republic there existed a "strong prejudice against people of colour." [69]

The immediate event that precipitated the 1863 Detroit riot was the alleged molestation of two girls by a Negro, William Faulkner, who owned an eating house. Mary Brown, white, and Ellen Hoover, black, both nine years old, accused the forty-year-old Faulkner of rape, and their testimony resulted in a guilty verdict. Faulkner was sentenced to life in prison. A part of the citizenry, mostly the Irish and the Germans, was aroused by the crime and, stirred by the *Free Press*, threatened to lynch the prisoner. Anticipating trouble, the sheriff had asked for militia reinforcements.[70]

> To keep from a rescue, and take him to jail,
> The soldiers were ordered to come without fail,
> But they were insulted and stoned at—pell mell—
> Till some of them fired and down a man fell.

Angry citizens gathered around when Faulkner was being taken back to the jail from the court house. The crowd menaced the fed-

[69] Voegeli, *Free But Not Equal*, p. 89; Williston H. Lofton, "Northern Labor and the Negro during the Civil War," *Journal of Negro History*, XXXIV (July, 1949), 253, 257, 262, 272; Eugene Converse Murdock, *Patriotism Limited 1862–1865: The Civil War and the Bounty System* (n.p., 1967), p. 2; Wood Gray, *The Hidden Civil War* (New York, 1942), p. 90; Albert A. Blum and Dan Georgakas, *Michigan Labor and the Civil War* (Lansing, 1964), pp. 13, 15; James William Massie, *America: The Origin of Her Present Conflict; Her Prospect for the Slave, and Her Claim for Anti-Slavery Sympathy* (London, 1864), pp. 66, 308.

[70] Norman McRae, *Negroes in Michigan During the Civil War* (Lansing, 1966), p. 34; *A Thrilling Narrative from the Lips of the Sufferers of the Late Detroit Riot, March 6, 1863* (reprinted Hattiesburg, Miss., 1945), p. 11.

eral troops, and one of the soldiers fired into the crowd, killing Charles Langer.[71]

> The mob, disappointed, now hied to a place
> Where some humble coopers, of the sable race,
> Were honestly working to earn their own bread,
> By rowdies were set on and left almost dead.

The crowd, frustrated in their attempt to lynch the convicted Faulkner, made their way from the jail to Beaubien Street in the Negro area of the city. Crying "kill all the d———d niggers," they attacked a cooper shop on Beaubien, just below Lafayette. The coopers managed to keep the mob out, but the shop was burned to the ground and Joshua Boyd, one of the men in the shop, died of the wounds he received.[72]

> Then they took the city without delay,
> And fired each building that stood in their way,
> Until the red glare had ascended on high,
> And lit up the great azure vault of the sky.

After destroying the cooper's shop and the dwelling next door, the mob spread out over Fort and Lafayette streets, burning and looting fifteen houses in the area. One victim, Louis Houston, recalled: "The mob went like a volcano, sweeping along the dwellings of colored people."[73]

> The sight was most awful indeed to behold,
> See women and babes driven out in the cold,
> And old aged sires, that fought for the land,
> Beat almost to death by a desperate band.

The wives of the coopers on Lafayette and other women and children in the area barely escaped with their lives as houses came tumbling down around them. The fanatical mob also hunted down old men; Ephraim Clark, the eighty-year-old sexton of the African Methodist Episcopal (AME) church, was badly beaten; and, while his home was being plundered, seventy-nine-year-old Richard Evans was shot in the head at close range by a pistol-wielding rioter.[74]

[71] Poem, "The Riot," by B. Clark, a Negro, in *Narrative of the Detroit Riot*, pp. 23–24.

[72] Ibid., p. 2.

[73] Ibid., pp. 3, 8.

[74] Ibid., pp. 8, 17.

Strange as it may be, yet 'tis true without doubt,
Mobs do not discriminate if once let out;
So when they had fired the huts of the poor,
They ran with the torch to their rich neighbor's door.

The mob directed its fury against all the blacks it came upon. The cooper shop's owner, Whitney Reynolds, hardly a competitor of the fearful Irish and Dutch dock workers and laborers, lost in the burning house $1,200 in cash and over $4,000 in property, the equivalent of more than ten years in wages of a laborer in the 1860s.[75]

A few whites in the area had attempted to disperse the mob, and a meeting of blacks at the AME church some days later thanked Police Officer Sullivan for having attempted to perform his duty in the face of the "inhuman and unlawful mob." The blacks also acknowledged the aid of J. and A. B. Tabor, proprietors of the Biddle House, a leading hotel, who had opened their doors to victims of the riot. Soldiers from Fort Wayne and the Twenty-seventh Infantry from Ypsilanti were needed before order was restored. The toll was devastating to the black community: two Negroes had been killed and more than a score seriously injured; thirty to thirty-five homes of Negroes had been razed; and more than two hundred blacks had been left homeless.[76]

While the 1863 riot destroyed much of black Detroit, it did not shake the renewed faith in American society brought about by the Civil War. The organization of colored regiments throughout the North and the formation of the First Michigan Colored Volunteers, for example, served to reverse the disorganization of the community that had set in during the 1850s and restored the faith of many blacks in the institutions of the larger society.

Michigan blacks, similar to their brothers elsewhere in the North,

[75] Ibid., p. 2; Edgar W. Martin, *The Standard of Living in 1860* (Chicago, 1942), pp. 407–416.

[76] *Narrative of the Detroit Riot*, p. 18; McRae, *Negroes in Michigan During the Civil War*, p. 36. Ironically, Faulkner was innocent and the girls later confessed that they had perjured themselves. The city council, by then Republican, made some restitution, providing Faulkner with a small restaurant. Silas Farmer, *The History of Detroit and Michigan* (Detroit, 1884), p. 348. Immediately following the riot, the Democratic city council refused to compensate the victims. *Narrative of the Detroit Riot*, p. 15. The mob, mostly Irish but partly German, went unpunished.

sought to serve in the Union army. When the first northern colored regiment, the Fifty-fourth Massachusetts, formed in April 1863, Michigan blacks enlisted in the ranks. Frederick Douglass caught the mood of those anxious to enlist in answering the question, "Why Should A Colored Man Enlist?" First of all, Douglass advised, enlistment proved that you were a man. Second, Negroes could gain the support of whites by enlisting. Third, Douglass feared a drift back to the whirlpool of pro-slavery days when Negro rights were sacrificed in the name of national unity, and he was concerned lest the Negroes might become victimized by such a drift: "The whole North will be but another Detroit," he wrote, "where every white fiend may with impunity revel in unrestrained beastliness towards people of color; they may burn their houses, insult their wives and daughters, and kill indiscriminately." Finally, Douglass recognized that it was a war for emancipation, "whether men so call it or not."[77]

Detroit blacks responded eagerly to the call for troops: when the War Department authorized Governor Austin Blair to raise a black regiment in July 1863, the city's Negroes were quick to join the First Michigan Colored Regiment. At first the enlistees were not offered any bounties and were paid three dollars a month less than white soldiers received. In December 1863, the regiment made a "grand tour" of Michigan towns, 250 men in uniforms and arms. After hearing the praises of their friends and relatives in all of the state's black settlements, the colored regiment went to the South, where in the spring of 1864 they became the 102nd United States Colored Infantry. By the end of the war nearly 1,500 blacks had seen service with the regiment in Michigan, South Carolina, and Florida.

Mustered out in Charleston on September 30, 1865, the soldiers arrived in Detroit shortly thereafter. One hundred and forty members of the regiment had died, including three officers. Although the regiment had been raised through the efforts of Detroit Negro leaders, none of the commissioned officers was black. The regiment nevertheless served to bind the black community together and won the respect of all but die-hard Negrophobes.[78]

[77] *Douglass' Monthly*, April, 1863, reprinted in Philip S. Foner, *The Life and Writings of Frederick Douglass* (4 vols.; New York, 1952), III, 340–344.
[78] George S. May, *Michigan and the Civil War Years 1860–1866: A Chronicle*

With the Republican party in the ascendant in the state and nation, and the black regiment in the field in the South, Michigan blacks renewed their fight for equality and enfranchisement. In October 1864, the National Negro Convention, meeting at Syracuse, New York, called for the creation of state leagues modeled after the National Equal Rights League. The Syracuse convention had created the league, and John D. Richards of Detroit served as one of the four members of the executive board. Two different groups responded to the Syracuse convention in Michigan: a January 1865 state convention of colored citizens met in Adrian and created the Michigan State Equal Rights League of Colored People with a bureau in Detroit, and another group met in convention in Detroit in September 1865 and organized the Equal Rights League of Michigan. Both conventions agreed on the necessity of pressing the struggle for enfranchisement and equal rights.

The Michigan State Equal Rights League of Colored People appeared to be the more active of the two leagues, and it sent a delegation to memorialize the legislature in the form of an ironic question that would be repeated by eighteen- and nineteen-year-old youths a century later during another war: "Are we good enough to use bullets, and not good enough to use ballots?" The petition went on to express the overwhelming sentiment of the black community, though the symbols used were those of the more affluent, the more secure: "In a republican country, where general suffrage is the rule, personal liberty, the right to testify in courts of law, the right to hold, buy and sell property, and all other rights, become mere privileges held at the option of others, where we are excepted from the general political liberty." The delegation from the league, John D. Richards, barber shop owner Robert Cullen, and carpenter James D. Carter, were invited to sit within the bar of the house of representatives in Lansing, but they declined, giving as a reason that "*they* were highly respectable, Christian gentlemen, and they feared that the evil communications of this body might seriously impair their usefulness." By "evil communications" the delegation probably referred to the long Negrophobic tradition among at least some members of the house,

---

(Lansing, 1964), p. 90; McRae, *Negroes in Michigan During the Civil War*, p. 48.

and by refusing "to sit within the bar," they were showing their contempt for those opposing black equal rights.[79]

In 1867 Michigan blacks won a major victory when, after a long fight stretching over three decades, the legal protection for school segregation was abolished in the state. In January 1867, former Governor Austin Blair filed a writ of mandamus in the Michigan Supreme Court ordering a white school in Jackson, Michigan, to admit a Negro student. Within a month, the question raised by Blair's writ appeared to be moot when the Republican legislature passed a bill, effective February 28, 1867, eliminating *de jure* school segregation in the state.[80]

Michigan black leaders continued their fight for equal rights and enfranchisement. With Radical Republicanism in power in Washington and Lansing, the granting of suffrage seemed to be only a matter of time. Although the 1867 Michigan constitution providing for Negro suffrage was defeated in April 1868, blacks continued to press for the passage of a constitutional amendment. By the time the Fifteenth Amendment was sent to the legislature by Governor Baldwin on March 3, 1869, the house had already passed a resolution putting the question on the ballot in November 1870.

Thus in April 1870, following the passage of the Fifteenth Amendment, Detroit blacks looked optimistically to the future. Although they recognized the persistence of Negrophobia, they announced that political equality had been won. When the Detroit black community celebrated the passage of the amendment on April 7, 1870, it turned out to be a massive, joyous event. When William Lambert wrote on April 7, 1870, "Freedom reigns to-day!" all the fears and tensions of the Negroes, all their hopelessness and despair seemed of the past. Michigan blacks looked forward to taking their rightful place in American society.

[79] *Proceedings of the Colored Men's Convention of the State of Michigan...* (Adrian, Michigan, 1865); *Proceedings of the National Convention of Colored Men Held in the City of Syracuse, N.Y., October 4, 5, 6, and 7, 1864...* (Boston, 1864), p. 36; Michigan, House of Representatives, *Journals*, 1865, I, pp. 158–164, 221.

[80] *Detroit Advertiser & Tribune*, Jan. 9, 1867, p. 1; *Acts of the Legislature of the State of Michigan 1867* (2 vols.; Lansing, 1867), I, 42–46. In spite of this act, Detroit's schools remained segregated until the 1870s and some Michigan communities continued school segregation into the twentieth century. See chapter 3.

Part II

Black Detroit

CHAPTER II
Patterns

EUROPEAN TRAVELERS in the New World would often visit Montreal and Toronto, then journey southwesterly through the Ontario triangle and cross the Detroit River to encounter the United States for the first time at the foot of Woodward Avenue in Detroit. The view of the city during the short fifteen-minute ferry ride across the river changed little from 1870 to 1915. Grim warehouses, small factories, and an occasional chimney billowing smoke lined the railyards and wharves on the edge of the river. The sight was impressive—it was, after all, what travelers expected of America. The slums and alleys, the unemployed and the poor were hidden from view when the ferry passed by the industrial riverfront, and the passengers disembarked on Woodward Avenue.

By the middle of the nineteenth century Woodward Avenue had replaced Jefferson Avenue as Detroit's major artery. Tree-lined and broad—a boulevard—Woodward bisected the city and stretched far beyond Detroit's ever-shifting northern boundaries. The avenue was both the city's major commercial street and its most fashionable residential boulevard. Campus Martius, a large open space on Woodward Avenue six blocks north of the river, was the heart of the city —later "downtown"—and the square led to a similar opening four blocks to the north—Grand Circus. This general region and its sur-

53

rounding area, the core of Detroit, remained a walking city, and its scale, in the eyes of the nineteenth-century pedestrian, seemed impressive and modern but not overpowering. Urban canyons were unknown in Detroit, and the city seemed open and clean.

Nearly all visitors to Detroit were quick to comment on the beauty of the city on the straits. A trip up Woodward Avenue, by horse-car before 1886 and by electric railroad after that date, rarely failed to impress the visitor. Neat stores, fashionable mansions, gracious lawns, and trim workingmen's cottages became the trademarks of the city. As the outer areas of the city developed in the late nineteenth century, Detroit became known as a city of single-family homes. The district within the boulevard encircling the city—Grand Boulevard—filled in first; and by 1900 settlement stretched far beyond it as real-estate agents platted subdivisions and builders constructed blocks of one- and two-story cottages. As the city grew rapidly, so did the areas with little frame houses and postage-stamp-sized "open grass plots in front." Detroit at any time between 1870 and 1915 was "considered to be one of the best examples of the modern American city."[1]

The electric railroad altered the pattern of Detroit city life. Before the 1880s the path of residences had progressively inched out from the core of the city, creating truncated arcs of settlement on the city's outskirts. Coincidentally, streetcars lessened the time and inconvenience of travel while the city was undergoing a great population increase. Land developers reacted quickly, and streets once beyond the realm of reasonable traveling distance from Detroit's core were now within the streetcar city. Settlement jumped out to the boulevard, and realtors developed the areas previously left vacant, such as those adjacent to Woodward Avenue. While the city's older families tended to remain in their Woodward and Jefferson Avenue mansions, the newspapers recognized that the better classes of people were moving to the ring areas of the city, settling on the boulevard and slightly north of it, as well as filling in vacant areas within the ring. Although industrial workers tended to live near the factories where

---

[1] J. W. Sullivan, "Detroit in the Van," *American Federationist*, II (December, 1895), 188; Great Britain, *Parliamentary Papers* (Commons), "Cost of Living in American Towns: Report of an Enquiry by the Board of Trade," 1911, 88: 173–181.

they worked, men in commerce, trade, and the professions found it no hardship, and indeed considered it beneficial, to escape the density, pollution, decay, and ethnic colonies of the core areas of the city. Distance was no longer a barrier since the streetcar had brought all points in the city closer together.[2]

The shift in population from the core of the city to the ring areas occurred at the time of Detroit's greatest population expansion. In 1884 Detroit's population was recorded at 132,956; six years later, in 1890, there were 205,876 people crowded within the city's borders. The movement to new subdivisions created vacant housing in the city's core, and foreign-language-speaking immigrants and other new arrivals found the vacated neighborhoods conveniently located, though not always reasonably priced nor warmly inviting. Nonetheless, the poorer classes—mostly black and foreign-born—settled in the once stylish neighborhoods within the center of the city, competing with commerce and trade for shelter and space in the city's oldest districts.

Detroit, like most American cities, was a conglomeration of ethnic and racial neighborhoods. In the 1860s, 1870s, and 1880s, Corktown, Dutchtown, Kentucky, Polacktown, and Piety Hill were common community names in Detroit. By the turn of the century less explicitly descriptive epithets would be used, but Detroiters still could identify the east side with the Irish, the St. Antoine district with Negroes, Gratiot with Germans, Hastings with Polish and Russian Jews, Hamtramck with Poles, and Paradise Valley with Italians. Neighborhoods were the benchmarks of late nineteenth-century Detroit; neither wards nor blocks were the living units of the city. Ethnic and racial groups clustered together in colonies whose areas overlapped and whose outermost limits were sometimes the same. Most Detroiters, certainly the poor but also the middle class, either by choice, necessity, or because of discrimination, sought people similar to themselves.

The ties of birth, culture, and language that bound together an ethnic colony also served as barriers to intergroup contact. Thus, within a common geographical area, ethnic and racial populations developed autonomous social systems. Overlapping and integrated,

[2] The real-estate columns of the *Detroit Tribune* from 1885–1895 reported this shift.

these small societies were the major components of Detroit life. The
result was that nineteenth-century Detroit was a mosaic of racial,
religious, and language groups. The locus of each overlapping tile
could be determined by a church, saloon, or group of stores, but each
district was diverse and mixed. The near east side of Detroit, from
Woodward to DeQuindre, from the Detroit River to the city limits,
reflected this ethnic mosaic.[3]

Detroit's near east side served as a port of entry and stopping-off
place for much of the city's foreign-born population. First the French,
then some of the Irish, and in their turn the Germans formed their
communities on the near east side. Later, in the 1880s and after, the
new immigrant groups—the Poles, Jews, Italians, Greeks, and Ru-
manians—repeated the pattern of the previous immigrants and settled
within the first few wards east of Woodward.

The French were the oldest ethnic group in the city. Originally
they had clustered near the river east of Woodward, but with the
post–Civil War expansion of the city, many of the French, mostly
second- and third-generation Americans, moved further east within
the city, close to many of the city's well-paying factories. The poorer
class of French, however, remained in the decaying waterfront district, which they shared with poorer Negroes and, after 1885, with
some poor Italians. The 1890s were the watershed of relatively large-

---

[3] The church, especially the Roman Catholic Church, was important in the
maintenance of ethnicity. In Newburyport, W. Lloyd Warner and Leo Srole
noted that "national differences are frequently and explicitly recognized in
reference to: (1) the national saints . . . ; (2) the traditions of the national
church; and (3) the national aspects of the national church's priesthood." For
many ethnic minorities, such as the Greeks, Armenians, Poles, French Canadians,
and Jews, who had lived within alien cultures in their native land, "their one
semblance of national organization . . . appeared in the only organized sub-system
of the group—the church." Warner and Srole, *The Social Systems of American
Ethnic Groups* (New Haven, Conn., 1945), pp. 156–157. In Detroit's near east
side, the French-language St. Joachim's and the Polish-language St. Albertus,
Sweetest Heart of Mary, and St. Josephat all marked the locations of ethnic
colonies. Later the synagogues Shaarey Zadek, Beth Jacob, B'Nai Israel, and
B'Nai David indicated the Jewish Hastings area, as the Church of San Francisco
announced the Italian quarter. Michigan Historical Records Survey, *Inven-
tory of the Church Archives of Michigan: The Roman Catholic Church,
Archdiocese of Detroit* (Detroit, 1941), pp. 8, 81, 82, 83, 89; Michigan Historical
Records Survey, *Inventory of the Church and Synagogue Archives of Michigan:
Jewish Bodies* (Detroit, 1940), pp. 15, 19, 20, 22, 24.

scale Italian migration to the city, and Paradise Valley, near the river, was the first Italian colony. A decade later a second colony north of Gratiot was founded. As Italian migration increased during the first fifteen years of the twentieth century, the two sections fused into one district.[4]

The Germans were the largest single foreign-language immigrant group in Detroit, and from 1870 to 1900 the Germans comprised one-third of the foreign-born population.[5] The beer gardens and lager establishments so prominent in nineteenth-century Detroit led some to view the city as a German *Staat*. The Germans seemed to "Americanize" and assimilate more easily than any of the other foreign-language groups, and they were greeted as an "industrious, thrifty, substantial and welcome class of immigrants." Although the Germans could be found throughout the city, the center of German life remained Gratiot Avenue or "Little Berlin." As a group, the Germans seemed to be better established and more upwardly mobile than most immigrant groups, and their neat workingmen's cottages were what most visitors saw when they adjudged Detroit a modern, progressive city of single-family homes. Well-to-do second-generation German-Americans—the more successful tradesmen and professionals—moved into the ranks of the city's upper classes. Less successful Germans

---

[4] *Eleventh Census 1890*, vol. 4, part II (Washington, 1896), pp. 219–221; *Detroit Sunday News-Tribune*, Sept. 6, 1896, p. 1; *Detroit News-Tribune*, Aug. 21, 1904, Supplement, p. 4; Gilbert Anderson, "A Study in Italian Residence Succession in Detroit, Michigan," (1935), typewritten copy in the Bureau of Government Library, University of Michigan, pp. 6, 7, Sheet I: Data; Lois Rankin, "Detroit Nationality Groups," *Michigan History Magazine*, XXIII (Spring, 1939), pp. 154–155; *Eleventh Census 1890*, vol. 4, part II, pp. 219–221; *Detroit News-Tribune*, Aug. 21, 1904, Supplement, p. 4.

[5] Albert Mayer, "A Study of the Foreign-Born Population of Detroit, 1870–1950," (1951), mimeographed paper in the Michigan Historical Collections, University of Michigan. The board of trade *Report* in 1909 noted that the great bulk of German immigrants "has become Americanized to such a degree that purely German institutions, such as churches, schools, press &c., do not appear to flourish." This is an exaggerated statement, but the Americanization programs of World War I made it true. The result has been that historians have overlooked the German element, the largest ethnic group in many American cities. The only broad study of Detroit's ethnic groups omits the Germans as does Glazer's and Moynihan's classic study of New York. Lois Rankin, "Detroit Nationality Groups," pp. 129–205; Nathan Glazer and Daniel Moynihan, *Beyond the Melting Pot* (Cambridge, Mass., 1963).

lived in Detroit's poorer sections and could be found, along with other ethnic and racial groups, rooming in subdivided houses or living among the warehouses near the river or in dilapidated small wooden tenements on the near east side.[6]

After the 1880s the Poles became the most visible ethnic group in Detroit, growing in population from approximately 27,000 in 1884 to an estimated 90,000 to 120,000 in 1909–1910. In the 1880s east-side Poles lived in a part of the Kentucky district, and the Polish population extended in a northeasterly direction from Indiana and St. Antoine streets. Before the turn of the century other Polish settlements could be found on the city's west side, close to the heavy industries. First employed as unskilled laborers in the city's construction trades, the Poles rapidly entered the railroad-car industry in the late 1890s and eventually moved into Detroit's new automobile industry. Heavy industry was outside of the city's core in the nineteenth and early twentieth centuries, and many Poles, following their jobs, settled nearby in one- and two-family row cottages. Unlike the Germans, the Poles tended to resist assimilation; a 1911 report described them as "yield[ing] much more slowly to American habits of life and speech."[7]

Woven into the east-side fabric of ethnic diversity was the city's Jewish population. In the late nineteenth century, as Jewish migration increased, the path of settlement of the city's Jews meandered into the side streets off St. Antoine, Hastings, and Rivard north of Gratiot. The texture of Jewish life in Detroit changed radically after the 1890s as the poorer and more ethnically aware Russian and Polish Jews began to arrive in large numbers. Jewish settlement after the turn of the century moved progressively northward toward Grand Boulevard, reflecting the increased affluence of many in the community.

[6] *Cost of Living in American Towns*, p. 173; *Detroit Post & Tribune*, Mar. 31, 1883, p. 2; *Detroit Sunday News-Tribune*, Oct. 21, 1894, p. 14; clipping, Feb. 3, 1896, in Friend Palmer's Scrapbook, II, 219–221 Burton Historical Collection; *Detroit News-Tribune*, Aug. 21, 1904, Supplement, p. 4; 1870 and 1880 manuscript censuses of Detroit.

[7] Sister Mary Remigia Napolska, "The Polish Immigrant in Detroit to 1914," *Annals of the Polish R.C. Union Archives and Museum*, X (1945–1946), 25, 30–31, 35; *Detroit Tribune*, Jan. 3, 1888, p. 4; *Detroit News-Tribune*, Aug. 21, 1904, Supplement, p. 4; *Cost of Living in American Towns*, p. 173.

Unlike the similarly upwardly mobile Germans, the Jews tended to remain clustered within a tightly woven ethnic community.[8]

As the source of migrants to America shifted from northern and western to southern and eastern Europe, new groups of immigrants came to Detroit. By 1910 the number of foreign-born in the city from Poland, Russia, Italy, Greece, and Hungary had surpassed the number of foreign-born from Britain, Ireland, and Germany. The tone and texture of the city's core changed as most of the older groups moved to the ring areas of the city while the newer migrants found shelter within the streets and blocks vacated by the working and middle classes of the old immigrant groups. Foreign-language churches became more prevalent than English-language churches on the city's near east side, and small shops provided a flavor of the old world. As the more affluent tended to move out of the area, only the poorer and downwardly mobile individuals remained. Money or spirit that might have led to the renewal of these areas was thus drained into the new, bright, single-family home tracts of the ring areas.[9]

Amid the changing ethnic and racial character of Detroit's near east side, the presence of most of the city's black population represented one of the few stable factors. Before the Civil War, Detroit's small black population had clustered in the area bounded by Randolph Street on the west to Hastings Street on the east, and by Gratiot on the north to the river on the south. Within a half-mile radius of Campus Martius lived most of Detroit's blacks, either in the waterfront district south of Jefferson or in the residential zone near the Negro churches. During the decade of the 1860s, when the black population increased nearly 60 percent, reaching 2,235 in 1870, blacks settled in relatively large numbers in the Kentucky district, twenty blocks north of Gratiot and St. Antoine. Detroit's black population scattered among mostly foreign-born whites within a narrow strip extending northward from the river; the area ranged from Randolph and Beaubien on the west to DeQuindre on the east and from the river on the

---

[8] *Detroit Post & Tribune*, Mar. 31, 1883, p. 2; Michigan Historical Records Survey, *Jewish Bodies*, pp. 11, 15, 19, 20, 22, 24; *Detroit Sunday News-Tribune*, Sept. 6, 1896, p. 1, Sept. 13, 1896, p. 13. There was also a group of Hungarian Jews on the west side in Delray. See Rankin, "Detroit Nationality Groups," pp. 147, 149.

[9] Mayer, "A Study of the Foreign-Born Population of Detroit," p. 24.

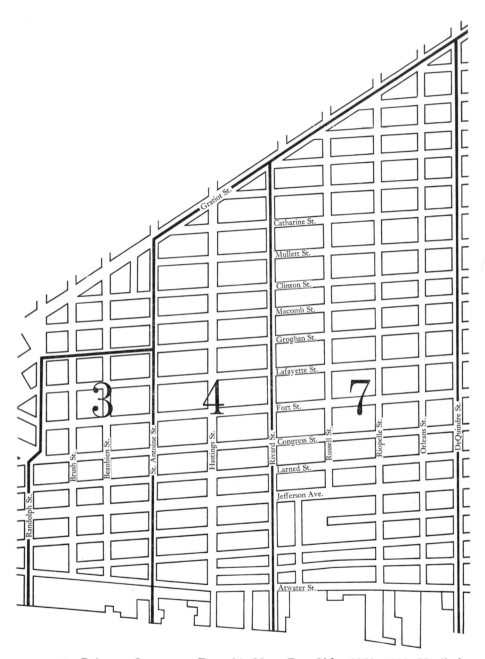

MAP 1 *Primary Streets on Detroit's Near East Side, 1850–1900. Until the redistricting of 1881 all of wards 3, 4, and 7 were within this district. Sometime after 1874 Lafayette Street was renamed Champlain.*

south to the edge of settlement short of the city limits on the north. In 1870 this area, Detroit's near east side, contained 84.7 percent of the city's blacks; in 1900, 84.5 percent; and in 1910, 84.8 percent.[10]

Throughout the late nineteenth century Detroit's black population was small in relation to the other ethnic groups. In 1870 black Detroit comprised only 2,235 people, or less than 3 percent of the city's total population. In the ensuing thirty years as the black population of the United States gradually began its shift to urban and northern areas, black Detroit increased nearly twofold, numbering 4,111 in 1900. The percentage of Negroes in Detroit declined, however, dropping to 1.4 percent in 1900 as the city as a whole grew from 80,000 population in 1870 to 280,000 in 1900.

In-migration provided much of black Detroit's population increase,

[10] This analysis of the Negro area, its boundaries and location, owes much to the research of Steven Serlin. He first identified this district in his senior honors thesis, "The Negroes in Detroit in the 1880's and Early 1890's," Department of History, University of Michigan, 1968. My information on the 1880 black population, unless otherwise noted, is derived from Serlin's file-index compiled from the 1880 manuscript census.

All of the data in this chapter are based on the decennial federal census, both the published aggregations and, when available, the enumerated manuscript schedules (1870, 1880). It is important to note, however, that the data at best are only a poor estimate. The undercount of Negroes in the South has long been noted, but the question of accuracy of the black count in the North has been neglected. A number of factors arose out of my work on the census that clearly revealed the schedules' weaknesses. A small number of blacks, mostly servants and waiters, were counted both at work and at home, and a few families were counted twice. The latter was most typical before the 1870 census when United States marshals served as enumerators and they were paid per head counted. Even more important, a larger number of blacks—possibly higher than 10 percent—were never enumerated. City directories, newspapers, court records, and association records indicate that a large number of Detroit black residents, or transients, at the time of the census were neglected. This category includes much of the criminal element, day laborers, alley dwellers, and probably those not home at the time. It is also possible that many census enumerators might have been hesitant to enter some of the notorious alleys and miserable dwellings that so often housed blacks. Another group, a few members of the black upper class, were occasionally designated "white" in the enumerated schedules, although the newspapers of the time make it clear that they were not passing. See Francis A. Walker, "Statistics of the Colored Race in the United States," *Publications of the American Statistical Association*, N.S., 11, 12 (September-December, 1890), 91–96; U.S. Bureau of the Census, *Negro Population 1790–1915*, pp. 26–28. For more recent periods see Reynolds Farley, "The Quality of Demographic Data for Nonwhites," *Demography*, V (1968), 1–10.

and Negroes came both from the surrounding region and from the South to settle in Detroit. A sizable proportion of the blacks in Detroit in the late nineteenth century were of foreign birth, nearly all of them migrants to Detroit from the Canadian hinterland. The federal census of 1870, taken after a decade of repatriation of American-born blacks and their Canadian-born offspring, recorded that 15.2 percent of Detroit's colored population was of foreign birth (see table 7). Of the 340 foreign-born, 325 or over 95 percent had been born in British America, and probably all of them were the Canadian-born children of Afro-American fugitive slaves or emigrationists who

TABLE 5   *Negro and Non-Negro Population,*
Detroit 1850–1910

Year	Negro	Non–Negro	Total
1850	587	19,845	20,432
1860	1,402	44,217	45,619
1870	2,235	77,342	79,577
1880	2,821	113,519	116,340
1890	3,431	202,445	205,876
1900	4,111	281,593	285,704
1910	5,741	460,025	465,766

SOURCES: *Ninth Census 1870*, I, 176 (for 1850, 1860, 1870); *Tenth Census 1880*, I, 420; *Eleventh Census 1890*, vol. I, part 1, p. 464; *Twelfth Census 1900*, vol. I, part 1, p. 661; *Thirteenth Census 1910*, II, 953.

TABLE 6   *Percentage Change in Detroit Negro Population 1850–1910*

Year	Negroes	Percentage Increase	Negroes in Detroit, %	Negroes in Michigan in Detroit, %
1850	587		2.9	23.7
		235.0		
1860	1,402		3.1	20.6
		59.3		
1870	2,235		2.8	23.8
		26.2		
1880	2,821		2.4	18.7
		21.6		
1890	3,431		1.7	22.5
		19.8		
1900	4,111		1.4	26.0
		39.6		
1910	5,741		1.2	33.5

TABLE 7 *Place of Birth of Detroit Negro Residents, 1870*

	Number	*Percent*	*Born in Other States, %*
Total population	2,235		
Foreign-born	340	15.2	
Native-born	1,895	84.8	
Born in Michigan	670	30.0	
Born in other states	1,225	54.8	100.0
Virginia and W. Virginia	338	15.1	27.6
Kentucky	302	13.4	24.6
Ohio	101	4.5	8.3
New York	66	3.0	5.4
Maryland	64	2.9	5.2
Tennessee	48	2.2	3.9
Indiana	35	1.6	2.9
All other states	271	12.1	22.1

SOURCE: *Ninth Census 1870*, I, 380–391.

had lived in the black utopian communities that had sprouted on the western Ontario frontier. A large number of these families had returned to the United States by the end of the Civil War, but a substantial community, nonetheless, remained in Ontario. In 1910, long after most of the Canadian-born blacks recorded in the 1870 census had either left the city or died, 904 black residents of Detroit or 15.8 percent of the city's Negro population had been born outside of the United States. Assuming that virtually all of them had been born in Canada, their presence in Detroit reflects that they were part of the steady stream of migrants who had come to Detroit out of the city's large hinterland in Canada and the neighboring states. In the late nineteenth century, blacks from Windsor, Chatham, and London, Ontario, and the adjacent rural communities joined the ceaseless flow of youths into Detroit, the city with the largest black population in the area. Canadian-born Negroes in nineteenth-century Detroit included Drs. Albert and William Johnson, Windsor-born brothers, and Chatham-born Michigan State Representative Joseph H. Dickinson, as well as many young servants, waiters, stevedores, and day laborers who came to the Michigan city in search of their fortunes.[11]

[11] Francis H. Warren (comp.), *Michigan Manual of Freedmen's Progress* (Detroit, 1915), pp. 53–54 (hereafter cited as *Freedmen's Progress*); *Michigan*

In 1870, 28.5 percent of Detroit's black population had been born in Virginia and Kentucky, and they represented 52.2 percent of the native-born blacks born outside of Michigan. In the next three decades, the proportion of southern-born Negroes in Michigan's population—and it is presumed for Detroit—declined. From 1870 to 1900, while Michigan's total black population rose 33.5 percent, from 11,849 to 15,816 people, the number of southern-born blacks diminished by 29.5 percent, from 3,752 to 2,647. From 1900 to 1910, however, the trend was reversed as the number of southern-born in Michigan's Negro population increased 9.4 percent in that decade. Presumably Detroit absorbed nearly all of these in-migrants since the outstate areas' black population declined 2.8 percent while the Detroit community grew nearly 40 percent.[12]

Though most of Michigan's southern-born blacks at the turn of the century were long-time residents of the state a selective but important migration of southern Negroes to Detroit had occurred in the 1880s and 1890s. Until about 1870 most of the southern-born blacks in Detroit had come from Kentucky or the cities of Virginia. Many of them, especially those born in Virginia, had come to Detroit as children with their parents. The result was that by 1900 a great many of the southern-born blacks had no memory of any place but Detroit. In the 1880s and 1890s, however, a small vanguard of blacks began to leave the cities of the South for Michigan and other northern states. Disillusioned as well as personally threatened by the deprivation of black rights and potential political oblivion that accompanied the end of Reconstruction, a small number of well-educated southern black leaders came to Detroit. Born in the West Indies and educated at Howard University, D. Augustus Straker had held elective office in South Carolina and had been the dean of law at Allen University in Columbia. Disheartened by the turn of events in the 1880s, he left the South for Detroit. Charles R. Roxborough, an attorney who was born in Cleveland but moved to New Orleans with his parents after the Civil War, came to Detroit in the 1890s. A graduate of Straight University in New Orleans, Roxborough had three

State Manual 1897–1898, p. 647; U.S. Bureau of the Census, *Negro Population 1790–1915*, p. 74.

[12] *Negro Population 1790–1915*, p. 68.

times been elected city attorney of Plaquemine, Louisiana, and had
also served as an assistant United States attorney in Tennessee before
growing discrimination led him to migrate northward. Physician
James W. Ames, a graduate of both Straight University and Howard
University and a teacher in New Orleans, came to Detroit in 1894
and later served in the Michigan legislature. Other blacks, such as
engineer John B. Lyle, Dr. A. L. Turner, and attorneys Lindsay E.
Johnson, Benjamin F. Lester, and William Hayes McKinney, received
their preliminary higher education in the South and attended professional schools in Michigan. Once in the state, they decided to remain
there.[13]

Detroit also attracted blacks from the surrounding areas. Like the
small-town and rural Negroes from western Ontario who sought out
economic opportunities in urban Michigan, blacks from the villages
and rural townships of Michigan and northern Ohio were drawn to
the city on the straits. Some worked in Michigan's seasonal industries
—mining, lumbering, and shipping; they sought temporary winter
employment in the city, returning to their primary occupations in the
North with the spring thaw. An indeterminate proportion came as
part of the centuries-old drift from hinterland to metropolitan city.
Young, single, and adventurous, they were the boarders and roomers
on Detroit's near east side. A few among them were relatively well
educated, arriving in the city with advanced degrees or seeking them
in Detroit's colleges and professional schools. Charles H. Mahoney,
born in Decatur, Michigan, and a graduate of Olivet College and the
University of Michigan Law School, came to Detroit after 1900. Robert C. Barnes, born in Mercer City, Ohio, and educated in his native
state, came to Detroit to start his own law practice. Mercer City,
presumably, had limited opportunities for a young black attorney.[14]

Still others came to Detroit because of family ties. Close relatives
would find Detroit attractive once a brother, sister, or cousin had
met with success in the city. The promise of marriage, whether
actual engagement or the distant hope of winning a mate, also brought

[13] *Detroit Tribune*, Aug. 6, 1887, p. 3; clipping, n.d., in C.M. Burton Scrapbook, XXX, 1, 6, Burton Historical Collection, Detroit Public Library; *Freedmen's Progress*, pp. 47–54, 85.

[14] *Freedmen's Progress*, pp. 45, 47, 48.

many young men and women to Detroit. Negroes in surrounding rural communities or in smaller Michigan cities such as Ann Arbor, Bay City, Lansing, Saginaw, and Ypsilanti had only a small number of possible mates to choose from, and the social whirl of black Detroit must have seemed exciting. A less desirable group migrating into the city was the traditional lowest stratum of society who found survival possible only in large cities. Whether it was London, Paris, New York, or Detroit, they joined the local world of vice and crime. Mostly white, but occasionally black, they were unwanted in all the big cities.[15]

Not all of Detroit's blacks remained in Detroit. Although more Negroes came to Detroit than were lost through emigration, some were not satisfied with the city. A few, aggressive and ambitious, sought other northern cities whose large Negro communities offered greater opportunities and a larger economic market than Detroit did. Detroit-born Jesse Binga wandered from place to place as an itinerant barber until his ambitions were fulfilled by the founding of the Binga Bank in Chicago in 1908. E. Franklin Frazier recorded a typical pattern in recounting the case history of the father of a Chicago school teacher. He had migrated to Detroit in the late nineteenth century, Frazier related, "from the small towns in Ontario, Canada, because wages were better and work more plentiful in the larger cities." Then, at the turn of the century he moved on to Chicago, "because it was larger than Detroit." Other blacks, similarly, simply outgrew Detroit. The political and public-service career of Robert A. Pelham, Jr., inevitably led him out of the state. A leading Negro Republican, Pelham found the opportunities limited in Detroit, and he left the city in 1900 to become a census clerk in Washington.[16]

[15] The Detroit *Plaindealer* reported on the social life of blacks in Detroit and its hinterland, and even the endless reports from the Michigan and Ontario small towns reveal the prominent role of black Detroit as a focus of social life for the entire region.

[16] Allan H. Spear, *Black Chicago: The Making of a Negro Ghetto 1890–1920* (Chicago, 1967), p. 74; E. Franklin Frazier, *The Negro Family in Chicago* (Chicago, 1932), p. 129; *Freedmen's Progress*, p. 91. Thus it is clear that, even during the period when the level of Michigan's black population remained around 15,000 in the 1880s and 1890s, it cannot be considered a stable group. Not only did shifts take place within the state, but there was a continuous out-migration as well as in-migration. In the 1880s, for instance, while Detroit's black

Detroit's near east side absorbed the city's increase in black population in the late nineteenth century. Throughout the period, the decennial census recorded no less than 83 percent of all blacks in Detroit
living within this area (see table 8). Blacks were even more heavily

TABLE 8 *Concentration of Detroit Negroes in the Near
East Side, 1860–1910*

Year	Detroit Negroes in Near East Side,* %	Percentage of Negroes in Area's Total Population
1860	82.5	5.2
1870	84.3	5.8
1880	83.0	5.6
1890	84.4	5.0
1900	84.5	5.0
1910	84.8	4.8

* Near east side: 1860, 1870—wards three, four, seven, six; 1880—
wards three, four, seven, six, eleven; 1890, 1900, 1910—wards one,
three, five, seven.

concentrated than ward statistics would indicate. In 1880, for instance,
the concentration of black residences in the near east side was even
greater than the 83 percent concentration of population. In wards
one and two in 1880 the census recorded 125 blacks as residents there,
yet eighty-two of them were waiters or servants who lived where
they worked. In the same year sixty blacks were recorded in the
fifth ward's population, yet fifty-seven were servants who lived in
their employers' households; the remaining three, including two law
students, were in boarding houses.

While the proportion of blacks to whites within the near east side
declined only slightly from 1870 to 1910, the district as a whole did

population rose 21.6 percent, Michigan total Negro population rose less than
1 percent, the outstate population declined 4 percent, and the state experienced
a negative rate of black net migration. Out-migration was also a characteristic of
periods of population increase: from 1900 to 1910, while the state's black population rose from 15,816 to 17,115, the number of Michigan-born Negroes living
in other states also increased, from 3,036 in 1900 to 3,384 in 1910. Simon Kuznets
and Dorothy Swaine Thomas, *Population Redistribution and Economic Growth
United States 1870–1950*, I: Everett S. Lee, Ann Ratner Miller, Carol P. Brainerd,
and Richard A. Easterlin, *Methodological Considerations and Reference Tables*
(Philadelphia, 1957), pp. 158–159; U.S. Bureau of the Census, *Negro Population
1790–1915*, p. 71.

TABLE 9 *Detroit Negro Population, by Ward, 1860–1910*

Year	West Side				East Side						
	9	8	5	1	2	3	4	7	6	11	10
1860	68	17	52	61	15	326	373	267	191		32
1870	32	7	54	83	49	183	464	553	683		127
1880		17	60	72	53	161	480	401	419	878	

(Ward)

Year	West Side												East Side					
	18	16	14	12	10	8	6	4	2	1	3	5	7	9	11	13	15	17
1890		42	38	52	17	30	22	56	75	532	1,379	602	381	150	31	13	11	
1900		85	44	24	22	41	44	57	108	434	1,855	812	374	119	30	40	18	4
1910	39	36	62	65	29	39	29	100	96	550	2,744	1,177	399	202	67	37	20	50

SOURCE: 1860–1870, 1890–1910—see table 5; 1880—manuscript census, 1880.

not keep pace with the city's large population expansion. The growth of residential ring areas in Detroit, following the development of electric street railways in the 1880s, and the development of satellite industrial communities in the city's eastern and western extremes caused a relative decline in population of the near east side. In 1870, 40.9 percent of Detroit's population lived in the area, but by 1910 only 21.7 percent of the city's people lived within the near east side's four wards. Despite this percentage decline, the number of people in the district increased during this period. In 1870 the area had 32,546 inhabitants and by 1880, though the zone was becoming increasingly commercial in the river end, the recent German migration had raised the population to 41,804. Thereafter, as population extended northward to the city's limits, and successive waves of immigrants made Detroit's near east side their home, the population soared. In 1890 there were 58,227 people living within the four-ward area; in 1900 the total reached 69,630; and in 1910 the new southern and eastern European migration pushed the population to 100,920.

Detroit's near east side was not homogeneous. Ethnic and racial groups mingled throughout the area, and many of the boarding and lodging houses in the zone catered to both blacks and whites. Often a semiskilled or unskilled immigrant worker lived next door to a Negro family, and tenements in the area frequently housed a variety of races and nationalities. An examination of the 1880 federal manuscript census of Detroit confirms that, even in the areas of highest Negro concentration, blacks and whites lived next to one another. In 1880, Macomb Street, between Riopelle and Orleans, had the greatest number of black residences on one street in the city—seventeen of its twenty-six residences were occupied by Negroes—but no other facing block fronts in Detroit had more than twelve black families. (See figure 1.) Even on Macomb Street, 35 percent of the residences were occupied by white families. Of the ten dwellings with whites, nine housed families with foreign-born members.[17]

Although blacks lived within a white milieu, they concentrated within small clusterings and, in most cases, lived at least a few doors away from other blacks, if they did not share the same dwelling or

[17] Serlin, "The Negroes in Detroit in the 1880's and Early 1890's," pp. 5–6.

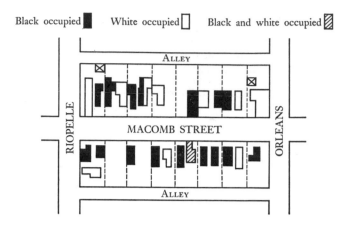

Black occupied ■   White occupied □   Black and white occupied ▨

FIGURE 1   *Residences Occupied by Blacks and Whites on Macomb Street, Detroit 1880.*

one adjoining that of another black man. In 1880 within the third and fourth wards—a sixty-four-block area—more than half the blacks in the wards lived in a zone of eight contiguous blocks between Fort and Catherine and St. Antoine and Hastings, and between Croghan and Clinton and Beaubien and St. Antoine. Even within this area blacks lived in small, heavily concentrated clusters. At 55–65 Mullet Street, between St. Antoine and Hastings, sixty-one blacks lived in five adjoining houses; at 56–66 Clinton Street, between Beaubien and St. Antoine, thirty-two Negroes lived in four of five contiguous houses; at 61–65 Croghan Street, between Beaubien and St. Antoine, twenty-three blacks lived in three connected houses; at 126–140 Lafayette Street, between St. Antoine and Hastings, thirty-six blacks lived in seven of eight adjoining houses; and at 183–191 Hastings, between Croghan and Lafayette, twenty-seven blacks lived in five contiguous dwellings. Thus more than half of the blacks in the eight-block area lived in only twenty-five of the more than 350 dwelling units in the area, and nearly a third of the blacks in the third and fourth wards who lived apart from their work lived in less than 1 percent of the housing available.[18]

The high concentration of blacks in a relatively small number of

[18] Blacks comprised 6.6 percent of the two wards' population.

dwelling units reflected, at least in part, the economically marginal life style of lower-class blacks. In the residential areas in which black day laborers and those in personal service could find housing, as in Detroit's third and fourth wards in 1880, single-family residences were the exception rather than the rule. Overall in these two near east side wards, forty-seven of the seventy-five black residences either boarded lodgers (twenty-five) or were multifamily dwellings (twenty-two). This held true as well in the Kentucky region north of Gratiot. Of sixteen black residences on Kentucky and Indiana streets in census enumeration district 309 in 1880, only four were single-family dwellings. As the census enumerator moved away from these focal streets, either northward or southward, he found that, among the black middle-class areas, single-family homes were the rule not the exception. Census district 305, between Gratiot Avenue and the Kentucky area, revealed that thirty-six of the forty-seven black-occupied dwellings contained only one family and no boarders. Similarly, all the black homes in the fashionable upper-class Negro district on Congress Street East were single-family dwellings.

In general, Detroit's near east side from the river to the Kentucky district was a relatively unattractive area. Although neat single-family cottages were the trademark of Detroit, small, wooden, two-family tenements and "shambling old sheds . . . propped and stayed by boards and stakes"—alley houses—seemed to dominate the near east side. In 1883 the Detroit Association of Charities reported that 70 percent of its cases were east of Woodward, most of them in this district of decaying and dilapidated buildings. The newspapers referred to the district as a "plague spot."[19]

In the 1870s and 1880s the sector south of Jefferson Avenue contained mostly poor Negroes, Frenchmen, and some Italians. It contained the notorious Potomac Quarter, once Detroit's vice area but by 1880 only a center for thieves and prostitutes. After 1880 the zone became more commercial as small factories and businesses spread northward from the river. By the turn of the century only the poor-

[19] Clipping, "Streets of Detroit," n.d., in C. M. Burton Scrapbook, III, 5, Burton Historical Collection, Detroit Public Library; Detroit Association of Charities, *Annual Report 1883* (Detroit, 1884), p. 13; *Detroit Post*, Dec. 17, 1884, p. 6.

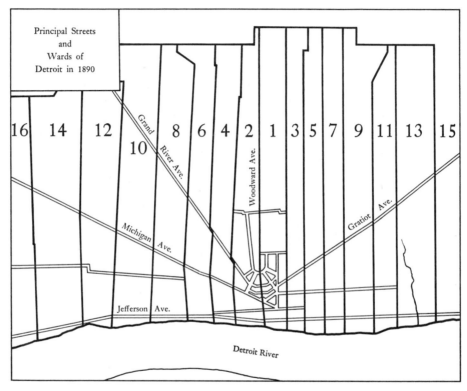

MAP 2 *Principal Streets and Wards of Detroit in 1890. Most blacks lived in wards 1, 3, 5, 7, and 9, the majority in the old "Near East Side" south of Gratiot Avenue.*

est Negroes, French, and Italians remained; the area had seen little of new building construction in a quarter of a century.[20]

The sector between Jefferson and Gratiot changed radically between 1870 and 1910. In the early years of the period it had contained many prime residential dwellings. The better class of whites and Negroes had lived on Fort, Larned, and Congress streets, adjacent to the eastern boundaries of the district, but by 1900 only a few of the older families remained. The area near Beaubien, "the Heights," was a major vice district, and many poor Negroes and immigrants lived in its decaying houses and tiny alleys. The once fashionable but now obsolete large wooden buildings were easily converted to multifamily dwellings, and the wide service alleys in the area north of Congress served also as housing sites. After 1880, as more immigrants moved into the area around Hastings in the center of the zone, well-to-do Negroes moved among the predominantly German streets near Gratiot, and by 1910 many had again moved into the upper reaches of the near east side.[21]

The blocks between Gratiot Avenue and the Kentucky district were populated mostly by the middle class. Tree-lined streets within a brief walk of Campus Martius had, at an early date, attracted many of the near east side's middle-class residents. In the 1870s the area was predominantly German; thereafter, "the better classes of the colored people" and Jews moved in among the Germans. Thus when St. Matthew's Protestant Episcopal Church was reorganized in 1880, the new brick church edifice was erected in the district at St. Antoine and Elizabeth streets. Similarly, Bethel AME moved to the corner of Napoleon and Hastings in 1889.[22]

Above the Gratiot district was "Kentucky." Negroes and the poorer Poles predominated in the area. They lived in small frame houses on small building lots on Kentucky, Indiana, and Illinois streets, between St. Antoine and Hastings. The crowded, wooden dwellings contrasted

---

[20] *Eleventh Census 1890*, vol. 4, part II, pp. 219–222.

[21] *Detroit Tribune*, Mar. 1, 1889, p. 4. The patterns discussed in this and the following paragraphs describe the general trend of black household clustering. The small number of blacks and their presence within a larger white population prevented the development of clearly demarcated *neighborhoods* with accompanying local institutions.

[22] *Detroit Post & Tribune*, Mar. 31, 1883, p. 2.

sharply with the area developed a few blocks to the west, on the other side of Russell Street. Part of the fashionable Woodward Avenue district, the blocks west of Russell were the site of large brick dwellings built on relatively spacious city lots. The open space which characterized these areas contrasted sharply with the crowded buildings of the Kentucky district.[23]

The northern areas of Detroit's near east side, above Kentucky, were opened to settlement by the development of the streetcar in the late 1880s. Streetcar tracks ran up Randolph to Catherine, then up Brush to Rowena, and then up St. Antoine, tying together the northern reaches of Beaubien, St. Antoine, and Hastings with the southern sector. Wealthier Negroes and the well-to-do among other ethnic groups settled on the northern suburban blocks, commuting southward to work. Mostly professionals, tradesmen, and white-collar workers filled the newly developed streets north of Kentucky.

For most of the poor, especially Negroes, alley dwellings were the curse of the lower end of Detroit's near east side. Nearly all the blocks between Jefferson and Gratiot were bisected by service alleys, originally designed to facilitate the removal of ashes, rubbish, and garbage, to provide access to stables, and to serve as a right of way for sewage systems. In the 1860s and 1870s some tenements were constructed in the alleys, and they were generally notorious for vice and misery. Close's Alley, a mostly colored quarter off East Fort Street, known for its filth and its immoral denizens, scandalized and terrorized much of the surrounding population in the 1870s and 1880s.[24] By the late nineteenth and early twentieth centuries, alleys were less known for their vice but had become more notorious for their misery.

Neither the alleys nor the dwellings in them were well suited to human habitation. The better-quality alley dwellings were erected as two-family wooden tenements that deteriorated soon after construction. The poorest Negroes were "found in the worst class of tenements"; most commonly these houses were of makeshift character, as former sheds and stables were converted into one-, two-, and three-family dwellings. Although the Fort, Congress, and Larned

[23] *Detroit Tribune*, Jan. 3, 1888, p. 4.
[24] *Detroit Post*, May 5, 1885, p. 5; *Detroit Tribune*, May 22, 1886, p. 4.

area contained most of the alley dwellings, by 1900 many had been constructed north of Gratiot in the region between Beaubien and Hastings. Because of the strong competitive pressure for housing in Detroit's near east side, Negroes and poor immigrants paid exorbitant rents for sheds and stables. In 1911 an alley house between Hastings and Rivard, occupied by two families and as many boarders and lodgers as they could secure, rented for $18 a month. Another alley dwelling a few blocks away, "built of rough boards in the chicken coop style of architecture," rented for $10 monthly. By comparison, in working-class areas in Detroit in 1909, older six-room dwellings fully serviced by utilities rented for $10 to $12 monthly, and new dwellings rented for $18 to $22 monthly. Still being used as garbage dumping grounds in 1911, and without any service facilities, the alleys were a serious health menace. Unsuccessful in their efforts to ward off filth, most residents soon resigned themselves to their insalubrious environment.[25]

A majority of Detroit's black families in the late nineteenth century probably lived in the small one- and two-family dwellings that dominated the streets of the near east side. Two or three families generally lived in what appeared from the street to be a one-family cottage. To make ends meet in the late 1880s, Mrs. Daniel Walker, a widow, thus sublet a portion of her little three-room house in Close's Alley to two other families. Most houses were subdivided, and a majority of working-class families took in boarders to help pay the rent. This practice was of special significance to Negroes because they paid more for housing than whites, even though they rented older, more obsolete, and less desirable dwellings.[26]

Though a considerable proportion of Detroit's citizens owned their own homes, most blacks were renters. In 1910 Detroit's 5,741 Negroes lived in 1,383 dwellings. Of the 1,332 of these homes on which information is available, 82.1 percent were rented. Of the 17.9 percent, or 238 homes, owned by their black occupants, only 127, or 9.5 percent

[25] Detroit Association of Charities, *Annual Report 1883*, p. 13; *Detroit Post*, Mar. 4, 1885, p. 3; *Detroit News-Tribune*, June 4, 1911, Magazine Section, p. 3; *Cost of Living in American Towns*, p. 182.

[26] Michigan Housing Commission, *Report* (Lansing, 1916), p. 34; *Plaindealer*, Oct. 24, 1890; *Cost of Living in American Towns*, p. xxi.

of the total Negro homes, were owned free of mortgage. In contrast non-Negroes in Detroit owned 41.5 percent of the homes they lived in, and 21.3 percent were owned free and clear.[27]

The story-and-a-half wooden frame building typified the rented homes on Detroit's near east side. Most often two-family, semi-detached dwellings, occasionally built in rows, these houses resembled badly constructed New England salt boxes. The homes were generally of the double-gabled type, with one gable on each side of the two-family dwelling and one window to each gable. The owner and his family might occupy the attic floor, "which is approached in the rear by a staircase between the two ground-floor dwellings." Toward the end of the nineteenth century, as the lower east side became less desirable residentially, the upstairs apartments as well as the street-level ones tended to be let. It was common practice to sublet apartments as well as to take in boarders, and two or more tenants frequently shared a house or an apartment.[28]

Blacks owned at least some of the rental housing. The Binga row on the southeast corner of Hastings and Rowena was no different from the other story-and-a-half row houses that were common on the near east side. Originally owned by a Negro barber, William Binga, the small row of houses fronting for ninety-five feet on Hastings Street exemplified what Detroiters referred to as tenements. Unrepaired and unpainted, the wooden facades rapidly deteriorated.

[27] To compute the non–Negro ownership, the number of Negro dwellings was subtracted from the total number of homes in the city in each category.

Negro: 1,332 homes reported information of 1,383 total.

Owned:	238	17.9%
127 free	9.5%	
110 encumbered		
1 no report		
Rented:	1,094	82.1%

Non-Negro: 96,970 homes reported information of 98,973 total.

Owned:	40,233	41.5%
20,625 free	21.3%	
19,391 encumbered		
217 no report		
Rented:	56,737	58.5%

Source: U.S. Bureau of the Census, *Negro Population 1790–1915*, p. 471; *Thirteenth Census 1910*, I, 1313.

[28] *Cost of Living in American Towns*, p. 181.

Although each dwelling unit was only the width of a door and a window, many of the residents took in boarders. In 1891 a syndicate of upper-class Negroes, headed by Dr. Levi H. Johnson, bought the dilapidated Binga row. The investors hinted at plans to tear down the houses and exploit the site's commercial value, but the tenement row remained unchanged.[29]

The attached building—a commercial structure with apartments above the ground floor—became increasingly prevalent in Detroit's near east side after the 1890s. Rarely more than three stories in height, these buildings first appeared on corner lots, with a saloon or grocery on the first floor. The three-story attached building at Beaubien and Macomb was typical. At first a grocery and later a saloon, the brick dwelling had a number of flats or apartments above the store. The entrance to the flats was on Macomb, and a house in the alley to the rear also shared the lot. Later on, additional commercial structures would be constructed adjacent to the original attached buildings. The side walls were generally blank, without windows, so that they could be joined to other buildings. Because the building basically served a commercial rather than a residential purpose, the structure maximized commercial space, and the store usually filled the entire lot. Unsanitary residential flats resulted; apartments usually had little access to air and less to light.[30]

Not all of Detroit's blacks in the near east side lived in lower-class neighborhoods. At the turn of the century some of the leaders in the Detroit black community lived in large three-story, brick, single-family dwellings on such tree-lined streets as Canfield, Alfred, Frederick, and Adelaide. These homes, with striped awnings, large lawns, and privet hedges, were common among Detroit's small upper- and middle-class black group. A 1902 newspaper feature on Detroit's Negro social elite printed photographs of the drawing rooms of Dr. W. E. Johnson on Canfield Avenue East, and of Bishop C. S. Smith on Columbia Street East. James H. Cole, reputedly Detroit's wealthiest Negro in the late nineteenth century, lived on Beaubien Street and his house was known for "its wide arches and great rooms." The neat, well-cared-for prime residential homes owned by Negroes, such as

[29] *Plaindealer*, March 20, 1891.
[30] Michigan Housing Commission, *Report*, p. 13.

those on Canfield Avenue, were, however, quite untypical of Negro housing in Detroit at the end of the nineteenth century.[31]

Some Negroes lived outside Detroit's near east side. In the 1880s a small Negro community was formed in the industrial Delray district, among some Irish and, later, Armenians and Hungarians. Probably they were engaged as day laborers and service workers. By 1891 there was a sufficiently large black community there to warrant an African Methodist Episcopal chapel on the southeast corner of Thirtieth and Jackson streets. Occasionally, Negroes in service occupations and other jobs elsewhere in the city were forced to live away from the near east side, but many upper-class blacks deliberately sought out white areas. Attorney Charles Roxborough, for example, settled in a Polish area, on Chene Street; his clients were mostly Polish and he spoke their language fluently. D. Augustus Straker, Detroit's leading black attorney in the late nineteenth century, lived on Bagg Street among expensive, fine homes. From time to time other upper- and middle-class Negroes settled on fashionable west side blocks.[32]

It appears that an unspoken caste line limited working-class blacks to the near east side. There is no contemporary evidence of whites ejecting a black family from the west side, but reports around the time of World War I acknowledged the traditional confinement of blacks to the near east side. One incident in the late nineteenth century, reported many years later, occurred when a black family succeeded in settling in the Irish district west of Woodward—Corktown. For a time they lived isolated and unmolested, but then, mysteriously, their house caught fire. The volunteer fire company answering the call responded to the captain's order to "Lave the nager's house be," and the men saved only the house next door. Blacks would rarely accept employment as servants in the district, and even black organizations and bands in political parades were subject to abuse when they marched in the area.[33]

[31] *Detroit News-Tribune*, Apr. 27, 1902, p. 7; clipping, *Detroit News*, May 16, 1907, in Burton Scrapbook, XXVII, 126.

[32] *Detroit City Directory 1893*, p. 50; clipping, n.d., in Burton Scrapbook, XXX, 1, 6.

[33] George Edmund Haynes, *Negro New-Comers in Detroit, Michigan: A Challenge to Christian Statesmanship. A Preliminary Study* (New York, 1918), pp. 9, 21–22; John Ihlder, "Booming Detroit," *Survey*, XXXVI (July 29, 1916), 449; *Detroit Saturday Night*, May 25, 1912, p. 14.

While blacks could find a home in the near east side, the white institutions in the area were not receptive to them. Settlement houses, which dotted the near east side, were typical of the zone's institutions that turned their backs on the black newcomer: they seemed to be more interested in Americanizing the foreign-language-speaking immigrant than in servicing and aiding the poor, black urban newcomer. Although blacks lived within the neighborhoods surrounding the settlements, none of the houses' activities serviced the native-born, English-speaking newcomer. Not until the Urban League founded a neighborhood house for blacks during World War I would Negroes find themselves welcome in an east side settlement. Some of Detroit's citywide welfare charities aided blacks as well as other groups, but organizations providing recreational facilities similar to those of the settlements barred Negroes; the YMCA, the *Detroit Free Press* Fresh Air Fund, and the city's orphanages, for example, were closed to black children.[34]

Thus, increasingly during the late nineteenth century, blacks clustered within a narrow area on Detroit's near east side. The third ward, a two-block-wide strip extending from the river to the city's limits, became synonymous with black Detroit. St. Antoine was its major artery. From 1890 to 1910, as the number of blacks in the ward nearly doubled, the proportion of Detroit Negroes living within this two-block-wide ward rose from 40.2 percent in 1890 to 45.1 percent in 1900, and 47.8 percent in 1910. At the same time the percentage of blacks within the ward increased from 9.7 percent in 1890 to 10.9 percent in 1900, and to 11.7 percent in 1910.

The high concentration of black population along the third ward's St. Antoine Street aided in the development of black business. The

[34] Robert A. Woods and Albert J. Kennedy (eds.), *Handbook of Settlements* (New York, 1911), pp. 142–144, and *The Social Service Directory of 1917* (Detroit, 1917), list the ethnic groups which the settlements intended to serve. See also *Detroit Tribune*, Jan. 5, 1890, p. 9; Mayor's Inter-racial Committee, *The Negro in Detroit* (Detroit, 1926), VII, 4, 10, 15; and Inquiry of the Detroit Association of Charities, June 30, 1909, Detroit Urban League Papers, Michigan Historical Collections. Fannie Barrier Williams of Chicago, sister of Detroiter George A. Barrier, complained in 1904 that "the poor colored people who came to the cities of the North are the only people for whom no directing agencies to save and protect have been arranged." "The Need for Social Settlement Work for the City Negro," *Southern Workman*, XXXIII (September, 1904), 504.

push of discrimination that limited Negroes to the near east side, and the pull of ethnocentrism that attracted Negroes to the area combined to create a suitable economic market for black business. Among the first black businessmen whose clients appeared to be exclusively Negro were the real-estate agents and promoters. In 1890 Fred W. Ernst and William W. Ferguson devoted their full time to their real-estate offices, and race leaders Dr. Levi H. Johnson, D. Augustus Straker, and others were involved in real-estate investment syndicates or ventures, such as the Detroit Industrial and Financial Cooperative Association. Although the development of black real-estate agents was a product of the high density of the Negro community, these men, in turn, were soon deeply involved in perpetuating the limited zone of black settlement, since they confined their activities to the near east side. They offered land and houses in the black district, and Negro development and building for Negroes were confined to the area. At least in one case, when a black held land outside of the near east side, as did Straker, he refused to rent to other blacks.[35]

St. Antoine Street, in the middle of the third ward, became the center of Negro life in Detroit. By 1910 a majority of Negro businesses would be located on St. Antoine—restaurants, newspapers, funeral parlors, pool halls, and small retail stores. The street became synonymous with black Detroit, whether it meant business, slums, or the fine residential district far to the north.

[35] *Plaindealer*, Jan. 3, 1890; May 2, 1890; July 25, 1890; Mar. 20, 1891; biographical sketch of Mrs. Bertha J. Scott in Bertha J. Scott Collection, in file "Negro," Historical Records Survey of Michigan, Michigan Historical Collections, University of Michigan.

CHAPTER III

Caste

DETROIT BLACK PEOPLE typically had limited social interaction with whites. Except for a small number of upper-class black families, few Negroes ever socialized with whites; contact was generally limited to school or work, and even there, prejudice and discrimination seemed inescapable. In 1864 William Webb, a black whitewasher, was employed by the mayor of Detroit. "We got into a little dispute about the work," Webb recalled nine years later, "and I talked to him with the best manners I could. He ran up to me, and told me to hush, that he did not allow niggers to talk to him."[1] Enfranchisement in 1870 would induce mayors to talk to Negroes, and the 1875 federal Civil Rights Act and the 1885 Michigan Civil Rights Act would remove the legal sanctions permitting discrimination in Michigan, but prejudice and proscription were to remain.

The American designation of race is a peculiar one, as Clarence Darrow, the famous trial lawyer, supposedly discovered in 1926. Three officials of the National Association for the Advancement of Colored People (NAACP) had called upon Darrow to engage him as counsel for Dr. Ossian Sweet, a Detroit Negro indicted for murdering a member of a white mob that threatened his house. The

[1] William Webb, *The History of William Webb Composed by Himself* (Detroit, 1873), p. 39.

NAACP officials found Darrow in bed "with all his clothes on," Arthur Spingarn recalled. Spingarn, of dark complexion, outlined the case to Darrow, who replied sympathetically:

> "Yes, I know full well the difficulties faced by your race."
> "I'm sorry, Mr. Darrow," replied Spingarn, "but I'm not a Negro."
> Darrow turned to Charles Studin, another member of the committee, and said, "Well you understand what I mean."
> "I am not colored either," replied Studin.
> The third man had blond hair and blue eyes. "I would not make that mistake with you," Darrow told him.
> "I am a Negro," replied Walter White, secretary of the NAACP.
> Darrow jumped out of bed. "That settles it," he cried. "I'll take the case."[2]

Darrow's uncertainty in identifying the racial designation of his visitors illustrates that the American division of black and white is an artificial one. Although biological theories have been used to defend and justify separation between black and white, the classification has not been a scientific one; it has been and continues to be a social designation. Individuals are assigned to one or the other caste, white or black, by social convention, not scientific logic. The general rule in nineteenth century Detroit was that children followed the caste of their parents. If their parentage was mixed, the children were considered to be of the subordinate caste.[3]

The social system that divided black and white in nineteenth-century Detroit was caste-like. The term "caste" is used here to designate the cross-cultural socio-historical concept that describes a particular type of social stratification. It is not confined to any one period or to any one society. Although it is most commonly applied to the Hindu-Indian status system, caste is employed here in its universal sense: "The essentials which distinguish castes from other types of social classes," according to Edward W. Pohlman, a scholar who has surveyed the use of the concept of "caste," "are (1) vertical immobility, both of the individual from one class (caste) to another

[2] Irving Stone, *Clarence Darrow for the Defense* (Garden City, N.Y., 1943), p. 470. The details of the story are, without doubt, apocryphal.

[3] For a recent exposition of these ideas see Michael Banton, *Race Relations* (New York, 1968).

and of the class group as a whole from one relative rank to another on the prestige scale; (2) class (caste) endogamy; (3) rigid class isolation and insulation." The word "caste" denotes the entire etiquette of relations between blacks below the upper class and all whites in nineteenth-century Detroit—from endogamy to occupational discrimination. Furthermore, it connotes a matrix of restricted life chances—the chances of a member of the black caste to live outside of the Negro area, to occupy a middle-prestige or well-paying job, or to participate in a wide range of the city's social institutions were virtually nil. On the other hand, the probability that a Negro would live in a Negro residential area, that he would be a servant or a day laborer, and that he would interact only with black institutions was extremely high in nineteenth-century Detroit.[4]

In general, blacks and whites in late nineteenth-century Detroit were separated into distinct castes. With the subordinate black caste never accounting for more than 3 percent of Detroit's population and comprising only 1.4 percent of its population in 1900, the caste structure of the community was not the most prominent feature of the city's social system. However, when one focuses on Detroit's black community or on areas that impinge on black-white interaction, the caste stratification readily becomes apparent.

Not all of Detroit's Negroes were of the black caste in the late nineteenth century. The city's upper-class blacks were a marginal group whose relative position in the social system was at some point between the white caste and the general black caste. Their life style and values incorporated characteristics of each of the two distinct castes, and they interacted with both groups. These upper-class blacks occupied this position by virtue of birth, wealth, education, occupation, and status; and none of them is known to have passed into the white caste in Detroit, nor do their ranks appear to have been increased by the upward mobility of any lower-class blacks after the

---

[4] Edward W. Pohlman, "Evidences of Disparity Between the Hindu Practice of Caste and the Ideal Type," *American Sociological Review*, XVI (June, 1951), 376. Pohlman's definition of caste is a consensus one, based on a survey "of over thirty representative sociologists and anthropologists who have dealt with the concept of caste." See Pohlman, "Hindu Social Class Organization and the Concept of Caste," Ph.D. dissertation, Ohio State University, 1949. See Appendix A, "A Note on 'Caste'."

Civil War, except through marriage. After the turn of the century, these marginal Negroes gradually disappeared as a group as migration from Detroit and death took their toll among them, and the remaining members threw in their lot with the new middle class.[5]

The ceaseless migrations of the foreign-born into the city during the nineteenth century failed to alter the caste system significantly. Unfamiliar with the social system that was unsanctioned in law, newly arrived immigrants tended, at least temporarily, to be outside of the system. Spatial and occupational mobility of second-generation Americans, however, clearly distinguished them in time as members of the white caste.

After the Civil War the Michigan Republican party, whose leadership was committed to black equality, sought to remove the legal sanctions protecting discrimination. Under firm Republican control, the state legislature passed a number of acts that provided for school integration and barred discrimination in public accommodations. The caste system, however, absorbed and cushioned the effects of legal changes wrought by the Republicans in their support of Negro rights, and discrimination and segregation remained. One permanent alteration in Detroit's caste system that resulted from legislative action was the integration of the city's public schools in the 1870s. Influenced by the momentum of Radical Republicanism, the Michigan legislature forced school integration upon a Detroit that generally wished to maintain a dual school system, and although at first caste taboos proved stronger than the law, the colored schools eventually were closed. The story of Detroit's resistance to integration, nevertheless, reveals the depth of white attitudes toward the Negro.[6]

Former Governor Austin Blair's application in 1867 for a writ to enter George Washington, a young black, in Jackson's public schools formally initiated the lengthy post–Civil War campaign to integrate public education in Michigan and Detroit. This assault on caste in Michigan's schools began the same year that the Radical Republicans in Congress opened their eight-year battle to abolish racial segregation in schools throughout the United States. Although the effort in

[5] See chapter 5.

[6] For legislation, see Franklin Johnson, *The Development of State Legislation Concerning the Free Negro* (New York, 1918), pp. 126–128.

Washington met with frustration and failure when the Civil Rights Act of 1875 failed to bar school segregation, the Michigan campaign met with a rapid success: within two months of Blair's petition to the state supreme court, a bill eliminating segregation had been passed by the legislature and signed by the governor. The Democratic Detroit Board of Education, however, remained obdurate and ignored the mandate of the overwhelmingly Republican state legislature.[7]

The grievances of Detroit blacks against the segregated schools were well founded. The Detroit school system offered twelve years of education for white children—two years each for the primary, secondary, and junior grades and three years each in the senior and high school levels—but only six years of schooling were provided for black children. Black politico John D. Richards, brother of the first Negro public school teacher in Detroit—Fannie Richards—charged that black children were excluded "after they have barely learned to read," and the president of the board of education admitted that the system was "manifestly unjust" to Negroes, since "no provision has ever been made, or opportunity, under our system, afforded them for advancing higher than the junior grade." Sarah Warsaw, among other black children, had sought more than six years of public school education, and she had to accept repeating the junior grade. The black schools were distant from much of Detroit's Negro population, and the board was slow in relocating them to the areas of highest black concentration; Colored School One in the fourth ward, and Colored School Two in the seventh ward left more than 40 percent of Detroit's black children in wards without public schools. A committee of Negro parents complained that young children were forced to walk several miles to attend a colored school.[8]

The 1867 School Integration Act would have removed these in-

<hr />

[7] Alfred H. Kelly, "The Congressional Controversy over School Segregation, 1867–1875," *American Historical Review*, LXIV (April, 1959), 537.

[8] *Detroit Tribune*, Feb. 5, 1872, p. 2, Jan. 11, 1871, p. 4; *Detroit Advertiser & Tribune*, Jan. 3, 1867, p. 3; *Twenty-Seventh Annual Report of the Board of Education* (Detroit, 1870), p. 7; *Detroit Tribune*, Jan. 16, 1868, p. 1, Feb. 2, 1869, p. 1. At least some black parents could afford to send their children to private academies to escape the segregated public schools; Alexander D. Moore sent his eldest son to the German-American seminary. *Detroit Tribune*, Jan. 5, 1890, p. 9.

equities if the board of education had complied with the law. City Counselor William Gray advised the board that the statute was valid and binding upon the city; he counseled the members that they could not continue to exclude and separate the black students. The board tabled Gray's report.[9]

The fall school term of 1867 began with the caste system intact in Detroit's public schools. Black children appeared at the single high school in Detroit and various ward schools, but were turned away. Negro parents appealed to the board of education, and in December the board appointed a committee to resolve the growing controversy. The committee reported that there was some uncertainty as to whether the 1867 statute barring segregation applied to Detroit, since the city's public schools had been created by a special act of the legislature rather than by the general state education act. The committee observed that in Detroit "a great majority of the people believe that the distinctive feature [of segregation] ought to be retained." Finally, the report recommended that if segregated schools were to be continued, the quality of the education and of the facilities of the black schools would have to be improved.[10]

In the face of increasing pressure from the black community, the board moved to improve the Negro school system. In early February 1869, after hopelessly awaiting a sign of the board of education's good faith, Detroit Negro citizens turned to open and more militant protest. The black community elected a committee to present their grievances. The board then authorized a search for a suitable building to replace Colored School Two and opened a new colored school in the upper part of the sixth ward. In April 1869, two years after the enactment of the 1867 integration statute, the board conceded the soundness of the black parents' complaints but it turned aside their demand for integration, arguing that the status quo best served the black students. "An abandonment of the separate colored schools at

[9] *Detroit Advertiser & Tribune*, Apr. 16, 1867, p. 1.

[10] The board analysis of popular opinion was no doubt shaped in part by the editorials and articles in the *Detroit Free Press*. Forest G. Wood, *Black Scare: The Racist Response to Emancipation and Reconstruction* (Berkeley, 1968), p. 138; *Detroit Advertiser & Tribune*, Sept. 3, 1867, p. 1, Dec. 3, 1867, p. 1, Dec. 17, 1867, p. 1.

present would be equivalent," the board of education contended, "to exclude colored children from school altogether." Transfers were impossible at this point, the board explained, because the term had already begun, and there were no vacancies in the white schools. The board's failure to consider the use of the colored schools in de-segregating the system indicated that the condition of the Negro schools was so poor that they would never be used by white students; the alternatives were to use the buildings for black children or not to use them at all.[11]

The board of education's arbitrary legal stance in defending segregation was undermined by the Michigan school integration statute of 1869 repealing and superseding the original Detroit school charter; the board, however, refused to comply. Black parents therefore turned to the courts to enforce the law and to end segregation, supporting as a test case the action of Joseph Workman, a black laborer who then brought suit for a writ of mandamus to compel the Detroit Board of Education to admit his child into the tenth ward school. The Michigan Supreme Court granted the writ and noted that both the 1867 and 1869 statutes were applicable to Detroit's public schools. The victory proved to be an empty one: though Cassius Workman was admitted to the white neighborhood school, a few weeks later two black children were denied admission to Barstow Union School in the fourth ward.[12]

The following semester, acting under board direction, school teachers continued to turn away black students from the ward schools. Black parents again turned to the courts, this time to compel the board to comply with the Workman decision. Threatened with the certainty of losing suits that were costly to defend and faced with the possibility of being heavily fined by the courts, the board moved to placate black parents. Although they resolved to accept the Workman decision, the board members showed no remorse over their previous resistance, and they defended their unwillingness to integrate the

[11] *Detroit Tribune*, Feb. 2, 1869, p. 1, May 2, 1869, p. 1, May 4, 1869, p. 1, Apr. 6, 1869, p. 1.

[12] Caroline W. Thrun, "School Segregation in Michigan," *Michigan History*, XXXVIII (March, 1954), 9; *People ex rel Workman* v. *Bd. of Ed. of Detroit*, 18 Michigan 400 (1869); *Detroit Tribune*, May 18, 1869, p. 1.

schools on the grounds that it heretofore had been "inexpedient to make any changes."[13]

The board's resolution to accept the Workman case decision was intended to forestall opposition; the schools remained segregated. Appeals to the courts only added to the frustration felt by the city's blacks. Obadiah C. Wood's attempt to enter his children in the white schools was met with vagarious responses, and black parents were left dismayed and angry. When Wood's children appeared to enroll in their local ward school at the beginning of the term they were denied admittance. By the time a writ was granted weeks later, the semester was already under way and the children could not be accommodated, since by then all of the available seats had been filled. The board of education flouted the law while frivolously remaining responsive to the advocates of caste in education. One parent was reported to have said that "he will fight before his children shall sit besides niggers."[14]

The 1870s initiated a new era in caste relations in Detroit. Renewed black militancy and an awareness of the power of political organization accompanied enfranchisement, and resulted in a heightened determination by the city's black leaders to accept nothing less than full integration. In January 1870, the officers of the black political clubs in Detroit sponsored a general meeting to press their cause. "Turn out," they called to fellow blacks, "not as slaves, but as American citizens, who have labored and toiled, fought and bled to save the life of the Republic, and to perpetuate a free Government, in which the Humblest citizen has rights which the most exalted are bound to respect." The Republican press endorsed the meeting, recognizing the "determined effort being made unjustly to exclude colored children from some of our public schools." They united to oppose the sham "integration" of the fourth-ward school: under the guise of

[13] *Detroit Tribune*, Oct. 5, 1869, p. 1, Oct. 7, 1869, p. 1, Oct. 12, 1869, p. 1.
[14] Ibid., Oct. 12, 1869, p. 1, Oct. 20, 1869, p. 3, Dec. 18, 1869, p. 3, Jan. 11, 1869, p. 4. The strong rhetoric of segregationists in Detroit during this period seemed to echo that of the local school trustees in Amherstburg, Ontario, across the river from Detroit, when Isaac J. Rice, a white missionary, reported in 1843 that the trustees "declared that rather than send their children 'to School with niggers they will cut their children's heads off and throw them into the road side ditch.'" Quoted in Robin W. Winks, "Negro School Segregation in Ontario and Nova Scotia," *Canadian Historical Review*, L (June, 1969), 172.

grading the students, all of the black children had been segregated into separate classrooms, but it was obviously a caste division as the color line was too carefully drawn. Blacks and Radical Republicans were further aroused by the treatment of black children attending white schools in accordance with court order, who were abused by their white classmates "without rebuke or correction from the teachers." The problem seemed clear: "among many of the lower classes of the white children," the *Detroit Tribune* noted, "a strong prejudice exists toward the colored children, either one natural with themselves or engendered by unwise counsels received from parents or friends." [15]

With resistance seemingly exhausted and with the crescendo of black protest, the Detroit Board of Education gave ground. It acquiesced to school integration while reminding the black citizenry that the presence of their children in white schools was unwanted by the community. In its annual report of January 1871 the board noted that "there are citizens who have objections to the two races mingling together in our schools." To parents of this persuasion, the board disclaimed its culpability in integrating the schools; it reported that it had been merely following the law. [16]

Detroit's school system had accepted integration as slowly as the courts would permit, resisting change at every point, and the dispute now raged over the integration of classrooms. In February 1871 the board finally pledged full compliance with the law and court orders but not without placing its actions within the framework of Detroit's caste system:

> A Colored man who has a prejudice against sending a child to a colored school ought not to complain because some white men feel in the same way. When the Fourth Ward school opened the first of this term, there were pupils enough enrolled to fill it and a surplus besides. A full corps of excellent teachers were placed in charge of the schools, but the white children withdrew almost in a body, parents refusing to send them because there were to be so many colored children in the building. As a temporary measure and one dictated by economy, and one with which we thought little fault would be found, we

---

[15] *Detroit Tribune*, Jan. 9, 1871, p. 2, Jan. 11, 1871, p. 4, Jan. 21, 1871, p. 4.
[16] Ibid., Feb. 9, 1871, p. 4, Jan. 24, 1871, p. 4.

placed the colored children in rooms by themselves, to induce the whites to return to school.[17]

The concluding scene in the integration drama was tragicomic. With the initiation of public school integration in Detroit in the summer of 1871, many whites could not endure black and white children sharing the same double desks. Responding to the anguish of white parents and teachers, the board of education appropriated scarce educational funds to replace the double desks with single ones.[18]

The law and the courts had been upheld, although belatedly, and in 1874 Mrs. Toussaint L'O. Lambert reported that "the mortification and slights which girls and boys were compelled to receive from their white school-mates for a while, have gradually diminished." Outside of Detroit, however, the vestiges of caste in education continued: in 1880 Michigan had eighteen segregated schools. Some school systems in the state, such as the one in Ypsilanti, remained segregated into the twentieth century.[19]

After the adoption of the school integration acts of the late 1860s, the enactment of federal civil rights legislation during the Reconstruction era, and the ratification of the Fifteenth Amendment in 1870, there remained but few legal supports for a system of caste in Michigan. When in 1883 the United States Supreme Court declared the 1875 federal Civil Rights Act unconstitutional, the burden of prohibiting caste distinctions was thrown almost entirely upon the states. De-

[17] Ibid., Jan. 24, 1871, p. 4, Feb. 7, 1871, p. 4.

[18] Ibid., July 14, 1871, p. 4.

[19] *New National Era and Citizen* (Washington), July 23, 1874, p. 1; *Compendium of the Tenth Census*, II, 1638; Harvey C. Colburn, *The Story of Ypsilanti* (Ypsilanti, 1923), pp. 213, 232; *Report of the NAACP for 1917 and 1918* (New York, 1919), p. 64. The Toledo, Ohio, black community, many of whose members had close ties of blood and friendship with Detroit blacks, met with more rapid success than did Detroit in the integration of schools. In a two-year fight, J. Madison Bell set into motion a chain of events that resulted in a new school board, which, under threat of court action, desegregated the public schools. The state government in Ohio proved more intransigent than the one in Michigan; the state law requiring segregated schools was not repealed until 1887. Leonard Erickson, "Toledo Desegregates, 1871," *Northwest Ohio Quarterly* (Winter, 1968–69), 5, 9, 10. On the other side of the border in Canada the battle was fought with less success; segregated schools were present in western Ontario until the twentieth century. Winks, "Negro School Segregation in Ontario and Nova Scotia," pp. 177, 182.

troit blacks condemned the Court's action as did the March 1884 Colored Citizens State Convention in Battle Creek. The necessity for civil rights legislation was reinforced the week of the state convention when a black-owned barber shop servicing only a white clientele refused to serve Detroit black politician and *Plaindealer* editor Walter H. Stowers. Robert Pelham, Jr., another *Plaindealer* editor, attended the April 1884 National Colored Men's Convention in Pittsburgh, which called for civil rights legislation. A civil rights bill was introduced in the 1885 legislature, and a mass meeting of the black community called for its enactment. The assemblage appointed three black politicos, Robert Pelham, Jr., attorney Thomas Crissup, and Wayne County Deputy Clerk Walter Y. Clarke, to present resolutions to the legislative judiciary committee. Michigan, like most northern states, passed a civil rights statute that closely resembled the unconstitutional federal act: "All persons are entitled to the full and equal accommodation of inns, restaurants, eatinghouses, barber shops, public conveyances on land and water, theaters, and all other places of public accommodation and amusement. . . ." An additional statute striking at caste distinctions, introduced by a black legislator, was passed in 1893, when life insurance companies were prohibited from considering race in fixing rates. The last vestige of the earlier black codes had been removed in 1883, when the Michigan legislature repealed the territorial statute, repassed in 1838, that had barred interracial marriage.[20]

Endogamy—the limiting of marriage to those within the caste—is one of the basic characteristics of a caste system and is a primary factor in perpetuating distinct castes. In Michigan, endogamy retained explicit legal sanction longer than any other social, political, or economic practice relating to race relations that was subject to state control.[21]

[20] *Detroit Post & Tribune*, Mar. 24, 1884, p. 2, Mar. 26, 1884, p. 4, Apr. 30, 1884, p. 4; *Detroit Post*, Mar. 11, 1885, p. 5; Gilbert Thomas Stephenson, *Race Distinction in American Law* (New York, 1910), pp. 90, 121, 138, 248; Johnson, *State Legislation Concerning the Negro*, pp. 126–128; *Detroit Advocate*, June 1, 1901, p. 2.

[21] In 1900 Senator Ben Tillman made use of the specter of miscegenation to turn a hostile student audience at the University of Michigan in Ann Arbor into a sympathetic crowd. The students greeted Tillman with hisses when he called a black student seated in front of him a "savage." Tillman responded: "When

Evidence is available of a number of prosecutions in Detroit of the state prohibition on intermarriage between blacks and whites. In 1859 a Negro minister, Rev. William Berry, was fined fifty dollars in police court for officiating at the marriage ceremony of a black man and a white woman. In 1874 Jeremiah Green (black) and Jane Cooper (white) were arrested for living together in violation of the miscegenation statute, but they were released when no one appeared to testify that they had been married in Michigan. The law barred mixed marriage ceremonies in Michigan, and if a couple were married out of the state their marriage would be valid in Michigan. The absurdity of the law was revealed in the Jones case, the last attempt to enforce the statute.[22]

In September 1881, James Jones, a black barber, and his white wife, Mary, were arrested for violating the 1838 miscegenation statute on a "charge of lewd and lascivious cohabitation" brought by Mary Jones's mother and brothers. The case aroused great interest among the black and Irish communities, and they filled the courtroom beyond capacity during the drawn-out proceedings. Police Court Justice John Miner bound the Joneses over to recorder's court, but he released them on $500 bail. As tension mounted over the issue, City Attorney Corliss argued that, although the statute "perhaps . . . was a relic of barbarism" and it was unfortunate that such cases were brought to trial, "he believed that as a matter of state policy such alliances should not be permitted. . . ." Many Irishmen agreed, and fears were voiced that the Corktowners would attack Jones when he was released on bail. To reduce the growing tension, Justice Miner suggested that the matter be terminated "by the parties interested going across the river and there be legally married." The couple remained in Detroit, however, and they were eventually tried in recorder's court, found guilty, and fined. A year later the Republican legislature repealed the 1838 act.[23]

---

that man who hissed gets ready to give his daughter in marriage to a Negro and proves by his actions, and not by his hisses, that he means business, I will apologize, and not before." The applause was "tremendous," and the audience was won over. *Cleveland Gazette,* May 12, 1900, p. 1.

[22] *Detroit Free Press,* Dec. 6, 1859, p. 1; *Detroit Tribune,* Apr. 10, 1874, p. 4.

[23] *Detroit Post & Tribune,* Apr. 20, 1882, p. 2, Apr. 21, 1882, p. 2, Apr. 28, 1882, p. 2, May 4, 1882, p. 8, May 23, 1882, p. 2, May 27, 1882, p. 2, Aug. 14, 1882,

Although the federal Civil Rights Act of 1875 and the Michigan Civil Rights Act of 1885 dealt directly with the elimination of segregation in public accommodations, many of Detroit's restaurants and hotels maintained the caste line. Nearly all the incidents stemming from the violation of the public accommodation statutes involved restaurants, an indeterminate number of which either excluded blacks or relegated them to back rooms. Segregated restaurants were designed to prevent whites and blacks from partaking in "the social ritual of eating together," since in most societies in the world the act of breaking bread "is a ritual symbol of brotherhood and at least of potential equality."[24]

In the late 1880s and early 1890s the number of reported incidents of discrimination against blacks in Detroit rose sharply. Some of Detroit's black leaders attributed this to a rise in prejudice against blacks: Robert A. Pelham, Jr., remarked in January 1890 that a "recent wave of prejudice ... seems to have struck Detroit within the past year." In all likelihood, however, prejudice was probably no greater in 1890 than it had been in 1880. If anything, the fifteen years of peaceful and mostly amicable integration in education and politics since 1875 had served to remove some of the stereotyped images of the Negro held by whites. Most likely, the increase in reported incidents of segregation during the 1880s and 1890s was a result of the growing affluence and militancy of many in the black community rather than of any sudden increase in prejudice.[25]

Few of Detroit's blacks were unlikely personally to be turned away

---

p. 2. Endogamy would remain as a social custom, and in the 1910s, efforts would be made in Michigan and other states to give the taboo of intermarriage legal sanction. The 1913 Michigan bill died in committee after the less-than-one-year-old Detroit branch of the NAACP mounted a strenuous campaign to defeat the anachronistic proposal. There were other ways, however, to deal with intermarriage without legal sanction. In 1900, in Larium, Michigan, a suburb of the mining camp of Calumet, when several white girls married some black men who had recently been brought there from Tennessee by a sewer contractor, the citizens of the town formed a vigilante committee "to rid the town of Negroes." *Crisis*, V (March, 1913), 245, V (April, 1913), 296–297, VI (May, 1913), 15; *Cleveland Gazette*, Mar. 24, 1900, p. 1.

[24] W. Lloyd Warner and Allison Davis, "A Comparative Study of American Caste," in Edgar T. Thompson (ed.), *Race Relations and the Race Problem* (Durham, N.C., 1939), p. 232.

[25] *Detroit Tribune*, Jan. 5, 1890, p. 9.

from a segregated facility. Nearly all of the city's Negroes, except for the upper class and the criminal element, lived within a restricted caste system. Confined to Detroit's near east side, most blacks interacted primarily with black organizations and with only a few integrated institutions. Most of the white social institutions that might bar blacks were either too expensive to attract these men and women or were outside the normal range of their activity. Most Negroes, presumably, were unwilling to venture outside the places where they knew they were welcome.[26] Upper-class blacks, on the other hand, were less restricted and tended to enter public accommodations outside the reach of other blacks, while the criminal element frequented establishments of the integrated Detroit underworld. As the number of professionals, white-collar workers, and small businessmen increased in the 1880s and 1890s, the probability increased that some blacks would attend Detroit's foremost restaurants and hotels.[27]

Though at times reluctant to do so, many of Detroit's hotels and restaurants seem to have complied with the 1875 Civil Rights Act. Walter Y. Clarke, a black delegate to a Republican convention, was at first barred from a Detroit hotel dining room in 1875, but he gained admittance when the question of his legal rights was raised. It soon became apparent, however, that subtle ways of noncompliance had developed. " 'I instruct my clerks to inform that class [blacks],' " said a Detroit hotel-keeper in 1877, " 'that they must pay double price for their entertainment if they insist on going to the first table.' " Other public places were more blatant: in 1882 the Kirkwood Hotel refused to accommodate the Fisk Jubilee Singers during a visit to Detroit. The manager of the hotel confirmed to the *Detroit Post & Tribune* that he excluded Negroes because it would hurt his business. In 1886 the regional assembly of black Knights Templar found that

[26] The hesitancy of Negroes to venture into new places was best expressed by novelist Jessie Fauset in 1922: "At noon I go for lunch. But I always go to the same place because I am not sure of my reception in other places. If I go to another place I must fight it through. But usually I am hungry. I want food, not a law-suit." "Some Notes on Color," *World Tomorrow*, V (March, 1922), 76.

[27] Most civil rights incidents reported in Detroit's newspapers after 1875 involved visitors to the city, and it is probable that Detroit blacks were more likely to press charges when faced with discrimination when accompanied by an out-of-towner. Under the circumstances, pride and embarrassment were likely to force a court test.

a few of the city's major hotels barred Negroes, and the 1888 Christian Workers' Convention in Detroit experienced an unpleasant confrontation with the color line when Rev. J. H. Hector, a black minister from California, was turned away from the dining room of the Hotel Cadillac.[28]

In 1888 black leaders sponsored a suit in circuit court to test the enforceability of the 1885 Michigan ban on segregation in public accommodations. Dr. W. H. Haynes, a Negro physician, and a white doctor had gone to Fred Soup's restaurant on Washington Avenue, but Soup refused to serve Haynes. Similar cases had afflicted the black community, and when William Lambert raised the issue at a meeting called to elect delegates to the 1888 state Afro-American convention, the assembly embraced Haynes's cause as a test case and appointed a committee to raise funds and to assist Haynes in pressing suit. Attorney D. Augustus Straker represented Haynes at the trial twenty months later. In court, Soup admitted discriminating against Haynes, but Soup's attorney argued that the restaurant owner had not violated the law because the dining room was not a public place; the eating-house, he argued, was unlicensed and a majority of its customers were regular boarders. The jury deadlocked eight to three (one juror was ill) in favor of Haynes. The judge thereupon took the case from the jury and found for the defendant. The decision in favor of Soup was based on the grounds that Haynes was not a citizen, that Soup's dining hall was not a public place, and that the public accommodations section of the 1885 Michigan Civil Rights Act was unconstitutional.[29]

While the Haynes case awaited trial, Straker initiated another court test involving segregation in a public place. On August 15, 1889, William W. Ferguson and M. F. Walker, the catcher on the Syracuse Negro baseball club, were refused service in the dining room of the fashionable Gies' European Restaurant, although a waiter offered to serve them in the saloon. At the trial, Edward Gies confessed to telling Ferguson that "we cannot serve colored people right at those

[28] *Detroit Tribune*, Mar. 6, 1875, p. 4, Aug. 20, 1877, p. 4; *Detroit Post & Tribune*, Apr. 3, 1882, p. 2; *Detroit Tribune*, Apr. 11, 1886, p. 5, Aug. 6, 1886, p. 4, Nov. 21, 1888, p. 5.

[29] *Detroit Tribune*, Apr. 18, 1888, p. 3; Detroit *Plaindealer*, Dec. 6, 1889, Apr. 18, 1890.

certain tables," but Circuit Court Judge George Gartner instructed the jury that separate but equal satisfied the provisions of the Michigan Civil Rights Act of 1885. Given Gartner's charge, the jury took only fifteen minutes to find in favor of the defendant.[30]

Stunned by the verdict, the *Plaindealer* compared the decision with "the line of the old 'Jim Crow car' bourbon doctrine." Black Detroit had looked to the abolition of caste distinction; instead, "it remained for a Democratic circuit judge in the city of Detroit . . . to rule that proscription is legal and that an intelligent, refined, wealthy Afro-American can be stowed away anywhere in a restaurant that a prejudiced or bigoted proprietor may choose."[31]

Although D. A. Straker, attorney for Ferguson and, previously, Haynes, was disheartened by the loss of the two civil rights cases, he believed that the courts, not the law, sheltered discrimination. The narrow construction of the law by judges, Straker remarked, "plainly aid[s] juries in subverting justice as we have seen done in Courts in the city of Detroit."[32]

Straker appealed the Ferguson-Gies case to the Michigan Supreme Court. H. F. Chipman, counsel for Gies, argued for the separate but equal doctrine, asserting that "public sentiment demanded that Gies separate his white and colored guests." The supreme court, however, vindicated Ferguson, Straker, and, by implication, Haynes. The court ruled that Judge Gartner had been in error: "The jury, under the defendant's own version of the transaction, should have been instructed to find a verdict for the plaintiff."[33]

Justice Allen B. Morse spoke for the unanimous court in ruling that "in Michigan there must be and is an absolute, unconditional equality of white and colored before the law. The white man can have no rights or privileges under the law that are denied to the black man." The court took notice of the caste system in existence: "Socially people may do as they please within the law, and whites may associate together, as may blacks, and exclude whom they please from their dwellings and private grounds." The court, however, had little sympa-

---

[30] *Plaindealer*, Oct. 17, 1890; *Ferguson* v. *Gies*, 82 Michigan 359–361 (1890).
[31] *Plaindealer*, Feb. 21, 1890.
[32] *Plaindealer*, May 23, 1890.
[33] *Plaindealer*, June 6, 1890; *Ferguson* v. *Gies*, 82 Michigan 361 (1890).

thy with these feelings, noting that it "does not commend itself either to the heart or judgment." "The prejudice against association in public places with the Negro, which does exist, to some extent in all communities, less now than formerly," declared Justice Morse, "is unworthy of our [white] race; and it is not for the courts to cater to or temporize with a prejudice which is not only not humane, but unreasonable." The supreme court reversed the jury's decision and ordered that only the question regarding the amount of damages to be awarded should be resubmitted to a jury. Straker returned to Detroit and reargued the case before a jury, but the panel disregarded the spirit of the supreme court's mandate and awarded Ferguson damages of only six cents.[34]

Incidents of restaurant discrimination continued to be reported in the Detroit newspapers, but rarely did blacks challenge these actions in court. One successful invocation of the civil rights statute occurred after letter carrier Frank Shewcraft, with a friend from Cincinnati, had been refused service at the Chamber of Commerce restaurant. Silas Watson, a black waiter, and John B. O'Neill, the restaurant manager, were found guilty in a nonjury trial in police court; Watson received a suspended sentence, and O'Neill was given a choice of paying a twenty-five-dollar fine or serving thirty days in the house of correction.[35]

As was true of Silas Watson, Negroes themselves were often compelled to draw the caste line against their black brothers. Blacks were most sensitive to segregation in barbering, a trade dominated by Negroes until near the turn of the twentieth century. White barbers rarely shaved or cut the hair of Negroes, and most black barbers with a white clientele would not risk serving blacks because they feared that this would "drive the white trade away." Black leaders lauded

[34] *Ferguson* v. *Gies*, 82 Michigan 366 (1890); *Plaindealer*, Jan. 30, 1891. In 1900 Ferguson personally settled a confrontation with a bigot. When a white man objected to Ferguson's eating with white people at a public restaurant, protested to the manager, and called Ferguson a "nigger," the black man demanded an apology. The white man refused, saying that "he would die before he would apologize to a blanked 'nigger.'" Ferguson knocked him down twice before he was restrained. "More power to 'Brother' Ferguson," remarked the *Gazette. Cleveland Gazette*, Apr. 7, 1900, p. 2.

[35] *Plaindealer*, Jan. 8, 1892; *Detroit Tribune*, Mar. 24, 1896, p. 5.

and praised Negro barbers who accepted both black and white customers, and the 1915 *Michigan Manual of Freedmen's Progress* praised the success and progressiveness of barber Henry Wade Robbins of Ann Arbor. His clientele, according to the *Manual*, included higher-class blacks and whites, and "Mr. Robbins has completely negatived the popular fallacy that in order to be successful in the barber business the boss was required to draw the color line in his patronage." Notwithstanding the success of barbers such as Robbins, and even though the 1885 Michigan Civil Rights Act specifically prohibited discrimination in barber shops, the color line continued to be observed in Michigan barbering.[36]

Although the caste line persisted in many of Detroit's public accommodations, blacks succeeded in removing the color barrier from the city's legitimate theaters. In the earliest days of Detroit, Negroes had been restricted to a cordoned section of the gallery or balcony in theaters. After the Civil War, Detroit Negroes attacked segregation in public auditoriums. In September 1866, George A. Johnson bought orchestra tickets for the theater in Young Men's Hall, but on the night of the performance the doorkeeper refused to admit Johnson and his guests, indicating "that colored persons were not admitted below, and that he must go into the gallery." Johnson sued the manager of the hall for breach of contract and was awarded twenty-five dollars and costs. Nine years later Walter Y. Clarke brought suit under the recently enacted federal Civil Rights Act of 1875 after a Whitney Opera House ticket agent had refused to sell him a reserved seat ticket. The color line in Detroit theaters was thereupon gradually eliminated, and by 1890 the theater was the one public accommodation in the city that black leaders agreed was free of discrimination.[37]

[36] *Detroit Post & Tribune*, Mar. 24, 1884, p. 2; *Detroit Advocate*, Apr. 20, 1902, p. 2, May 11, 1901, p. 2; Francis H. Warren (comp.), *Michigan Manual of Freedmen's Progress* (Detroit, 1915), p. 123 (hereafter cited as *Freedmen's Progress*).

[37] *Detroit Journal & Michigan Advertiser*, Apr. 24, 1833; *Detroit Advertiser & Tribune*, Sept. 14, 1866, p. 3; *Detroit Tribune*, Oct. 15, 1875, p. 4, Oct. 18, 1875, p. 4, Jan. 5, 1890, p. 9. While Detroit's opera houses and major halls drew no color line, the small theaters and movie houses that arose after 1900 would institute a caste line by either confining blacks to a specified section or barring them altogether. In 1914 the Detroit NAACP would make this practice one of

The caste line in Detroit was strongly buttressed by a widely held white view that blacks were inferior. The opponents of Negro suffrage had based their opposition on this assumption, and generally the city's newspapers continued to reflect this view after 1870. The newspapers divided blacks into three groups: (1) upper-class blacks—professionals and politicians—who were rarely identified as Negro; (2) "respectable" Negroes; and (3) the overwhelming majority of blacks, who were generally identified with the traditional nineteenth-century designation "(col'd)." The last group, according to Detroit's newspapers, was the Sambo, Topsy, or Uncle Tom of southern folklore.

Detroit's newspapers described the life of black Detroit in sarcastic and patronizing terms. The *Detroit News-Tribune*, which regularly included features dealing with street life in Detroit, reported in 1896 on "A City Plantation," a coal refueling station for steamboats employing Negroes. At the dock, the *News-Tribune* commented, "they pass day after day, eating and sleeping, working and playing, apparently as happy and as jolly though they were back on the old plantation itself." The *Detroit Evening News* found that "there is always material for the humorous, the grotesque, the speculative and the sad" among the gay, singing, "half dressed pickaninnies" in the black areas. The *Detroit Free Press*, when not directly harping on black inferiority or raising the specter of a black invasion or miscegenation, depicted Negroes in a satirical manner, mocking their customs, organizations, and churches.[38]

Whites, rather than anticipating any Negro improvement or uplift, expected blacks to act like inferiors and thus to confirm white stereotypes. "To be a good Negro in some men's estimation," black attorney Walter H. Stowers wrote in 1903, "one must lose his self-respect. He must cringe and crawl and fawn in the presence of the 'superior race' or he is a bad actor and must be dealt with by men who have red blood in their veins and often on their hands, too." Ten years earlier Stowers

its major targets, and it would bring fourteen lawsuits against theater discrimination, of which it would win four. *Crisis*, II (June, 1911), 53, VIII (July, 1914), 141.

[38] *Detroit News-Tribune*, Sept. 27, 1896, p. 18; clipping, *Detroit Evening News*, May, 1890, in C. M. Burton Scrapbook, III, 4–5, Burton Historical Collection, Detroit Public Library; *Detroit Free Press*, Nov. 3, 1881, p. 8.

had collaborated with his friend William H. Anderson, under the pseudonym "Sanda," in writing *Appointed: An American Novel.* The first of many novels written by Negroes that attacked lynching in the South, *Appointed* is set in Detroit in its earlier chapters. The novel relates the story of the educated and cultured young Afro-American, John Saunders, and his schoolmate and white employer's son, Seth Stanley. A graduate of the University of Michigan, John Saunders had been unable to find a job as a civil engineer but, through the intervention of Stanley, he finally secured employment as an assistant bookkeeper and part-time servant "subject to his [Stanley's] call when he thought he needed a valet to accompany him on his rambling trips." Stanley's friends were astonished by Saunders's breeding, that a black man "seemed so intelligent." These whites rationalized that Saunders was unique among Negroes; they refused to allow him to affect their stereotyped view of the uniform character of blacks as a whole. In time, a journey to the South ends in Saunders's being lynched by a "motley" mob.[39]

There was more than a ring of truth to the career of the fictional John Saunders: his life closely paralleled that of Anderson, one of the authors of *Appointed*. Anderson had been born in Sandusky, Ohio, and had come to Detroit in 1873, when he was sixteen. A graduate of Detroit High School, he later received an LL.B. from the Detroit College of Law but never practiced law. A bookkeeper, he was one of the few nineteenth-century Detroit Negroes to work for a leading retail store in a capacity other than porter, messenger, or elevator operator. Presumably the novel reflects Anderson's frustrations in encountering white prejudice and his inability to fully pass over the caste line.[40]

William Anderson's writings confirm Laura Haviland's observation of the "necessity of a few strokes of the reconstruction brush north

[39] *Detroit News-Tribune*, Sept. 6, 1903, p. 4; Sanda [Walter H. Stowers and William H. Anderson], *Appointed: An American Novel* (Detroit, 1894). Vernon Loggins attributed the novel to Stowers in his authoritative *The Negro Author: His Development in America to 1900* (New York, 1931), pp. 325, 405n, but contemporary accounts gave credit to both Stowers and Anderson, and the Detroit Public Library's copy was donated by the joint authors. *Detroit Sunday News-Tribune*, Nov. 7, 1897, p. 24; Sanda, *Appointed*, pp. 35–36, 41, 176.
[40] *Detroit Sunday News-Tribune*, Nov. 7, 1897, p. 24.

of Mason and Dixon's line, as well as south of it, to obliterate the color line." Often Negrophobia in Detroit took the form of willful and malicious violence committed against blacks or their property, frequently under the guise of good-spirited fun. Occasionally, Negro day laborers and whitewashers were hired for a day's work, only to find that the "contractor" and his work orders were bogus. Similar practical jokes at the expense of blacks were considered great sport in Detroit.[41]

Sometimes whites assaulted blacks on the street, without provocation and apparently without motive. During the late nineteenth century "gangs of rowdies," often composed of Irishmen, would invade the Kentucky district, insulting black women and children and beating the men. In 1870 some toughs kicked and beat laborer Henry Faucett and another black man as they left the Detroit Opera House. Not surprisingly, policeman John Hogan arrested Faucett for disorderly conduct. Frequently blacks accused the all-white police force of harassment and brutality. Time and again Detroit newspapers carried reports of the arrest of unidentified or suspicious-looking Negroes, charged with vagrancy or held allegedly as burglars until it could be discovered whether or not any of their possessions were stolen goods. A Negro woman was thus arrested for carrying a rocking chair on a public street. Hugh Carter, later a deputy sheriff, was arrested in his sister's backyard when two apple peddlers harassed them. Harris, his brother-in-law, interceded, asking the police officer why he was arresting Carter, whereupon Harris was beaten. When Mrs. Harris attempted to protect her husband she also was arrested. Sometimes, however, the blacks were able to obtain justice. In 1892, William Larue, a black barber, who had been arrested in September 1891 on a complaint of disturbing the peace, successfully pressed a charge of harassment against patrolman George A. Foran. Witnesses testified that Larue had been walking quietly with friends, and the board of police commissioners agreed that Foran had been guilty of harassing the barber and they fined Foran $100.[42]

---

[41] Laura S. Haviland, *A Woman's Life-Work* (Cincinnati, 1882), p. 451; *Detroit Tribune*, Aug. 18, 1869, p. 1, Sept. 23, 1870, p. 3.

[42] *Detroit Tribune*, Dec. 25, 1871, p. 4, May 27, 1870, p. 3, Jan. 17, 1873, p. 4, Nov. 8, 1869, p. 1; *Plaindealer*, Apr. 11, 1890, Jan. 15, 1892, Jan. 22, 1892. In

Blacks also continued to meet interference in exercising their voting rights. The question of black suffrage had always been a partisan one—with the Republicans in favor and the Democrats against—and the election boards, when Democratically controlled, sought to turn away black voters. In 1872, John Hedgman, a Canadian-born black, sought unsuccessfully to vote in Detroit. His parents had escaped to Canada from slavery in Virginia, and Hedgman had moved to the United States about 1857, when he was twenty years old. He had never applied for United States citizenship, but claimed that he was an American citizen because his parents were citizens. In accordance with the Dred Scott ruling, the Michigan Supreme Court decided that his parents had not been citizens of the United States, as they were legally slaves at the time of his birth. The provisions of the Fourteenth Amendment granting ex-slaves United States citizenship did not apply in this case, the court stated, because the amendment was not retroactive in its effect, and Hedgman's parents were not covered by the relevant provision because they were outside of the country when the amendment became effective. The case is indicative of the sentiment in Michigan at that time "against the Negro's exercise of the voting franchise." [43]

Blacks did not register to vote in Detroit with any great sense of security until the late 1880s. The Democrats annually accused the Republicans of importing blacks from Windsor to vote in Detroit, whereas the Republicans charged the Democrats with registering "foreigners"—mostly Irishmen—and "repeaters." Democratic efforts to thwart black voting were so widespread in 1884 that the federal government had to intervene to enable Negroes to register and vote.

1911 blacks would charge that the Detroit police were "attempting to drive colored men from business who have white patrons and in general exercise an unwarranted supervision over colored and white people who meet in any way." Two years later policemen would begin unlawfully detaining black men seen in the company of white women. The police were ill equipped to distinguish between a light-skinned Negro woman and a white woman, and "in one instance a young colored boy was arrested in company with his mother, a very fair colored woman." They both were subjected to humiliating treatment at the police station. *Crisis*, II (May, 1911), 6–7, V (August, 1913), 188.

[43] *People ex rel Hedgman* v. *Bd. of Registration*, 26 Michigan 51 (1872), *Detroit Tribune*, Oct. 23, 1872, p. 1, Oct. 24, 1872, p. 1; Charles S. Mangum, Jr., *The Legal Status of the Negro* (Chapel Hill, N.C., 1940), p. 373.

In late October 1884, Democratic election inspectors in a number of wards refused to register eligible black voters, among them Charles Webb, a well-known Detroit Republican. The United States supervisors of elections, appointed under statutes aimed at ensuring free elections in the South, were obstructed in their duties and were denied access to the registration books in their efforts to protect Negro suffrage in the election. United States District Attorney Finney announced that "the colored voters are being intimidated generally." On election day some black voters were turned away by election officials and were eventually able to vote only because of the intervention of United States marshals.[44]

The caste line was also in evidence in Detroit's occupations. Most blacks were confined to menial or service employment; few of the city's well-paying industrial or white-collar jobs were open to them. More important, the caste system limited black access to instruments of occupational mobility as apprenticeships, higher education, and unskilled factory jobs remained closed to them.[45]

The effect of the caste system, then, was to assign most, but not all, of Detroit's blacks to an inferior status. Those born within the subordinate caste had little hope of escaping its consequence. Their place of work, their street of residence, and their range of social activities were all limited by the large number of Detroit institutions closed to the black caste. In essence, children of the caste were predestined to experience the limited life chances of their parents.

[44] *Detroit Post*, Oct. 24, 1884, p. 8, Oct. 28, 1884, p. 5, Oct. 29, 1884, p. 5, Nov. 5, 1884, p. 5.
[45] See chapter 4.

CHAPTER IV

Work

I

NINETEENTH-CENTURY DETROIT had been an important, but not major, industrial center. Midcentury factories had produced cigars and shoes; thereafter, exploitation of natural resources in Michigan and along the Great Lakes had led to the growth of Detroit's chemical and iron and steel industries. In the 1880s the city on the straits became a major freight-car builder, foreshadowing its future as the center of the automotive industry. In 1881 the Michigan Car Company's Detroit plant covered twenty-five acres, employed 2,000 men and produced 6,000 freight cars per year. Later the city shifted from railroad car to automobile production and the history of Michigan and Detroit became intertwined with the development of the internal-combustion engine.[1]

The meteoric rise of manufacturing in Detroit, especially of the automotive industry, required an extraordinary supply of labor, and the tide of immigration into the United States between the Civil War and World War I filled this need. More than a majority of Detroit's factory workers from 1890 to 1910 were foreign-born, and some factories almost exclusively employed them; in 1910 all but 106 of 3,750

[1] Victor S. Clark, *History of Manufactures in the United States, 1860–1914* (Washington, 1928), pp. 34, 126, 129, 131, 185, 339, 341–342, 685, 687, 696.

laborers in Detroit's car and railroad shops were foreign-born whites. A large number of Detroit's industrial plants were ethnically organized, and many employers hired only one ethnic group: prior to World War I Dodge Brothers relied exclusively on Polish employees. Some factory managers were prejudiced against particular groups; others favored a single community. When industry became rationalized around the turn of the century, homogeneous work forces seemed even more desirable. A basic managerial guide warned employers to avoid general "help wanted" advertisements and to secure "from men already employed names of friends who they think would make desirable workmen."[2]

Black workers remained outside of Detroit's ethnically organized factories. In 1890 there were no blacks in the brass and ship industries, and only twenty-one blacks were found among the 5,839 male employees in the tobacco, stove, iron, machine, and shoe industries. Ten years later only thirteen Negroes worked in Detroit's book, shoe, brass, chemical, furniture, gas, iron and steel, machine, stove, tin, tobacco, and wire factories—industries employing 10,498 males. Of the 36,598 men reported in the 1900 census to have been engaged in manufacturing and mechanical pursuits, only 139 were Negro, and of these, forty-seven were in the building industry. In 1910 only twenty-five Afro-Americans were recorded among the 10,000 mostly foreign-born, semiskilled operatives and laborers who worked in Detroit's automotive factories.[3]

The ethnic organization of Detroit's factories would be shattered by World War I when the severe labor shortage forced the industrial plants to recruit workers of any nationality, of any background, of

[2] John Marshall Ragland, "The Negro in Detroit," *Southern Workman*, LII (November, 1923), 534, 536; *The Library of Factory Management*, IV, *Labor* (Chicago, 1915), 30. Gerd Korman discusses ethnically organized factories in a city similar to Detroit in *Industrialization, Immigrants and Americanizers: The View from Milwaukee, 1866–1921* (Madison, Wis., 1967), pp. 66–67.

[3] In 1913 the resistance against hiring blacks in factories, especially young men who sought to learn a trade, was so great that it took more than six months of combined effort by the Society for the Prevention of Cruelty to Children, the Poor Commission, and the YMCA to procure a manufacturing-plant job for a fifteen-year-old Negro boy "of unusual mechanical ability who wanted to learn a trade to support his mother and six younger brothers and sisters." *Crisis*, VI (May, 1913), 41.

any color. The entry of blacks into Detroit's factories, however, would have only a slight effect on the seemingly fixed Negro occupational structure. Nearly all black industrial workers entered the city's factories at the bottom of the work ladder, and, in spite of their new industrial roles, they remained, as before, in the city's lowest-paying, least-secure, unskilled jobs. These tasks, and those in the service trades, shared certain common characteristics: they required neither education nor technical training, and the employer made only minimum demands upon the integrity, judgment, and trustworthiness of the employee. The work of the unskilled common or day laborer was similar to that of the semiskilled laborers—dock hands, teamsters, hostlers. The semiskilled and unskilled workers were hired on a daily basis in generally seasonal occupations. They were sometimes referred to as children of poverty. They were constantly threatened by the high pressures of competition, "for behind the unskilled," noted Edith Abbott, "is the whole 'reserve army of industry,'—the immigrants, the vagrants, and the 'unemployable'. . . ." Blacks in Detroit, as elsewhere, were destined to watch the army of industry pass them by, steadily climbing above them on the occupational ladder.[4]

Some black professionals and Negroes seeking a white-collar career faced an equally dismal future. Many black professionals were unable to pursue their careers in Detroit. John Saunders, the hero of Walter Stowers's and William H. Anderson's novel, *Appointed*, reflected the experiences of the authors, who, for a long period of time, were professionals without practices. Attorney Stowers worked as an editor, deputy sheriff, and government clerk for a quarter of a century before he opened a law practice, and Attorney Anderson never practiced law. Although black professionals and clerical workers increased in number after the turn of the century as the black community in Detroit developed its own economy, the picture still

[4] George Edmund Haynes, *Negro New-Comers in Detroit, Michigan: A Challenge to Christian Statesmanship. A Preliminary Study* (New York, 1918), p. 12; Mayor's Inter-racial Committee, *The Negro in Detroit* (Detroit, 1926), III, 15; Edith Abbott, "The Wages of Unskilled Labor in the United States, 1850–1900," *Journal of Political Economy*, XIII (June, 1905), 322–324. The department of labor reported that Detroit had a greater demand for *unskilled* labor than any other city in the United States. *Reports of the Department of Labor 1919* (Washington, 1920), p. 987.

remained bleak: "He may be a janitor, but cannot be a clerk," D. A. Straker wrote in 1901, "he may be a porter on a steam-car, but not a conductor; he may sweep the lawyer's office, but cannot become his law-partner, his typewriter, or his stenographer; he may buy of the merchant, but cannot become his clerk; he may carry the hod, but cannot contract for the building." Of nearly 15,000 male clerks, commercial travelers, agents, bookkeepers, cashiers, and accountants in Detroit in 1910, only forty-six were black.[5]

Black women fared no better than the men. In 1910, 87 percent of the employed black women were employed in domestic and personal service. There was not a single black among the 1,186 telephone operators in the city; among the 2,081 saleswomen in stores in Detroit, only 1 was black; among 1,474 women clerks, 3 were Negro; and of 7,106 office clerical workers, only 10 were black. It is probable that these 14 Negro women with white-collar jobs were employed in black businesses. Black women were also excluded from most of Detroit's factories until World War I.[6]

II

From the Civil War until World War I the largest proportion of black workers in Detroit was engaged in service occupations. Though the economy of the city changed radically during this period, becoming a great center of automobile factories and foundry and machine shops, Afro-Americans remained highly concentrated in the least-rewarding and lowest-status occupational group: personal and domestic service.

Most black women worked as domestics. In 1870 nearly 56 percent of employed black women in Detroit worked as servants; in 1890,

[5] D. Augustus Straker, "Greater Opportunity for the Civic Development of Mankind," *Colored American Magazine*, II (1901), 191.

[6] In effect, black women were being excluded from the rapidly expanding commercial world. Office and telephone work opened up new directions for women outside the world of the factory—yet black women could find work in these occupations only with black employers. In 1910, Graham Taylor, in a survey of telephone companies, reported that the applications of colored women were rejected on the basis of their color alone. "Industrial Survey of the Month—The Telephone Girl," *Survey*, XXIV (April, 1910), 61.

51 percent; and in 1910, 43 percent. By comparison, in 1890 approximately one-third of the employed white women were servants, and by 1910 only one-eighth of the whites were domestics. Although blacks comprised 2.6 percent of the female work force in 1890 and 2 percent in 1910, they made up 4 percent of the servants in 1890, and over 6 percent in 1910. Similarly, black men constituted less than 1.5 percent of the male work force, yet they comprised 20 percent of the male servants in the city.[7]

The problems and trials of servitude changed little during the nineteenth century. From the publication of the earliest housewife's guides in the 1840s to the establishment of public employment agencies in Michigan in the early twentieth century, the "servant problem" or "girl question" was synonymous with domestic service. Nineteenth-century homes tended to be large—chores were performed by manual labor, and households required care and maintenance beyond the ability of one woman. A large number of households employed servants, and those unable to afford hired help might offer board and lodging to a young girl, in exchange for housework. Theoretically the girl would be an apprentice housekeeper, learning skills to be applied later in her own home. In reality she was a servant.[8]

Since the early decades of the nineteenth century, domestic service has been viewed as a variety of servitude. In the 1840s Catherine Beecher observed that servants objected to being called "servant," associating the word with slavery. Beecher linked service with a fall in fortunes and advised housewives to take a Christian approach to the servant problem; in treating servants, she counseled, "let a mother or daughter conceive of their own circumstances as so changed, that the daughter must go out to service."[9]

Not all domestic guides sympathized with the servant. In *House and Home: A Complete Housewife's Guide* (1889), a typical house-

---

[7] 1870 manuscript census; *Eleventh Census 1890*, II, 664–665; *Thirteenth Census 1910*, IV, 503–505.

[8] Catherine E. Beecher, *A Treatise on Domestic Economy for the Use of Young Ladies at Home and at School* (3rd ed., New York, 1845), p. 205; *Annual Report of the Department of Labor of the State of Michigan 1911*, p. 28 (hereafter cited as *Labor: Mich*).

[9] Beecher, *Treatise on Domestic Economy*, pp. 205–208.

wife's bible which circulated toward the end of the century, Marian Harland complained that the present generation of girls felt that domestic service was beneath them. "The middle-aged mother or aunt of the smart colored damsel," Harlan counseled, "furnishes us with the best 'help' to be had in this, or any other country, and speaks of herself and her congeners in her honest self-respect, as 'servants.' " Marian Harland, like so many other Americans, understood that no American in the 1880s except middle-aged blacks had known actual servitude.[10]

The disadvantages of domestic service far outweighed the benefits of steady work and the acquisition of housekeeping skills. First of all, servants had comparatively less independence than those in other occupations. The work day was long, and generally, except for the one day off per week, the servant remained on call around the clock. Second, a domestic lived in isolation, generally lacking companionship and with limited time for social contacts. Third, a domestic suffered much abuse because her employer arbitrarily determined her living and her working conditions. Finally, no promotions or advancement were possible except in some hotel positions. It was thus not the work that was objectionable "but the conditions under which the work is performed."[11]

Domestic service was synonymous with social inferiority. "The feeling that employment in domestic service involves social inferiority," the United States Industrial Commission reported in 1901, "is practically universal. . . ." Significantly, the stigma of inferiority attached to the individual, not just to the occupation, an unfortunate distinction shared only by the dockworker. In service—unique among mass occupations—the individual was hired, not the labor of the individual. Thus a "badge of social inferiority" was placed upon the servant "in characters as unchangeable as are spots of a leopard." For a woman, part of the badge might be the cap and apron of a domestic;

[10] Marian Harland, *House and Home: A Complete Housewife's Guide* (Philadelphia, 1889), pp. 93–94.

[11] *Report of the Industrial Commission on the Relations and Conditions of Capital and Labor*, XIV (Washington, 1901), 757–758; Lucy Maynard Salmon, *Domestic Service* (New York, 1897), pp. 141–147; Mary V. Robinson, *Domestic Workers and Their Employment Relations* (Washington, 1924), p. 1.

but for all it was the form of address—servants were called by their Christian names.[12]

"Every family, however lowly in the financial scale," Russell McLauchlin recalled of his youth before World War I on Alfred Street in Detroit, "had a hired girl." Domestic servants did housework as well as errands for the family, and visitors to the early-morning produce markets in Detroit encountered black servants bargaining for their employers' provisions. The more desirable domestic tasks went to white servants, whereas more strenuous tasks and those involving less of an intimate relationship with the employing family were commonly reserved for blacks. By the turn of the century the foreign-born were generally preferred as servants because they were considered to be of a "better class" than the native-born blacks.[13]

Russell McLauchlin remembered that on Alfred Street the seamstress was a *Miss* Van Horn, his family's "hired girl" was Irish, and his family's laundress was always a colored girl. Negroes were engaged as domestic laundresses on a large scale; from 1870 to 1910, about one-fifth of Detroit laundresses not in commercial laundries were black. The work was more physically strenuous than housework, and a laundress shared none of the advantages of domestic work. Overall, the occupation was even less desirable than housework.[14]

Men filled nearly all of the well-paying and higher-status jobs in Detroit, shunning domestic service not only because of the low pay and harsh working conditions, but also as an occupation hardly befitting the paternal role of the male in American society. The great industrial expansion between the Civil War and World War I reduced the proportion of men who were forced to accept work as domestic servants, but the industrial caste line barred blacks from the factories and therefore the percentage of Negroes in service increased. In 1870 blacks comprised only 9 percent of all male servants in Detroit, whereas by 1910, 20 percent of the 946 male servants, constituting nearly 9 percent of the entire black work force, were Negro.

[12] *Report of the Industrial Commission*, XIV, 759; Salmon, *Domestic Service*, pp. 154–158.

[13] Russell McLauchlin, *Alfred Street* (Detroit, 1946), p. 45; William Morris, *Letters Sent Home* (n.p., [1874]), p. 247; Salmon, *Domestic Service*, pp. 91–92.

[14] McLauchlin, *Alfred Street*, pp. 40, 48, 87; U.S. Bureau of the Census, *Statistics of Women at Work* (Washington, 1907), pp. 240–243.

By contrast less than ½ of 1 percent of employed white males in 1910 were servants. The cause of this discrepancy was evident to blacks: few occupations other than service tasks were open to them.[15]

The status of hotel and restaurant work was closely related to that of domestic service. In 1870 nearly 13 percent of the black male work force worked as waiters, and in 1910 nearly 17 percent served meals. Although some restaurant owners would not hire Negroes as waiters, blacks were the largest single group in the trade. In 1910 over 48 percent of all waiters in Detroit were black.[16]

"Social and caste prejudice," according to D. A. Straker, were responsible for the black overrepresentation among waiters. Excluded from the trades, they sought employment as waiters in hotels and restaurants. Waiters worked long hours and were expected to behave in a servile manner, and they served many masters: they had to please customers, head waiters, and proprietors. An 1893 study reported that there were few occupations other than waiting in which employees took so much abuse. Although the prestige of some hotel employees was high—the hotel clerk was considered a professional man and paid accordingly—the status of hotel waiters was extremely low. In restaurants, only dishwashers received less pay: even porters and elevator operators were paid higher wages than waiters. A skilled tradesman could earn more than three times the hourly wage of a waiter in Detroit.[17]

[15] 1870 manuscript census; *Ninth Census 1870,* I, 785; *Thirteenth Census 1910,* IV, 553–555; Detroit *Plaindealer,* Nov. 22, 1889. It is important to note the age distribution of the thirty male servants in Detroit in 1870:

Under 15	3	36 to 45	2
16 to 25	16	46 to 55	1
26 to 35	5	Over 56	3

Although the distribution is skewed toward the lower ages, it is clear that not all of the black servants were young men with at least the hope of rising above the servant class.

[16] 1870 manuscript census; *Thirteenth Census 1910,* XIV, 553–555. Want ads frequently read "WANTED—FIRST CLASS WHITE WAITER," and one Detroit restaurant owner declared "I wouldn't have a Negro waiter in the house." *Detroit Tribune,* Apr. 27, 1887, p. 6, Apr. 11, 1886, p. 5.

[17] D.A. Straker to the Editor, *Detroit Tribune,* July 5, 1895, p. 8; "Condition of Bakers, Waiters and Miners," *Social Economist,* V (November, 1893), 285; Jefferson Williamson, *The American Hotel: An Anecdotal History* (New York, 1930), p. 170; *Labor: Mich 1916,* pp. 468–469, 501–505, 529. For a waitress's

Head waiters were a breed apart from restaurant and dining room waiters, and the social distance between the two was great. Head waiters were well paid, had relatively high status and sometimes national reputations, and actually ran the hotel dining room—hired and fired, distributed work, and fixed the hours and wages. They had their own national organization, the Head and Second Waiters' Association, and its president, W. Forrest Cozart, wrote a weekly column for the *Freeman*. The difference in social levels between the head and second waiters on the one hand, and the ordinary waiters on the other, was so great that when supervisory positions opened, the hotels would seek experienced men outside of Detroit rather than promote waiters within the city. In 1900 Russell House took over two months in selecting a head waiter, finally hiring H. T. Eubanks of Cleveland, Ohio, after men from Brooklyn, New York, and Indianapolis had turned down the job. Three years later, head waiter Henry Williams of the Hotel Cadillac advertised nationally for a second waiter rather than promoting someone on his staff. Among the requisites: a man "not too dark in color."[18]

Waiters had little job security, and the few attempts made at unionization among them in Detroit before World War I failed dismally. In 1884 an attempt to organize a waiter's union proved abortive. Five years later a few black waiters formed an occupationally based Waiter's Benefit Association but it seems to have been short-lived. Because waiting required no previous experience, troublesome waiters could easily be replaced. When twelve Afro-American waiters struck the Griswold House Hotel in 1882, the *Detroit Post* reported, "They were struck from the pay roll and twelve other waiters struck a job." Similarly, in 1892, black waiters struck the Hotel Cadillac "just before the dinner hour"; the strikers were fired and new men hired, while "the dinner was delayed somewhat."[19]

---

thoroughly negative view of the profession see Frances Donovan, *The Woman Who Waits* (Boston, 1920).

[18] Indianapolis *Freeman*, Nov. 24, 1900; *Hotel World*, reprinted in *Freeman*, Jan. 10, 1903.

[19] *Detroit Post & Tribune*, Mar. 28, 1884, p. 2, Apr. 2, 1884, p. 2; *Plaindealer*, Jan. 24, 1889; *Detroit Post*, June 4, 1885, p. 5; *Annual Report of the Bureau of Labor and Industrial Statistics of the State of Michigan 1893*, p. 1212 (hereafter cited as *BLS:Mich*).

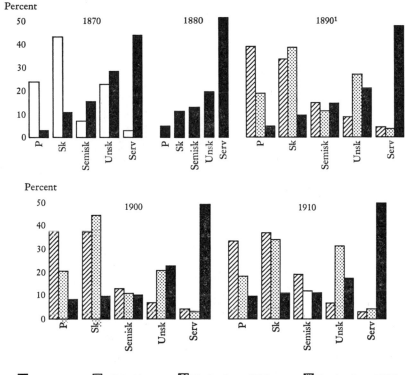

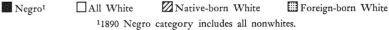
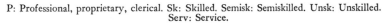

■ Negro[1] □ All White ▨ Native-born White ▦ Foreign-born White

[1]1890 Negro category includes all nonwhites.

P: Professional, proprietary, clerical. Sk: Skilled. Semisk: Semiskilled. Unsk: Unskilled.
Serv: Service.

FIGURE 2 *Occupational Distribution, by Percent, of White and Black Males, Detroit, 1870–1910.*

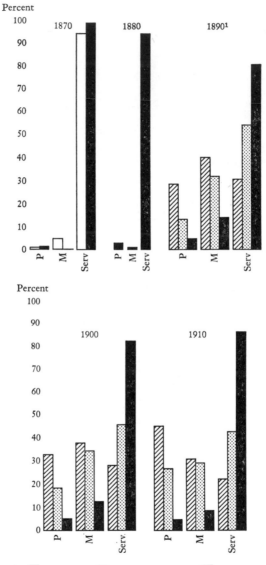

FIGURE 3 *Occupational Distribution, by Percent, of White and Black Females, Detroit, 1870–1910.*

Innumerable other black men and women worked in service occupations similar to those of domestic servant, laundress, or waiter. Hotels were staffed with such black workers as porters, scrubwomen, dishwashers, bellboys, and chambermaids. These employees worked more hours for less pay than did the workers in the semiskilled and skilled occupations. For unskilled blacks and recent immigrants, however, other job opportunities were either limited or nonexistent.

Barbering was unique among domestic and personal service occupations in that it necessitated acquired skills and offered the opportunity of upward mobility through shop ownership. The service began to flourish in the United States in the 1840s when men's hair styles underwent a radical change. Long hair, folded under at the back of the head, lost favor and the half shingle or short cut became popular and required regular clipping. At first only a hotel service, barbering quickly expanded, and shops appeared throughout the business districts of American cities. Though barbering required some skill, the period of apprenticeship was short—a teen-ager might learn the trade within a year's service as a part-time apprentice and part-time sweeper. Once a journeyman, a barber realistically could hope to establish or acquire his own shop.[20]

Although barbering was considered a profession, barbers were highly sensitive about their low status as personal service workers. Like waiters, they worked long hours for low pay, catering to the whims of the customers. Barbering shared with other service occupations the potentially degrading customer-servant relationship and the isolation of domestic servants. Many barbers were literally journeymen—transients traveling from one town to another, commonly with the hope of establishing their own shop. They were able to enjoy few of the amenities of community life, partly because the steadily employed among them worked the longest hours of any occupation. In 1886 a census of Detroit barbershops reported that barbers averaged more than thirteen working hours a day, and they worked Saturday

[20] M. J. Vieira, *The Tonsorial Art Pamphlet, Origin of the Trade, the Business in America and Other Countries* (Indianapolis, 1877), p. 12. For the career of a border-state barber from apprentice to business man see J. M. Hazelwood, "How to Establish and Maintain the Barber Business," Report, *Fifth Annual Convention, National Negro Business League 1904* (Pensacola, Fla., [1904]), pp. 104–107.

night and all day Sunday. Of the forty-seven men surveyed, only three owned their own homes, and only one had a bank account.[21]

Stigmatized as a service occupation, barbering further was held in low prestige because it was a black and later a foreign-born profession. In the late nineteenth century, ironically, Detroit blacks were slowly pushed out of barbering, the one service occupation that offered them a direct path to middle-class status. In 1870, 55 percent of Detroit's 138 male barbers were black. By 1890 the number of black barbers had risen by nearly half, but blacks then comprised only 24 percent of the male barbers as compared to the 30 percent of the male barbers who were foreign-born, and the additional 24 percent who had at least one foreign-born parent. Thereafter, as the number of barbers increased approximately 50 percent in each decade, the absolute number of black barbers decreased. In 1910 only 78 or 7.3 percent of Detroit's barbers were black.[22]

The declining number of black barbers was due to increased competition from the foreign-born, the tightening color line in barbering, and discrimination against black barbershop owners. Large-scale immigration to the United States threw thousands of foreign-born, in Detroit and elsewhere, into competition with Negroes for low-paying, low-status service tasks. Although barbering was the only task among the service occupations that required prior training, it was the skill that the largest number of Italians had brought with them to the United States. Blacks were also hurt by the restrictive color line common in barbering. By the late 1880s few help-wanted advertisements for barbers failed to specify "white only," and black barbers were gradually restricted to a Negro clientele. Moreover, technological changes in shaving slowly released barbers from some of the stigma attached to a service occupation. Prior to the invention of the safety razor, men went to a barbershop more often for a shave than for a haircut. Shaving was more of a service task and required less skill than the cutting of hair. Once King Gillette invented the safety razor (around the turn of the century), however, men went to the barbershop less often, and the service acquired a slightly more

[21] *BLS:Mich 1886*, p. 296.
[22] 1870 manuscript census; *Ninth Census 1870*, I, 785; *Eleventh Census 1890*, II, 664; *Twelfth Census 1900*, II, 544; *Thirteenth Census 1910*, IV, 554.

Binga row on the southeast corner of Hastings and Rowena streets, shown about 1890, was originally owned by a Negro barber, William Binga. Each dwelling unit was only the width of a door and a window, and the small row of houses exemplified what Detroiters referred to as tenements. (Burton Historical Collection, Detroit Public Library)

Story-and-a-half wooden buildings such as this one at Clinton and Macomb streets usually housed two families. It was common practice to sublet apartments as well as to take in boarders. (Burton Historical Collection, Detroit Public Library)

Larned Street, Detroit, c. 1890. The better class of whites and Negroes once lived on Larned, Fort, and Congress streets, adjacent to the eastern boundaries of the Kentucky district, but by 1900 only a few of the older families remained. (Burton Historical Collection, Detroit Public Library)

Black business began to develop in Detroit from the 1880s into the twentieth century. Numbers of black men were owners of small shops and stores such as this grocery at Rivard and Fort streets, c. 1900. (Burton Historical Collection, Detroit Public Library)

This three-story brick building at Beaubien and Macomb streets was typical of the "attached building"—a commercial structure with apartments above the ground floor—that appeared in Detroit's near east side after the 1890s. (Burton Historical Collection, Detroit Public Library)

Robert A. Pelham, Jr., was the leading black politician in Detroit from 1882 to the end of the century. He was active in the 1896 Republican National Convention and held various government appointments on the state and national level. While working for the Bureau of the Census he invented the first tabulating machine used in the census of manufactures, and compiled the "mortality" and "home ownership" sections of the monumental demographic volume, *Negro Population in the United States 1790–1915*. (Simmons, *Men of Mark*, 1887)

D. Augustus Straker was a prominent member of Detroit's black elite for nearly two decades. Born in Barbados, he studied to become an Episcopalian clergyman but later turned to the law, graduating with honors from Howard University in 1871. He was dean of law at Allen University before moving to Detroit in 1887, where he built a distinguished career in politics and letters. (Simmons, *Men of Mark*, 1887)

Organization of the weekly *Plaindealer* in 1883 was an important landmark in the history of black Detroit. The founders are shown here:
Standing, from left, Robert A. Pelham, Jr., Walter H. Stowers, William H. Anderson; seated, Benjamin B. Pelham, Byron G. Redmond.
During eleven years of publication the *Plaindealer* was a champion of
race unity, promoter of black business, and leading force in Republican
politics. It had a Midwest circulation of about 2,500 subscribers. (Warren
[comp.], *Michigan Manual of Freedmen's Progress*, 1915)

This drugstore at 717 Rivard, photographed c. 1919, was owned by Dr. Albert H. Johnson and his brother, Dr. William E. Johnson. Apartments on the second floor were rented to other middle-class blacks. (Warren [comp.], *Michigan Manual of Freedmen's Progress*, 1915)

At the turn of the century some of the leaders in the Detroit black community lived on tree-lined streets in large, single-family houses such as these on Canfield Avenue. (Warren [comp.], *Michigan Manual of Freedmen's Progress*, 1915)

An alley scene in Detroit, 1911. Many blocks in the near east side were bisected by service alleys, originally designed for access to stables and removal of rubbish and garbage. Later, tenements such as these were built in the alleys. (*Survey*, 1911)

impersonal character and hence became a more desirable profession for whites. Finally, the number of black shop owners declined as barbershops, especially hotel barbershops, became more profitable and the shop owner became more of a businessman and less of a boss or foreman barber. In 1884 one-quarter of the barbershops in Detroit were Negro-owned; by 1908, fewer than one-fiftieth had Negro owners. In the 1860s, 1870s, and 1880s the leading and most lucrative hotel barbershops were black-owned; few of these shops remained in black hands by the turn of the century. As old leases in hotels expired or owners died, Negroes were unsuccessful in their attempts to lease the hotel shops. With the color line clearly drawn in barbering, it was inevitable, through attrition, that blacks would disappear from the trade. By 1910 the black barbers in Detroit were cutting only black men's hair.[23]

III

Detroit has been an important lake port since the 1830s. During the nineteenth century Lake Erie ships arrived at Detroit with manufactured goods and passengers from as far east as New York, and Huron and Superior vessels steamed into the harbor with raw materials—ore and lumber—from Michigan and Wisconsin. The lake boats in the Detroit harbor had to be loaded, unloaded, reloaded, fueled, and refueled. Dock workers worked feverishly in the ships' cargo and fuel holds, but spent much time idly awaiting the arrival of the vessels.

The annual city directories and decennial federal censuses conceal that a significant segment of Detroit's black males were engaged

[23] Eliot Lord, John J. D. Trenor, and Samuel J. Barrows, *The Italians in America* (New York, 1905), pp. 63–64; *Detroit Tribune*, June 22, 1887, p. 6, May 18, 1887, p. 6; *Detroit City Directory 1908*; *Plaindealer*, June 13, 1890. For the story of the safety razor, see *The Gillette Blade*, I (February, 1908). There is no evidence that Michigan's barber license law had any effect on restricting black entry. Barbers were first licensed in Michigan in 1869 but the state board estimated that, in 1913, when the old law was revised, about 45 percent of the state's barbers were unlicensed. Those denied journeymen licenses received apprentice cards. *Biennial Report of the Michigan State Board of Examiners of Barbers 1913–1914* (Lansing, 1915), pp. 3–5.

in loading and unloading lake vessels along the Detroit River. In 1880 the manuscript census schedules recorded four black dock hands; yet Detroit's newspapers had regularly reported Negroes' working the wharves and piers prior to the Civil War, and the number of black longshoremen had increased during the war. Few longshoremen or their wives, however, would admit that the head of the household was employed on the docks. In New York City just prior to World War I, Charles Barnes found that longshoremen's wives told the census enumerators that their husbands were employed as laborers or shipping clerks. As working men, the reputation of dock workers was among the lowest, and Barnes concluded that "they were ashamed of the occupation." What was concealed in the public record, however, could not be concealed in society: the broken fingers and gnarled hands of a regularly employed longshoreman could not be hidden.[24]

Though not a desirable occupation, dock work had an indispensable attraction for black workers: stevedores hired blacks, and the work required no previous training or experience. Men did not aspire to be longshoremen; they simply drifted down to the docks when no other work was available. Dock workers would appear for work early in the morning to await the arrival of the ships, and then the men worked in gangs, hired on the spot by a boss or stevedore. The hiring process—the shape-up—was quick and highly discriminatory. A few men would get the nod from the boss as they stood in a semi-circle around the pier, and they would be hired. The rest would await the next shape-up, most likely in a nearby saloon.[25]

Those lucky enough to be tapped for work were hired on an hourly basis. The day laborer and the domestic were at least hired for a full day's work, but not the longshoreman. When the hold was unloaded and the baggage taken off the boat, the men were paid. They

[24] Charles B. Barnes, *The Longshoreman* (New York, 1915), pp. 17–18. The status of longshoremen in Detroit was so low that the *Plaindealer* of July 25, 1890, in reporting the suicide of the once regularly employed Edward Dempsey, declared, "It is claimed he was out of heart at loss of steady employment, and the enforced work of a stevedore and deck hand."

[25] Commission on Industrial Relations, *Final Report and Testimony*, III (Washington, 1916), 2054–2055, 2172; E. Franklin Frazier, "A Negro Industrialist Group," *Howard Review*, I (June, 1924), 203.

then returned to the waterfront saloon or pier shack to await the next vessel and the next shape-up. The hourly pay was relatively high but the annual compensation was low. Although longshoremen were paid twice the hourly wage of street-railway employees in Detroit in 1897, they probably earned less than half as much annually. With the best of weather conditions, the port of Detroit was open only eight months of the year, and few dock workers managed to eke out more than seven months' work. An 1899 report on longshoremen in Bay City, a Lake Huron port sheltered in Saginaw Bay, eighty-seven miles north of Detroit, revealed that dock workers there were paid at the rate of four dollars a day but averaged only one dollar per work day. Detroit probably was no different, and increasing industrialization of the city around the turn of the twentieth century probably served to widen the wage, security, and prestige gap between longshoremen and other workers.[26]

Refueling of steamers was the least attractive work task among the many undesirable chores of the longshoremen. Since the lake steamers could stop at any time to refuel, coal handlers had to be on call twenty-four hours a day. If dock hands who were engaged in refueling were married—it is doubtful that very many were—they would have had to live near the docks in the notorious Potomac Quarter. The bachelors passed their days working, eating, sleeping, and gambling on a wharf surrounded by coal and water. Not surprisingly, refuelers were nearly always black men.[27]

It is possible that as many as 30 percent of Detroit's male black population engaged, regularly or occasionally, in dock work. In 1894, Longshoremen's Union No. 5392, a local of Afro-Americans employed in loading and unloading coal and raw materials from vessels, claimed 300 members, which would have been nearly one-third of

[26] Commission on Industrial Relations, *Final Report*, III, 2054–2055; Barnes, *Longshoreman*, p. 57; *BLS:Mich 1898*, pp. 87, 171; *BLS:Mich 1899*, p. 100; *BLS:Mich 1900*, p. 48. Work on the docks, and on the lake boats—another relatively large black occupation—guaranteed winter unemployment. Because they lacked security, longshoremen and sailors would ask to be sent to the house of corrections during the winter months so that they would be assured of at least shelter and board. *Detroit Tribune*, Dec. 18, 1871, p. 4, Mar. 26, 1872, p. 4, Jan. 18, 1875, p. 5.

[27] *Detroit Sunday News-Tribune*, Sept. 27, 1896, p. 18.

the total black male work force at the time. A few years later the growing International Longshoremen's Association (ILA) claimed 143 dues-paying members in Detroit in two locals. The proportion of blacks in the ILA reflects to some degree the proportion of blacks working on the waterfront; in the 1890s probably one-fifth of Detroit's dock workers were black. There are no statistics to indicate the changes over time in the racial composition of longshoremen as a group, but it is possible that blacks comprised a larger proportion of dock workers in the 1870s and 1880s than they did in the 1890s and the first decade of the twentieth century. It is likely that the immigrants who arrived in Detroit after 1890—the Poles and Italians—replaced many blacks on the docks.[28]

I V

The uniformed municipal services were closed to blacks until the 1890s. Black citizens of Detroit long had agitated for representation on the police force, but their efforts were met with resistance and deception. In 1886 when three Negro candidates passed the required examinations for the position of policeman, threats of immediate resignations and a general police strike kept the force lily white, although Bernie Chappee, a black patronage appointee, worked at police headquarters as a clerk and eventually rose to the position of chief clerk. In 1890 a number of Afro-Americans applied for appointment as patrolmen, supported by black politicians and the Detroit *Plaindealer.* Joseph Stowers, brother of the *Plaindealer* editor, became a probationary policeman in the spring of that year, but he was dropped from the rolls after he had served for two months. Three years later L. T. Toliver, brother of the attorney and realtor of Harry T. Toliver and Company, became the first regular black police officer on the force. Under the continued pressure of black politicians, most notably Wayne County Circuit Court Commissioner D. A.

---

[28] *Detroit Tribune,* Sept. 27, 1894, p. 5; *Detroit Sunday News-Tribune,* Oct. 21, 1894, p. 19; *BLS:Mich 1896,* pp. 250–251. In 1902 there were sixty blacks in the longshoremen's local. W. E. B. DuBois (ed.), *The Negro Artisan* (Atlanta, 1902), p. 161.

Straker, two more black patrolmen were appointed in 1895. There-after Negroes remained on the force though their representation was never more than token. In 1910 only seven of Detroit's 657 police-men were black.[29]

Blacks had some success in gaining appointment to the city's street railways, but virtually no success in becoming firemen. After break-ing the caste line in the police department, Straker turned his at-tention to the street-railway companies, and some blacks were hired on the cars despite the opposition of the motormen and even though it meant the firing of a white employee who then threatened that "if any colored men were put on the Michigan Avenue cars he would find them going toward the river." In 1900 reporter James Samuel Stemons found that Detroit was only one of three northern cities with black street-railway employees. Cleveland and Indianapolis were the other two cities. Integration of the street railways in all three cities did not, however, advance beyond the token stage. Unlike the con-ductors and motormen, the firemen, hewing to their lily-white heritage, successfully resisted integration. In 1910 only one of De-troit's 623 firemen was black.[30]

V

It had become apparent to blacks by the 1890s that as a group they had fared badly in competition with immigrants. Black residents of Detroit's near east side discovered that, although their immigrant neighbors had come to the city without jobs, without skills, without even the knowledge of English, they eventually secured better hous-ing and better jobs than did Negroes. "First it was de Irish, den it

[29] *Detroit Tribune*, Jan. 5, 1890, p. 9, Jan. 31, 1886, p. 4; *Plaindealer*, July 31, 1891, July 11, 1890, March 3, 1893; clipping, *Detroit News*, Jan. 7, 1945, in "George W. Carmichael," "Negroes," Reading Room File, Burton Historical Collection, Detroit Public Library; clipping, *Detroit Informer*, June 9, 1898, "Alfred W. Wilson," in file "Negro," Historical Records Survey of Michigan, University of Michigan (hereafter cited as NHRSM); *Thirteenth Census 1910*, IV, 554.

[30] *Detroit Tribune*, July 22, 1895, p. 5, Feb. 6, 1896, p. 5; James Samuel Stem-ons, "The Industrial Color-Line in the North," *Century Magazine*, LX (July, 1900), 478; *Thirteenth Census 1910*, IV, 554.

was de Dutch," observed a black whitewasher in 1891, "and now it's de Polacks as grinds us down. I s'pose when dey [the Poles] gets like de Irish and stands up for a fair price, some odder strangers'll come over de sea 'nd jine de faimily and cut us down again."[31]

The ability of many immigrants to improve their living conditions and better their jobs while most blacks remained poor servants and domestics pained Detroit's Negro leaders. In the late 1880s and for the next decade, Detroit blacks joined in the protests against immigrants that were voiced throughout the United States and especially in the Midwest. The *Plaindealer's* editorials complained of the "influx of foreigners of the lowest classes," of arrivals "of the most dissolute and depraved classes," and openly supported restrictions on immigration. Dissatisfied with the limited character of the anti-immigration legislation passed in the 1880s, the Republican editors of the *Plaindealer* charged both major political parties with "cowardice" for not turning away the "ignorant, penniless, and sometimes criminal hordes of immigrants that are landed at Castle Garden by the thousands each week." "Common sense," declared the weekly, "demands the restriction of foreign immigration."[32]

D. A. Straker and Robert Barnes, two of Detroit's leading black attorneys and politicians in the 1890s and 1900s, added their voices to the rhetoric of nativism that spread across America after 1886. As the Detroit Negro who had led the fight against the caste line in the municipal uniformed services, the skilled trades, and the city's factories, Straker questioned the equity of granting immigrants relatively well-paying jobs in Detroit while native-born Afro-Americans were limited to menial occupations. Because many of the black gains in the late nineteenth century were tied to the influence of Negroes in the Republican party and because a Democratic or reform victory diminished the amount of patronage received by blacks, conflict soon developed between the black Republicans and Irish Democrats.

In the 1890s the nativistic and anti-labor American Protective As-

[31] Clipping, *Detroit News*, May 24, 1891, in C. M. Burton Scrapbook, III, 138, Burton Historical Collection, Detroit Public Library.

[32] John Higham, *Strangers in the Land* (New York, 1965), pp. 53, 77, 81; *Plaindealer*, Apr. 11, 1890, Aug. 22, 1890, May 29, 1891, Sept. 20, 1889.

sociation (APA), which was especially strong in Michigan, welcomed Negro support. Barnes, black Republican, one-time law partner of Straker, and, after 1905, associate of former *Plaindealer* editor Walter H. Stowers, spoke before APA groups in Detroit. Addressing APA Council No. 108 in Mayor's Hall in Detroit in 1891, Barnes played on the xenophobic and anti-Catholic prejudices of his audience. A year later, before APA Council No. 9, Barnes called for "slumbering America [to] awake!" He warned his sympathetic listeners that their own patriotic attitudes permitted them to be "hoodwinked" by the multitudes landing on American shores. The new arrivals "assume to put on the role of American citizenship—but in truth, only to hide their treasonable garments with a mental reservation to be true and true only to the Pope sitting at Rome. . . ."[33]

Stung by continued discrimination and the severity of the caste line, Detroit blacks failed to sense the irony of their xenophobic stance. They held deeply the American faith in an open society, but they mistakenly sensed that their interests lay with the native born American groups. The apparent polarization of municipal politics, which cast the Democrats in the role of the party of the foreign-born while the Republicans united the native-born, strengthened the blacks' sense of identification as a native-born group. These feelings were further reinforced by the competitive relationship of blacks and immigrants. Since immigrants entered the labor market at the bottom of the occupational structure—the level at which most blacks remained —the two groups were in head-to-head competition. Through the years many of the foreign-born rose to better-paying jobs and more secure futures while Negroes remained at the bottom. Understandably the blacks lashed out at the immigrants, blaming them as the cause of blocked mobility. Though the immigrants, as a group, acceded to the caste system, they can hardly be accused of bringing it to America in the late nineteenth century. It is hard to believe that, if the valve had been closed, if the flood of immigration had been stopped, blacks would not have remained at the lowest level of the

[33] Higham, *Strangers in the Land*, pp. 81, 86; copies of Barnes's APA speeches, "The Duty of the Hour" (1891) and "Slumbering America—Awake!" (n.d.), in "Robert C. Barnes," NHRSM.

occupational ladder. It was the caste system, after all, that severely restricted the employment opportunities of the city's blacks.

VI

Until the 1930s, when the National Industrial Recovery Act enabled unions to gain a foothold in the city, Detroit was a bastion of the open shop. Most locals enjoyed only an ephemeral existence, and those that managed to survive were weak. An organizer for the barbers' union in 1910 found the Detroit labor movement "in very bad shape." "There is hardly a craft in the city," he wrote, "that is organized." [34]

Negroes and labor unions remained far apart. First of all, most blacks were in occupations ignored by unions; servants, waiters, and day laborers remained outside of the nineteenth-century American labor movement. Second, when blacks expressed an interest in organizing—Detroit Negroes were represented at the 1869 Colored National Labor Union—whites did not evidence much interest. When nearly two decades later, in the 1880s, the Knights of Labor openly courted blacks, no Afro-Americans in Detroit would join the organization because, according to the *Plaindealer*, previous rebuffs at the hands of trade organizations had made Detroit blacks suspicious of the Knights. D. A. Straker articulated the black attitude toward unions: "The 'ostensible object' of labor unions," he wrote in *The New South Investigated*, "is to protect labor against the oppression of capital," but their "hidden purpose is to shut out and keep shut the doors of industry against a class of people on account of their race, color and past condition." Although opposed to unions that discriminated, Straker endorsed those "which truly have for their end and purpose, reform in the use of capital." [35]

[34] *Journeyman Barber*, VI (July, 1910), 171.

[35] *New National Era*, Jan. 13, 1870, Jan. 18, 1871, p. 2; Sterling D. Spero and Abram L. Harris, *The Black Worker* (reprinted New York, 1968), pp. 24–27; Sidney H. Kessler, "The Negro in the Knights of Labor," M.A. thesis, Columbia University, 1950, p. 54; Straker, *The New South Investigated* (Detroit, 1888), pp. 98, 186. In 1886 the Knights announced plans for the organization of a segregated colored assembly in Detroit but there is no evidence that it was actually established. *Detroit Tribune*, Oct. 27, 1886, p. 5.

By the turn of the century most of Detroit's union locals either excluded blacks or admitted them in segregated locals. Detroit blacks were represented in a segregated longshoremen's local and were members of integrated musicians', engineers', carpenters', and letter carriers' locals. The barbers' local in Detroit had been integrated in 1889, but in 1909 when it was reestablished after a period of dormancy it was all-white. In essence, the admission of blacks to unions in Detroit was not a major issue because few Negroes were occupationally eligible for membership. Skilled Negro tradesmen who had migrated to Detroit from southern Ontario were ineligible for union membership unless they had taken out citizenship papers, since most unions required American citizenship as a prerequisite to entrance. Moreover, Detroit locals adhered to the caste system that blocked Afro-American access to the skilled and semiskilled crafts. Straker charged, "it is well known that the rules of trades unions make it exceedingly difficult, if not impracticable, for a colored youth applying to learn a trade, to be received as an apprentice." "The ironclad barriers" were such, wrote Straker to the editor of the *Detroit Tribune*, "that not one in a hundred is admitted." In responding to Straker's charges, the head of the printers' union did not deny the black man's accusation but instead took shelter in the A. F. of L.'s blanket condemnation of discrimination. The ban against black apprentices was so widespread that in 1887 the Republican *Tribune* found it expedient to appeal to Negro voters by endorsing the Republican candidate for treasurer, Thomas Tuite, as a man who had "defied public opinion by taking a young colored boy as an apprentice in his plumbing and gas fitting establishment. . . ."[36]

The exclusion of Detroit blacks from labor unions, either through occupational ineligibility or discrimination, left them at a serious economic disadvantage in comparison to white union members. Be-

[36] Gerald N. Grob, "Organized Labor and the Negro Worker, 1865–1890," *Labor History*, I (Spring, 1960), 169; DuBois, *Negro Artisan*, p. 130; Glen E. Carlson, "The Negro in the Industries of Detroit," Ph.D. dissertation, University of Michigan, 1929, p. 193; *Detroit Evening News*, Sept. 7, 1903, p. 1; *Plaindealer*, Mar. 4, 1892, Dec. 27, 1889; *Journeyman Barber*, V (October, 1909), 338; F. E. Wolfe, *Admission to American Trade Unions* (Baltimore, 1912), pp. 100–101; *Detroit Tribune*, July 5, 1895, p. 8; *Detroit Sunday News-Tribune*, July 7, 1895, p. 6; *Detroit Tribune*, Nov. 7, 1887, p. 4.

fore the initiation of the twentieth-century welfare state, national and international unions were the major purveyors of social security —death, sick, and jobless benefits. A survey of sixty-seven national unions paying benefits shortly after the turn of the century found sixty-three paying death benefits, twenty-four giving sick benefits, and six offering out-of-work insurance. The Commission on Industrial Relations concluded in 1915 that trade union members were "never found among the applicants for charity during periods of unemployment." In contrast to union members, however, the only insurance available to most blacks was the small lump-sum death benefits offered by their fraternal associations.[37]

Since sick, unemployment, or retirement benefits were unobtainable, at least some Detroit Negroes relied on the medieval custom of buying old-age security by transferring all of their assets to a relative or friend in return for "food, raiment, shelter, medical care and other necessities until death." Few blacks, however, had the assets to buy this kind of security and most of them, like some of their white neighbors, worked until death.[38]

VII

For most blacks the caste line served to block channels of occupational mobility. Confined mostly to domestic and personal service and unskilled labor, Detroit's Negroes found nearly all other work closed to all but the upper class. Thus there were only two avenues of upward mobility available to ambitious Afro-Americans. They could

[37] James B. Kennedy, *Beneficiary Features of American Trade Unions* (Baltimore, 1908), p. 17; *BLS:Mich 1907*, pp. 342, 355; Commission on Industrial Relations, *Final Report* (Washington, 1915), p. 175. The cigar makers—one of the leading trades in Detroit, a trade without black craftsmen—received the highest benefits among unions. Death benefits were paid both for the member and nonmember spouse, out-of-work benefits were begun in 1889, and sick benefits, disability payments and loans were readily available to members. Helen L. Sumner, "The Benefit System of the Cigar Makers' Union," in John R. Commons (ed.), *Trade Unionism and Labor Problems* (reprinted New York, 1967), pp. 527, 529, 533, 534. For benefits of Michigan unions see the annual *BLS:Mich*.

[38] Julia Lambert to Deborah Willoughby and Frances Saunders, March 20, 1863, Lambert Papers, NHRSM.

enter the public service by exploiting the Republican party's commitment to the Negro, or they could become independent businessmen by turning away from the white world and capturing the black retail market. Because the upper class monopolized the patronage received from the Republican party, the black business world offered the only available route.

Detroit's earliest black businesses had been based on services or skills provided for a white clientele. While the Civil War years saw the destruction of some of these shops in the riot of 1863, the wartime period proved to be a boon to at least two Detroit Negroes. James H. Cole took advantage of the wartime exigencies in rising from stable boy to the owner of a livery and grain store servicing the army. Dr. Samuel C. Watson came to Detroit in 1863, established one of the most successful prescription drugstores in the city, and quickly rose to the forefront in black political activity. Born in South Carolina in 1832, Watson had been orphaned at age nine and became the ward of a Washington, D. C., Presbyterian minister. An 1857 graduate of Western Homeopathic College, a Cleveland medical school, Watson had previously attended Phillips Academy in Andover, Massachusetts, Oberlin College, and the medical school of the University of Michigan. Although he had practiced medicine in Chatham, Ontario, upon graduation from medical school, and in Toronto from 1861 to 1863, and in between had followed the path of gold fever across Canada to the gold fields of British Columbia, his forte was business and politics and he met with immediate success in Detroit. A leading Detroit citizen, the heavy-set, light-skinned, mutton-chopped Watson served on both the board of estimate and the common council of Detroit, and in 1884 served as a delegate to the Republican National Convention, the first Negro delegate from the North.[39]

After the Civil War black businesses continued to develop along the same lines as in the two decades before the war, with service to whites the basis of most black business. Barber shops remained the

---

[39] "James H. Cole," in Fred Hart Williams and Hoyt Fuller, "Detroit Heritage," typewritten MS in Fred Hart Williams Papers, Burton Historical Collection; *Plaindealer*, Mar. 18, 1892; "Samuel C. Watson, M.D.," in William J. Simmons, *Men of Mark, Emminent, Progressive and Rising* (Cleveland, 1887), pp. 860–865; *Detroit Evening Journal*, Dec. 25, 1885, p. 1.

single most important black business, and by 1884 they comprised more than 25 percent of Detroit's 120 barber shops. Other new businesses resulted from the entrepreneurial development of traditional black occupations. A few Negroes made the jump from proprietor of a disorderly house to operator of a saloon; others advanced from cook or waiter to restaurant owner. Wilson Beard opened a laundry; Henry C. Clark went from yard work to a lawn-mowing business; and Reuben Davis, by successfully contracting with the Detroit and Milwaukee Rail Road to provide them with janitorial service at a depot, employed several cleaning women and became a contractor.[40]

Until the turn of the twentieth century black professionals had limited opportunities to practice their trade; a few were successful but some turned to other roles. Dr. Benjamin Clark, a black physician, practiced in Detroit from 1858 until his death in 1891, but his clientele was mostly white. Dr. Samuel C. Watson never practiced medicine in Detroit, and Dr. Joseph Ferguson, who also came to Detroit during the Civil War, served for many years as a city physician. Black attorneys fared no better; until the beginning of the twentieth century a majority of Negro lawyers in Detroit pursued other vocations.[41]

The organization of the *Plaindealer* in 1883 by five young men— Robert A. Pelham, Jr., Benjamin B. Pelham, Walter H. Stowers, William H. Anderson, and Byron G. Redmond—was an important landmark in the history of black Detroit. Except for a brief period in the 1890s after the weekly *Plaindealer* ceased publication, Detroit has not been without a black newspaper since 1883. The *Plaindealer* was the first Detroit race paper to last longer than six months, and its eleven years of publication with a circulation throughout the Midwest that ranged from 2,100 to 2,500 subscribers proved that Detroit could provide a base for a Negro weekly. A leading force in Republican politics, the *Plaindealer* also served to boost the growth of black

[40] *Detroit City Directory 1884–1885*; *Detroit City Directory 1875–1876*; M. Marguerite Davenport, *Azalia: The Life of Madame E. Azalia Hackley* (Boston, 1947), p. 23; *Detroit Evening Journal*, Dec. 25, 1885, p. 1; *Detroit Advertiser & Tribune*, Dec. 19, 1866, p. 3.

[41] *Plaindealer*, June 26, 1891, Mar. 18, 1892, Nov. 4, 1892. The 1900 census reported six Negro lawyers in Detroit, yet there were at least ten blacks with law degrees; in 1910 eleven were recorded in the census, yet at least sixteen blacks in Detroit held LL.B.s. After 1900 the number of black attorneys began to rise sharply as black business activity generated a demand for legal services.

business. After the cessation of the *Plaindealer* and before the great migration of World War I, George R. Nevels's *National Indepen-dent*, Francis H. Warren's *Detroit Informer*, D. A. Straker's *Detroit Advocate*, and William P. Kemp's *Detroit Leader* served to unite De-troit's black community and to provide support for the city's black businessmen.[42]

The 1880s appear to be a major turning point in black business in Detroit, although it is impossible to date the change precisely. The chances for blacks to appeal to the white market—and even the desire of a few—seem to have diminished, and blacks began to turn to the Negro market. While the increasing concentration of black popula-tion along St. Antoine Street would be tied together inextricably with the growth of black business, the two occurrences were related only casually. The growth of black business was a function of ideology and caste, not population growth. The simultaneous appearance of migrants from the South and black businesses in Chicago and New York has led other observers to conclude that the population increase was responsible for the business growth. The Detroit black com-munity in this period also received migrants from the South, but it experienced no large increase in population and yet it, too, underwent a growth in black business. The rise in the level of black business activity resulted, not from the increased market (although this was an enabling factor), but from the aggressiveness and ambition of Detroiters and the new arrivals on the one hand, and their blocked opportunities in business, white-collar jobs, and factory work on the other hand.

The *Plaindealer* pushed the theme of patronizing race business and so would the *Detroit Informer* and its competitors and successors. "If our colored business men are to receive our patronage," declared the *Plaindealer*, "they should . . . show themselves to be interested in the race and . . . give us as much in quality and quantity for our money as we could get elsewhere." The weekly called for the adoption of "the Republican policy of protecting home industries and patronizing our

[42] The earlier, unsuccessful black papers included the short-lived *Western Excelsior* of 1848, the *Popular Era*, which appeared from May to November, 1879, and the *National People*, which first circulated a month prior to the ap-pearance of the *Plaindealer*, and lasted only two months thereafter. Silas Farmer, *The History of Detroit and Michigan* (Detroit, 1884), pp. 675, 681, 682.

business men until they have had a chance to catch up with their competitors." While the *Plaindealer* was boosting race unity, it never strayed far from self-interest: "A colored lawyer or doctor who never attends a colored church, fails to patronize colored business men, refuses or neglects to aid colored newspapers, has little title to our patronage and support." A leader in some of the conspicuous successes that blacks achieved in the political arena, the *Plaindealer* called on its constituency to "carry the same methods in mercantile life and use your solid trade as you use an almost solid vote in political affairs."[43]

The development of black businesses in the 1880s, 1890s, and the first decade of the twentieth century—moving companies, coal yards, lumber yards, drugstores, groceries, funeral homes, restaurants, candy stores, news-dealerships, hotels, and saloons—was reflected in the growth of black financial and realty agencies. There were three realty agencies in Detroit in 1890 where none had existed a few years before: W. W. Ferguson, Fred W. Ernst, and H. T. Toliver and Company. The Toliver Company not only engaged in real-estate transactions and the collection of rents but also served as a small-loan institution. In 1890 black leaders founded the Detroit Industrial and Financial Cooperative Association, a joint stock company authorized to buy and sell houses, lend money, build homes "for the laboring classes . . . and otherwise engage in industrial affairs for the benefits of the association and the welfare of the race." Encouraged by this development, the *Plaindealer* called for the establishment of an insurance company to complement the new association. In spite of the weekly's enthusiasm, however, there is no record that the Industrial and Financial Cooperative Association developed beyond the organizational stage. The black community was simply not large enough until after World War I to support such black-oriented enterprises. This did not, however, prevent the formation several years later of the equally unsuccessful Industrial and Protective Association and Michigan Co-Operative League.[44]

[43] *Plaindealer*, Nov. 21, 1890, Sept. 2, 1890.
[44] *Plaindealer*, Jan. 30, 1890, May 2, 1890, Nov. 21, 1890, June 5, 1891, July 25, 1890, Jan. 23, 1891; *Detroit Sunday News-Tribune*, Oct. 24, 1897, p. 24; Charles Alexander, "The Michigan Co-Operative League," *Alexander's Magazine*, II

Although nearly all black businesses in Detroit were small, requiring a minimum of capital and inventory, capital was available in
Detroit's black community. Wealth, except in a few notable cases,
had resulted from real-estate investment and speculation; by 1900
much of it was inherited. Many of the earliest black families such as
the Lamberts had acquired extensive real-estate holdings in what was
to become Detroit's downtown business district, and the Virginian
families that migrated to Detroit in the 1840s and 1850s also had
acquired much realty. After the Civil War, real estate was the major
source of investment among Detroit blacks, and successful barber shop
owners, businessmen, and professionals placed much of their assets in
land. As land values in the center of the city and the near east side
rose sharply in the closing decades of the nineteenth century, the net
worth of some blacks of modest means rose into the $10,000 to $75,000
range. When James H. Cole died in 1907, the *Detroit News* estimated
that he was worth nearly $200,000—his assets consisting of large
property holdings, stores, dwellings, and a moving business which
he co-owned with his sons. After 1900, as the black business community expanded northward up St. Antoine, modest residential lots
became prime commercial land, and the value of realty holdings
multiplied.[45]

The turn of the century saw a sharp rise in the number of black
retail businesses and the foundation of business corporations such as
the Home Oil Company and the Ernst-Thompson Regalia Company.
Most of the black capital, however, continued to flow into realty investment: the purchase of dwellings or stores, or the construction of
apartments and business structures. Real estate remained the principal
investment of the Cole family, and the James H. Cole Realty Com-

---

(Oct. 15, 1906), 17–21. Dominated by outstate Michigan blacks, the league
brought together ambitious businessmen and realtors with the conviction
"that it is absolutely necessary that the best men and women of the race co-
operate for the benefit of the masses...."

[45] *Negro in Detroit*, IV, 18–19; calendar of tax receipts, title transfers, and
ledger book in the Lambert Papers, NHRSM; *Detroit Evening Journal*, Dec.
25, 1885, p. 1; *Detroit News-Tribune*, Apr. 27, 1902, p. 7; clipping, *Detroit News*,
May 16, 1907, in Burton Scrapbook, XXVII, 126; Francis H. Warren (comp.),
Michigan Manual of Freedmen's Progress (Detroit, 1915), p. 114 (hereafter
cited as *Freedmen's Progress*).

pany was the kingpin of the family's enterprises. The Lamberts, Watsons, Strakers, and other families also invested primarily in real estate, much of it in white neighborhoods. Some blacks, like Lomax B. Cook and James D. Carter, found real-estate investment and speculation so profitable that they gave up their shops to devote full time to land transactions and the collection of rents. William Ferguson sold the Ferguson Printing Company in 1890 to concentrate on real-estate sales and investment.[46]

The large black investment in real estate made a mockery of the *Plaindealer*'s call to Negroes to support black business. Wealth channeled into realty created no new jobs for blacks and was of little overall benefit to Detroit's black community. Without adequate financial institutions the wealthy black families had no mechanism for investing in employment-creating institutions, even had they been interested in doing so. And they were not. The black businessmen, politicians, and professionals of the period controlled the institutions in the black community. They not only headed the black economic, religious, social, and political institutions and directed the civil rights movement of the late nineteenth century, but they also served as the link between the black and white communities. Their successes and victories, however, were personal. Political involvement and patronage benefitted mainly their offspring, not the hundreds of Negro domestics and personal servants. The old families sought to eliminate the caste line in white-collar occupations and skilled crafts, but they did not use their wealth for the benefit of the entire black community, and their sons mostly shunned the business world for the government payroll. The few Detroit-born blacks of the generation of 1900 who owned businesses—and only a handful did—inherited them, like Watson's Drug Store or the Home Moving and Storage Company.

By 1900 it was clear, in Detroit as in Chicago, that the black community was being transformed by the growth of black business in spite of the indifference of the black leadership. St. Antoine was becoming a major business thoroughfare—a black business street. Small

[46] *Plaindealer*, June 27, 1890; *Freedmen's Progress*, pp. 114–115; deeds, Jan. 11, 1878, July 12, 1878, Lambert Papers, NHRSM; "Bertha J. Stewart Scott," NHRSM; *Detroit Evening Journal*, Dec. 25, 1885, p. 1.; *Plaindealer*, Nov. 4, 1892.

Negro businesses, with few employees and run by relatively recent arrivals to Detroit, were slowly crowding out white businesses and residential buildings. As the black population increasingly massed in the side streets adjoining St. Antoine, Negro hopes of capturing the black dollar on the main street became a reality. The Etcombe Hotel on St. Antoine at Beacon, and Roy's Hotel on Champlain near Beaubien—later Day's Hotel, the "Largest Colored European Hotel in the West"—symbolized the growth of the new businesses and the resultant pride in the institutions of the community.[47]

The majority of black businessmen in Detroit after 1900 were relative newcomers to the city.[48] They were ambitious and aggressive men, and they seemed less interested in the community's cultural activities than were some of the long-time residents. A few of the new businessmen, such as Francis H. Warren, attorney, Democrat, and editor of the *Informer*, and lawyer Charles H. Mahoney, were well educated and came from the Michigan hinterland. Probably more typical, however, was Thaddeus W. Taylor, a native of Jackson, Mississippi, who had worked for many years in the barber supply industry and succeeded in 1900 in establishing his own manufacturing company. Similarly, Harrison and Wallace Williams came to Michigan around 1910 from Louisiana and opened a coal, wood, and express business in Detroit. The mortality rate among the black businesses was high, but stores did not remain vacant for long as new shops replaced the unsuccessful ones. The frequent turnover in business was probably a function of undercapitalization and lack of management experience.

The newcomers would create a new community spirit, a sense of black community. Most of the old leaders, with their close ties to the white community, were outside of this new community. When the *Leader*, on December 25, 1910, printed a Detroit Afro-American Business Directory—a guide that listed black businesses and professional men catering to the Negro market—many of the old established attorneys, physicians, pharmacists, expressmen, contractors, and other

[47] *Detroit City Directory 1900–1908*; *Freedmen's Progress*, pp. 33, 48, 125, 127.
[48] *The Negro in Detroit*, IV, 17–18.

Afro-American business owners were missing. Catering primarily to whites, these men were outside of the *Leader*'s world.[49]

The newcomers also created their own community institutions. They established new saloons and saloon-based social clubs, organized new churches, and founded new sects. Unwelcome in the old fraternal societies of the city, they formed new lodges and brought new fraternal orders to Detroit. After World War I the newcomers were to assume control of nearly all of Detroit's black community institutions.

VIII

The caste system affected black occupational activities at least as much as any other institution in Detroit. The rigidity of the black occupational structure from 1870 to 1915 is particularly startling in view of the rapid industrialization of the American economy during this period. Black workers were frozen in mostly menial work tasks and the occupations within which they eked out a living offered neither the promise of advancement nor promotion. Security, home ownership, self-respect, and rising expectations were realities for those who walked through the gates of the massive factories in the Detroit area, but no blacks were allowed there.

By and large, the black community won no major victories against the caste system in the late nineteenth century. The inroads made were small and mostly benefitted a small group of blacks. Significantly, blacks themselves failed to build any black institutions that would have alleviated some of the harshest effects of the caste system. Those with the means and capital were primarily interested in integration or in real-estate investments. Those who came later to the city and established a black business community were probably too self-centered and too profit-oriented to exert a great part of their energy against the caste system. Tragically, all of the successful blacks believed too much in the American dream, in the openness of American society, and they failed to imitate the patterns of ethnic cohesiveness that surrounded them.

[49] *Detroit Leader*, Dec. 25, 1910, p. 4.

CHAPTER V
Class

THE SOCIAL AND ECONOMIC INSTITUTIONS of Detroit's black community served more to divide than unite the city's blacks. No single organization other than the political clubs had a broad communitywide membership that significantly cut across class or clique lines. The patterns of black social interaction reflected the class divisions in the community.[1]

With but few exceptions, church membership was an excellent measure of class standing in black Detroit. Black congregants in white churches were among the elite of the black community, as were the parishioners of St. Matthew's, whether they were of the old upper class or the new middle class. Although a few families of the elite group, mostly descendants of the migrants from Virginia in the 1840s, maintained membership in Bethel African Methodist Episcopal (AME) Church, most black Methodists were of the black community's middling class.[2] The Baptists, on the other hand, were drawn predominantly from the lower part of the working class and from the lower class, although most members of the lower class were not churchgoers.

[1] This chapter in particular owes much to August Meier, whose criticisms and insights over the past few years have greatly influenced and improved this analysis of the black class structure in Detroit.

[2] By "middling class" I mean the small middle and large working classes.

135

A small group of prestigious black community leaders attended white churches in Detroit. A few families had attended white Episcopalian churches during the period of St. Matthew's dormancy in the 1860s and 1870s, and they remained attendants at their parish churches after the black Episcopalian mission had been reestablished. Other blacks, especially the elite who lived in an integrated world, were drawn to fashionable white churches, and their membership reflected their involvement with the white community. Among the black leaders who at one time or another belonged to white churches were city councilman Dr. Samuel C. Watson and state legislators William W. Ferguson and Dr. James W. Ames. Dr. Benjamin Clark and Walter H. Stowers, among others, also attended white churches.[3]

Black congregants of white churches were few in number, probably never exceeding 1 or 2 percent of the membership of the Negro churches. Within the black community, African Methodism was the largest denomination, and Bethel AME had the largest congregation. Baptists comprised the second largest denomination, and the oldest black church in Detroit, the Second Baptist, was second in size to Bethel. Episcopalianism, the third major religious affiliation within the black community, had only one black church in Detroit before World War I—St. Matthew's.

Although only a small part of the black community's church membership—probably no more than 10 percent at any time—belonged to St. Matthew's, the church (a mission until 1907) served nearly all of Detroit's Negro upper class. In 1902, the *Detroit News-Tribune* headlined an illustrated story on the Negro elite with the caption: "Detroit's Most Exclusive Social Clique, The Cultured Colored '40.' " Fifty-one families and individuals comprised the newspaper's black society register, of whom thirty-one were Episcopalians, twelve were African Methodists, and four were Baptists. The four remaining families, plus two with memberships at one time in black

[3] *Journal of the Proceedings of the Forty-eighth Annual Convention of the Protestant Episcopal Church in the Diocese of Michigan: 1882* (Detroit, 1882), p. 64 (hereafter cited as JoPEC:Mich); *Detroit Post*, Dec. 23, 1884, p. 5; "William Ferguson," in file "Negro," Historical Records Survey of Michigan, University of Michigan (hereafter cited as NHRSM); Detroit *Plaindealer*, June 26, 1891; Frank Lincoln Mather (ed.), *Who's Who of the Colored Race 1915* (Chicago, 1915), pp. 6, 256.

churches, worshiped at white churches. Similarly, of the ten Detroit Negroes listed in Frank Lincoln Mather's 1915 *Who's Who of the Colored Race*, half were Episcopalians, three were Methodists, and two belonged to white churches.[4]

St. Matthew's had much to recommend it as an elite church. It was a "high church," a religious body with much prestige even in the white community. The services were dignified and reserved, and the church offered a quiet, traditional mass. Whether deservedly or not, the Episcopalian church had a "reputation for exclusiveness and non-co-operation with other Protestant bodies," and this added to its prestige. Its lay officials and congregants were welcomed by their white Episcopalian brethren, thus giving St. Matthew's parishioners an entree into the white world that was unknown to the overwhelming majority of black church members. As the first colored Protestant Episcopal church west of the Alleghenics, St. Matthew's was tradition minded, and, as a church, it took pride in the men it had sent into the ranks of the clergy—including the Rt. Rev. James T. Holly, Bishop of Haiti and the first Negro bishop of the Protestant Episcopal Church (PEC) in the United States—and in the rectors of the mission church, who were the best educated of the black clergy in Detroit. The first black minister of the revived St. Matthew's mission was Charles Thompson, a former professor of theology at Straight University and a graduate of Oberlin College. In 1893 Rev. Joshua B. Massiah succeeded Thompson, who had served three years as rector. Born in Barbados of a wealthy family, Massiah had attended Oxford University and General Theological Seminary in New York City. From 1906 to 1911, George Bundy, a graduate of the Detroit College of Medicine, was pastor. When Bundy resigned in 1911 to practice medicine in Detroit, the Rev. Robert W. Bagnall, a graduate of Bishop Payne Divinity School and Temple University, replaced him.

[4] *Detroit News-Tribune*, Apr. 27, 1902, p. 7; *Who's Who of the Colored Race 1915*. Of the fifty-one persons listed in the *News-Tribune*, the church affiliation of thirty-two was determined directly from church publications or records and newspaper reports, and that of the remainder was estimated on the basis of information concerning a relative's religious affiliation, membership in church-affiliated societies, or similar data. Publications of the various Detroit black churches can be found in the Detroit Public Library, as can the receipt book of the Rector's Aid Society of St. Matthew's, 1896–98, in the Burton Historical Collection.

Bagnall would organize the Detroit chapter of the National Association for the Advancement of Colored People (NAACP), and in 1921 he would leave St. Matthew's and the ministry to become the NAACP branch director.[5]

Congregants came to the Episcopalian parish at Elizabeth and St. Antoine from throughout black Detroit, whereas all of the other black religious societies, including Bethel AME, were predominantly neighborhood churches. The black elite—the old families, the professionals, the race leaders—dominated the list of vestrymen. Most of the social activities of the Detroit upper class centered on St. Matthew's, and the weddings held in the chapel highlighted each social season. The newspapers acknowledged the position of St. Matthew's as the church of the higher classes, and the luxurious weddings with expensive clothes, fashionable carriages, and abundant bouquets of flowers were reportedly attended by the "150 . . . in the blue book of colored society in Detroit."[6]

In the late nineteenth century, St. Matthew's cultivated its reputation as the church of the elite. William Lambert and the rest of the Lambert family had been the moving force behind black Episcopalianism in Detroit, and they played the largest role in St. Matthew's organization and daily affairs. They lent their large prestige to the mission, as well as assuming a considerable portion of the financial obligation after reorganization of the church in 1880. Deeply religious, the Lamberts did little overtly to make St. Matthew's an elite social organization although they attracted their closest friends

[5] Frank S. Mead, *Handbook of Denominations in the United States* (New York, 1956), pp. 179–183; George F. Bragg, *History of the Afro-American Group of the Episcopalian Church* (Baltimore, 1922), 117; "St. Matthew's 75th Anniversary," *Michigan Churchman*, XXIX (November, 1924), 9; "A Brief History of St. Matthew's Church" (1926), in "R. W. J. Jeffrey" file, NHRSM; "African Churchmen," NHRSM; D. Augustus Straker, *A Trip to the Windward Islands, or Then and Now* (Detroit, 1896), p. 67; *Detroit Sunday News-Tribune*, Nov. 21, 1897, p. 22; Allan H. Spear, *Black Chicago: The Making of a Negro Ghetto 1890–1920* (Chicago, 1967), p. 65; Francis H. Warren (comp.), *Michigan Manual of Freedmen's Progress* (Detroit, 1915), pp. 52–53 (hereafter cited as *Freedmen's Progress*).

[6] St. Matthew's Episcopal Church, *Centennial Celebration 1846–1946* [Detroit, 1946]; *Plaindealer*, June 19, 1891, July 31, 1891, Oct. 2, 1891; *Detroit Evening News*, Nov. 25, 1903, p. 1.

to St. Matthew's—a circle that inscribed much of the black elite. Among those drawn to St. Matthew's were the Johnsons—physician Albert H. and dentist William E., sons of physician Levi H. Johnson—the Fergusons—attorney William W. and physician John C., sons of physician Joseph Ferguson—and others such as William H. Anderson, county clerk Benjamin Pelham, stenographer Charles Webb, attorney William Swan, and Eliza Wilson, president of the Phillis Wheatley Home. After William Lambert's death in 1890, St. Matthew's appeared to have consciously sought to preserve its elite role and slowly erected barriers to membership. At a time when black migration from the South was expanding at a rapidly increasing rate, St. Matthew's instituted pew rentals—at first this applied only to some pews, but by 1906 all were offered for rental—and the church doors were closed to the black poor and the urban newcomer. Black Detroit knew, Rev. Edward Daniel of St. Matthew's wrote in 1923, that St. Matthew's had been "out of sympathy with the new arrivals. . . ." Instead, the romanesque chapel at St. Antoine and Elizabeth streets attracted the elite—"those who fancy themselves to the intelligentsia and of the better paid workmen and businessmen"—a group conscious of their role as community leaders and separate from "the masses of the laboring classes."[7]

When some of the new middle class would begin to dominate the black community's institutions after the turn of the century, they would be drawn to St. Matthew's much as the old elite had been a generation before. The new leaders would eliminate the overt snobbishness of St. Matthew's while retaining its high status and prestige, and their ascendancy would be marked by the rectorate of Rev. Robert W. Bagnall.

Until the Second Baptist Church rebuilt its edifice to accommodate the southern migrants after the turn of the century, the Bethel AME chapel was of a scale that dwarfed the other black churches. The

---

[7] Joseph H. Johnson, *In Memoriam: William Lambert, Sermon Preached at St. Matthew's Church* (reprinted from *Michigan Church Life*, July, 1890); *JoPEC:Mich 1903*, p. 127; *JoPEC:Mich 1907*, p. 197; Mayor's Inter-racial Committee, *The Negro in Detroit* (Detroit, 1926), X, 9–10; Edward W. Daniel, "St. Matthew's Need—A Challenge," *Michigan Churchman*, XXVIII (December, 1923), 22; *Freedmen's Progress*, pp. 134–135.

massive brick walls supporting the romanesque chapel and spire symbolized the strength and endurance of the mother church of African Methodism in Michigan. Located on Lafayette Street between Brush and Beaubien until 1889, when its new building at Napoleon and Hastings opened, Bethel AME was most distinctly identified with the interests of black people.[8]

Both the doctrine and practices of the AME followed those of the other Methodist churches, and laymen were deeply involved in running the church. The Methodist policy of biennially rotating ministers served to make lay power paramount and to increase the secular awareness of the church. From its beginnings Bethel was active in the education of black youth in the city, and in an effort to serve the recent migrants who had moved in and near the Kentucky district after the Civil War, it formed Ebenezer AME in 1871, on Calhoun between Beaubien and St. Antoine streets. In 1889 Bethel itself moved northward, closer to its middling-class constituency. Appropriately, Bethel's relatively large church hall served as the primary meeting place for black organizations, and during political campaigns its chapel hosted as many election meetings as it did religious services. Nondenominational social organizations such as the Queen of Sheba's Royal Council affiliated with Bethel, and the new middle-class-oriented organizations such as the Association of Colored Women's Clubs of Michigan would hold their first meetings there. Dedicated to humanitarian causes, and race conscious, Bethel AME was the first Detroit organization to do social-service work among Negroes. It early recognized the plight of the southern migrant to the city, and welcomed the newcomers, founding a social service department in 1911 and adding a labor and housing bureau a few years later.[9]

[8] *Eleventh Census 1890*, IX, *Report on Statistics of Churches in the United States* (Washintgon, 1894), 5, 41, 49; *Freedmen's Progress*, p. 131; Michigan Historical Records Survey, *Inventory of the Church Archives: African Methodist Episcopal Church, Michigan Conference* (Detroit, 1940), pp. 3, 8; *A Historical Sketch Published on the Occasion of the Eightieth Anniversary of Bethel A.M.E. Church, Detroit, Michigan, 1841–1921* [Detroit, 1921].

[9] Mead, *Handbook of Denominations*, p. 152; *History and Directory of the Churches of Detroit, Michigan* (Detroit, 1877), pp. 232, 234; A. L. Turner and Earl Moses, *Colored Detroit 1924* (Detroit, 1924), p. 51; *Historical Sketch Bethel A.M.E.*

Few of the black professionals, leading businessmen, or race leaders belonged to Bethel before the 1890s, nor did any significant number of the numerous servants or day laborers worship there. One complete nineteenth-century Bethel AME membership roll exists (1877), and it recorded nearly 70 percent women membership. The women members included a few laundresses, servants, cooks, and washwomen, but 69 percent of those members identified in the 1880 census were housewives, a somewhat higher percentage than the 60 percent citywide average. By contrast, at St. Matthew's a decade later, only 10 percent of the women congregants were working women. The male members of Bethel were mostly in unskilled or service occupations, although a plasterer, a carpenter, and a rag peddler were included. Among the husbands of female members, some of whom held church offices even though they were not themselves carried on the church rolls, were a secondhand dealer, a fish dealer, a livery stable keeper, a tailor, two carpenters, a plasterer, a bricklayer, a teamster, a factory worker, several laborers, a janitor, and a dock worker. These were the occupations of the middling class of the Detroit black community of 1880.[10]

After 1880, as migrants from the South and the hinterlands of Detroit came into the city and as the middling class of the black community grew larger, Bethel AME grew in membership, adding to its rolls a few of the more important new arrivals in the city—such as D. Augustus Straker. Membership by a race leader in a white church, or in St. Matthew's during the period of pew rental, sometimes aroused resentment among Detroit Negroes. The old elite seemed unconcerned about this matter, but the new leadership, the new middle class, dependent upon black patronage and support, could not afford to alienate any groups within the black community, and so they would gravitate toward Negro institutions. Increasingly after 1890, it appears that some race leaders thus tended to identify with black churches and particularly with Bethel AME. Attorney Robert C. Barnes, contractor William Ellis, and Robert Pelham, Jr., associated

[10] The Bethel membership is recorded in *History and Directory of the Churches of Detroit*, pp. 235–236. Other figures and occupations are derived from the 1880 manuscript census.

themselves with Bethel. The AME service, uplifting yet dignified, probably appeared reserved in comparison with the more fundamentalist, southern-based churches. It was likely that, for many black migrants, the AME would mean a large step upward in status. This would be particularly true of most of the migrants from the South who had been members of the more emotional southern Baptist churches.

Founded as a mission in 1871 by Bethel, Ebenezer AME served the middling class of the black community who had moved into the district north of Gratiot. Services were first held in a public hall but the next year the congregation acquired a frame building, and in 1873 they hired a full-time pastor. In 1874 Ebenezer purchased the adjacent Second Congregational Chapel, retaining the old hall as a rectory. Located a few blocks south of the heart of the notorious Kentucky district and somewhat removed from the more fashionable areas of the walking city of the 1870s, Ebenezer AME appealed to poor but respectable working-class families. Its congregation was more homogeneous than that of Bethel, whose members represented a broader occupational and social spectrum.[11]

Ebenezer AME appeared to be basically a family church. The 1877 membership list recorded at least twenty instances in which both husband and wife were members, whereas only three such cases appeared on Bethel's rolls. The number of families participating was actually much higher, although it is difficult to determine or even estimate the exact number. One indication is that a number of Bethel male office-holders were not recorded as members. Nonetheless it is significant that more families tended to enroll at Ebenezer than at Bethel. Ebenezer's women members were less likely to work outside the home than were Bethel's members; only 14 percent of Ebenezer's women members identified in the 1880 census were gainfully employed. Unlike Bethel, whose male congregants included skilled craftsmen as well as petty merchants, 96 percent of Ebenezer's men worked as unskilled or day laborers or in a service capacity. Only one member worked as a tradesman (carpenter), and one was self-employed (rag

11 *One Hundred Years at Bethel* [Detroit, 1941], p. 4; Michigan Historical Records Survey, *A.M.E. Church*, p. 11; Silas Farmer, *The History of Detroit and Michigan* (Detroit, 1884), p. 577.

peddler). Similarly, nonmember husbands of women congregants at Ebenezer were all unskilled or day laborers.[12]

Two other African Methodist churches were established in Detroit, but their activities and even their presence were rarely recorded in the black press or in city directories. Brown's Chapel, affiliated with the AME, was organized in 1891 to serve the growing Negro settlement in Springwells on the far western fringe of Detroit. The pastor, Lillian F. Thurman, was the daughter of Lucy Thurman, a noted black temperance and church worker, and the *Detroit News-Tribune* reported that she was the only woman Afro-American preacher in the United States. The other African Methodist church, Zion African, was affiliated with the AME Zion denomination which, though similar to the AME in ritual and service, did not flourish in Detroit before World War I and was one of the smallest black churches in Detroit.[13]

The Baptist Church was the second largest black denomination in nineteenth-century Michigan and Detroit, and it would become the major sect during the great migration of World War I. More fundamentalist than the AME, the Baptists attracted the poor and the newcomers from the South. One indication of the wealth of the members was that in 1897 the Michigan African Methodists were able to supply parsonages for fifteen of their twenty churches, whereas the black Baptists could furnish only two parsonages for their twenty-one churches in the state.[14]

The Second Baptist Church was the oldest black religious society in Michigan and it remained on Croghan (later Monroe) Street in the old Negro district, adjacent to the vice area and amid the small factories and boarding houses. In 1870, George French, long-time deacon at the Second Baptist and one of its founders, organized the Zion Baptist Church in his home on Macomb between Riopelle and Or-

---

[12] Ebenezer membership roll for 1877 in *History and Directory of the Churches of Detroit*, pp. 239–240. Among the families attracted to Ebenezer were the Andersons; both William and his white wife, Mary, belonged to the church.

[13] *Detroit Sunday News-Tribune*, Dec. 26, 1897, p. 13; Farmer, *History of Detroit*, pp. 577–578.

[14] *Freedmen's Progress*, p. 132; A. A. Owens and Harvey C. Jackson, "Report on Negroes in the State of Michigan," *Annual Report of the Bureau of Labor and Industrial Statistics of the State of Michigan 1899*, pp. 328–329.

leans. The church, however, failed to attract new members and even lost some of its original congregants. In the mid-1870s it relocated on Calhoun Street in the Kentucky district, with Joseph White, a day laborer, acting as the pastor. The church acquired neither a regular minister nor a permanent home, and it faded away during the 1880s. Built largely on the personal following of French, and attracting only day laborers and working women, nearly all southern-born, Zion Baptist was the forerunner of the storefront churches of the twentieth century. Shiloh Baptist Church, on the other hand, was organized to serve Second Baptist members living in the district above Gratiot. Although it remained within the shadow of the Second Baptist, it met with the success that eluded Zion. Founded in 1881 by a group of twenty-five, mostly from the Second Baptist, Shiloh served as a neighborhood church and drew its membership entirely from the "masses of the laboring classes." [15]

The black leadership in nineteenth-century Detroit castigated the emotionalism of the Baptist service and disparaged the church's southern, lower-class membership. In 1891 the Detroit *Plaindealer* sharply criticized the southern custom in which the minister harangued the congregation after an insufficient Sunday offering. To the Episcopalian and African Methodist editors of the *Plaindealer*, this practice was not befitting a northern church and violated the true spirit of charity. The elite also thought poorly of the educational qualifications of the Baptist ministers, some of whom earned doctorates of divinity but who had rarely attended a college other than a Baptist seminary. Not all of the Baptist ministers fitted well the stereotyped view held by the upper class, although this seemed to have had little effect on the stereotype. Arthur D. Chandler, minister of the Second Baptist from 1893 to 1902, held B.A. and D.D. degrees and had been a professor of ancient languages at the Negro state university at Louisville. His tenure at the Second Baptist was successful; within his first year in Detroit he had held the "most successful spiritual awakening in the history of the church and of the denomination in the state." The new middle class, by contrast, treated the Baptists sympathetically, looking favorably upon the Baptist church as a black-controlled in-

[15] Farmer, *History of Detroit*, pp. 607, 609–610; *History and Directory of the Churches of Detroit*, p. 33; *The Negro in Detroit*, X, 10.

stitution. The *Detroit Leader* identified with the new middle class and thus assigned editors to cover the affairs of the Baptist and the AME churches, but it ignored St. Matthew's.[16]

Since most black Baptists in Detroit were probably poor or recent arrivals from the South, the Baptist congregations exhibited little of the drive and social awareness that the membership of St. Matthew's and Bethel AME displayed. Baptists rarely belonged to organizations other than the church, and before the twentieth century the church did little to meet the nonreligious needs of the congregation. The most prominent congregants of the Second Baptist were the members of the Cole family, and they provided much of the secular initiative in the church. In his rise to wealthiest black man in Detroit, James Cole retained his Baptist affiliation, and the family brought social organizations to the Second Baptist that were similar to those at St. Matthew's and Bethel, but—like the Ladies Aid Society, for example—they were almost exclusively Cole family organizations. Only with the waves of southern migrants after 1910 would the character of the church change, and, at the urging of some, begin to meet the social as well as the religious needs of the urban immigrants.[17]

Below the Baptist churches in prestige were the congregations of the Church of God. A black congregation that held services in a converted frame residence on Chene Street became the first Church of God in Michigan in 1884, although it did not acquire a clergyman until 1917. The denomination had been formed about 1880, originating as a movement within existing churches. Its adherents rejected the overburdened organization of the other denominations and relied rather on an informal membership and a congregational system. Believing that they were returning to the true faith, they stressed baptism by immersion, "the divine inspiration of the Scriptures," and the "personal return of Christ."[18]

[16] *Plaindealer*, Aug. 21, 1891; *Freedmen's Progress*, pp. 81–83, 131–135; M. E. D. Trowbridge, *History of Baptists in Michigan* (n.p., 1909), p. 326; Henry Thompson to Chandler, August 21, 1893, letter of recommendation for Chandler from Second Baptist Church, Detroit, March 20, 1902, in "Arthur D. Chandler," NHRSM; *Detroit Leader*, Dec. 23, 1910.

[17] *Detroit Sunday News-Tribune*, Jan. 9, 1898, p. 13; *Freedmen's Progress*, p. 134.

[18] Michigan Historical Records Survey, *Inventory of the Church Archives of*

About twenty years later, coincidentally with the growing southern migration to Michigan, fundamentalist and spiritual churches would begin to appear in greater numbers in Detroit. Many urban newcomers would turn to religion to provide a sense of community, an intimacy among neighbors, that they probably had shared in the South but could not find within the established institutions of the northern city. The traditional churches were probably too large, too impersonal, and too distant to satisfy the emotional needs of the newcomers. Sometimes the migrants would reject the traditional religious denominations, forging new cults with nonconventional doctrines and activities, including faith healing. Often the new churches would be built around the personality of a single man, and rarely would they survive beyond the lifetime of the pastor. Typical of these churches was the Holiness Church of Living God, founded in Detroit in August 1909. The leader, "Bishop" J. B. C. Cummings, who had been organizing his temple for about a year, finally acquired a two-story frame house on Wilkins, near Beaubien, and announced his presence on a cloth banner stretched across the facade of the building. Born in Georgia and raised in Tennessee, Bishop Cummings led his "brethren and sistern" in fundamentalist worship.[19]

Before World War I the black press ignored the existence of the fundamentalist churches, and the elite and middling classes evidenced a similar lack of concern. When questioned on the matter, elite Negroes tended to respond that Detroit was overchurched, and they implied that the storefront church ministers were out for personal gain. Many viewed the Church of God and the cults as harmful and dangerous. Unsympathetic to the life style of the lowest classes, John Dancy,

---

Michigan: Church of God Michigan Assemblies (Detroit, 1941), pp. 1, 2, 10; Mead, *Handbook of Denominations*, pp. 62–63.

[19] Henry Allen Bullock, "The Role of the Negro Church in the Negro Community of Detroit," unpublished sociology paper, University of Michigan [1935]; clipping, *Detroit Journal*, Sept. 14, 1909, in C. M. Burton Scrapbook, XXXV, 37, Burton Historical Collection, Detroit Public Library. For a discussion of the fundamentalist and cult churches, see E. Franklin Frazier, *The Negro Church in America* (New York, 1966), pp. 47–67. In 1911, before World War I, the first black Catholic church would appear—St. Peter Claver. An effort had been made in the late 1860s to construct a black Catholic church but it had been unsuccessful. *Detroit Tribune*, Jan. 9, 1869, p. 3; Michigan Historical Records Survey, *The Roman Catholic Church*, p. 98.

head of the Detroit Urban League after 1918, believed that the Church of God churches did "more to retard Negroes than anything else." Dancy's position, probably reflecting the attitude of much of the black elite, was in response to the rejection by the fundamentalists of the major trend of the traditional black denominations after the turn of the century: the secularization of the church. At a time when St. Matthew's, Bethel AME, and Second Baptist were showing concern for the urban newcomers and initiating social services, the rural migrants were seeking more spiritual and fundamentalist churches.[20]

Only fraternal and beneficiary societies were as widely spread among the Negroes in Michigan as were the churches. In 1897, the two largest organizations, the Masons and the Odd Fellows, had twenty-three chapters in the state's black communities, and the Masons had an additional eleven Knights Templar commanderies. In the following fifteen years, additional Negro orders appeared in the state and in Detroit; black people organized chapters of the Knights of Pythias, True Reformers, Shriners, and the Brothers of Friendship, many accompanied by women's auxiliaries.[21]

The Masonic order was both the largest and oldest secular organization among Negroes in Michigan and Detroit. Negro Masonry dates back to the 1780s when the British Grand Lodge chartered a chapter for Negroes in Boston. Whites regarded the black organization as "spurious" or "clandestine," but black Masonry spread nonetheless, reaching Michigan in 1859. In 1864, St. Paul, the fourth lodge in the state and the first in Detroit, was organized. Hiram Lodge was founded in 1869, followed within a few years by Mount Pavan and Unity Lodges and by the Eureka Commandery of the Knights Templar. By 1888, when Pythagoras Lodge was formed, only Hiram and Mt. Pavan remained in existence. A decade later Hiram and Pythagoras were the only surviving chapters, both with relatively large memberships.[22]

[20] John Dancy to F. Marian Woods, September 28, 1928, Detroit Urban League Papers, Michigan Historical Collections, University of Michigan; memo of conversation between John Dancy and James Couzens, September 6, 1920, James Couzens Papers, Library of Congress, Washington, D.C. Larry Engelmann furnished me with a copy of this memo.

[21] Owens and Jackson, "Report on Negroes," pp. 329–330.

[22] W. H. Grimshaw, *Official History of Freemasonry Among the Colored People in North America* (New York, 1903), pp. 67, 77–78, 236, 238, 239;

The nineteenth-century Masons were essentially a fraternal society; if lodges offered death or disability benefits they were of secondary importance to the social nature of the organization. Primarily, Freemasonry offered fellowship, ritual, and a Mason hall, all of which provided a sense of cohesion and community. Judging from the annual listings of officers, and an occasional membership roster, Masonry attracted a broad spectrum of the black community in Detroit, although it was primarily an association of the middle and working classes. Although a large number of the elite were Masons—William Lambert, clerk John Lyle, James Cole, Walter Stowers, and James W. Ames, for instance—rarely did contemporary reports note their presence at a Masonic event nor did they hold Masonic office. With their orientation toward integration and white institutions, it is probable that the elite belonged to Masonic lodges in order to maintain some social connections with the bulk of the black middling classes; nearly all the elite among the Masons were active in politics.[23]

Until around the 1890s, the middle and working classes tended to dominate the leadership of Detroit black Masonry. Officers included postal clerk Henry Thompson, carpenters Henry Vena and George Kersey, barbers Edward P. Harper, William Mumford, and John Langston, plasterer Richard Wright, waiters Stephen Robinson and Jerry Williams, and painter William Mitchell. In the first decade of black Masonry in Detroit, physician Joseph Ferguson was a leading member; thereafter it appears that no other Detroit professional man held a Masonic office in Detroit until the 1890s when Robert C. Barnes held office. Businessmen and those politically active comprised much of the officer lists—men such as James H. Cole, barber shop owner and later restaurateur Daniel Mills, and lawn-mowing contractor Henry C. Clark. In the 1890s an additional number of black businessmen and professionals became identified with Masonry as the new middle class began to rise. Men such as Dr. James W. Ames, attorney Walter Stowers, and lumberyard owner Frank May joined the

---

Detroit Tribune, Mar. 12, 1869, p. 3; Turner and Moses, *Colored Detroit 1924*, p. 43. The Detroit city directories regularly reported information on the lodges.
    23 Officers' lists of the lodges appeared in the Detroit city directories, and minutes of the Wolverine consistory from 1904 to 1906 can be found in "R. W. J. Jeffrey," NHRSM.

society. It seems that many within the new middle class understood the value of membership in the Masons. Like the old elite, they realized that political careers necessitated broad social connections within the black community, but they also appreciated the economic benefits of identifying with black interests and belonging to organizations such as the Masons.

Unlike Freemasonry, Odd Fellowship was primarily a benevolent movement. Organized in 1843 under charter of the English Grand Lodge, the Negro Grand United Order of Odd Fellows (GUOOF) spread slowly until the Civil War, and then expanded seventy-two-fold in the next four decades. It was the most rapidly expanding black society. The beneficiary features—death and sick benefits—attracted members, whereas the ceremonial and fraternal aspects were of secondary significance.[24]

Paradoxically, Odd Fellowship in black Detroit seemed to attract those who needed the beneficiary features least, while those who needed them the most were attracted to Masonry. In 1885 a group of mostly middle- and upper-class blacks organized the first GUOOF chapter in Detroit, the Zach Chandler Lodge, in memory of the late white Michigan abolitionist senator, a politico with whom many of the black Odd Fellows had worked. In its early years, the Odd Fellows Lodge enrolled more professionals and white-collar workers than did the Masons. Among its members were AME minister J. R. F. Browne, attorney D. Augustus Straker, William Lambert, clerk Edward Watson (son of Dr. S. C. Watson), and physicians James W. Ames and Levi H. Johnson. Physician Benjamin Clark, an Afro-American never otherwise associated with a black organization in the city, was also a member.

Although a beneficiary society, Zach Chandler Lodge developed into a nonceremonial social club, an adjunct of black elite society. Since nearly all of the charter members were already close friends, the benevolent organization merely gave structure to the existing informal social relationships. Soon after its inception the men acquired a social hall on Monroe Street, and in 1887, when the membership had grown to seventy, they moved to larger quarters at Catherine and

[24] Albert C. Stevens, *The Cyclopaedia of Fraternities* (2nd ed., New York, 1907), pp. 235–236.

Hastings. They frequently hosted banquets and social affairs, and the entertainment often included an orchestra. Zach Chandler Lodge occasionally sponsored a community-wide event, and all of respectable black Detroit, as if summoned, would appear. Azalia Smith, a school teacher and later a concert singer, attended the first New Year's ball sponsored by the GUOOF chapter and reported that nothing like it had occurred before in Detroit. "Talk about a crowd!" she wrote her fiancé, "Everybody was there. I don't mean the tough element, but everyone else."[25]

By the turn of the century it appears that Zach Chandler Lodge became less of an elite club and more of a beneficiary society. No professional men were listed as officers, and the social affairs were no longer mentioned in the city's newspapers. Significantly, when Arthur Turner and Earl R. Moses published *Colored Detroit 1924*, which included a history and directory of black Detroit, they recalled the history of black Masonry and the Negro Elks, but made no mention of the Odd Fellows.

As the Detroit black community grew in numbers and the working and lower classes increased, more and more black men and women sought to gain and maximize economic and psychological security by acquiring insurance against death and illness. Working men, whether black or white, obtained these benefits primarily through trade unions or beneficiary societies rather than through established insurance companies. Since both trade unions and insurance companies discouraged black participation, Negroes sought membership in beneficiary societies.

Increasingly, the new lodges organized in Detroit were southern in origin. A chapter of the Negro Elks, a basically northern society would be formed in 1905, but otherwise the societies had their beginnings and their headquarters in the former slave states. The Knights of Pythias, United Brothers of Friendship, Good Samaritans, and the True Reformers began to appear in Detroit in the 1890s and after, offering life insurance and sick benefits. It is likely that they attracted men and women from the working and lower classes, especially the

[25] *Detroit Tribune*, Sept. 28, 1887, p. 4, Oct. 26, 1887, p. 4; quoted in M. Marguerite Davenport, *Azalia: The Life of Madame E. Hackley* (Boston, 1947), p. 57.

growing number of new arrivals in the city. It is interesting to note, however, that a fraction of the old elite, men who would be throwing in their lot with the black-oriented middle class, found their way into leadership positions in a few of the new lodges. All of these men were active black politicians, and it is probable that their participation in nonelite-based beneficiary and fraternal societies reflected their desire to plant roots within the black community. In 1905, when the Wolverine Lodge of the Improved Benevolent and Protective Order of Elks would organize in Detroit, a few political leaders such as Dr. James W. Ames, attorney Robert J. Willis, and newspaper editor Francis H. Warren would be found among the overwhelmingly working-class membership of the chapter.[26]

The fraternal and beneficiary societies and the churches had relatively broad roots in the black community in comparison with the seemingly endless numbers of other voluntary associations. The participants in the numerous groups shared not only like interests and friendship but a common background and community standing. In black Detroit, the innumerable organizations and institutions served to make visible the social stratifications of the black community. A few of the associations, like the upper-class men's clubs, were specifically designed to emphasize social distinctions, but most of the clubs, like the upper-class literary societies, merely imparted a formal structure to existing patterns of association, which would have continued in any event.

Around 1890 a group of elite blacks, politically aware and socially conscious, organized the first black men's club in Detroit—the Sumner Club. The officers included D. Augustus Straker, Dr. Levi H. Johnson, and attorney Robert J. Willis. Significantly the bylaws of the club prohibited the members from indulging in the working- and lower-class entertainments of card playing, gambling, and drinking. Modeled after the Michigan Club, a mostly white social-political club to which some Sumnerians belonged, the Sumner Club was political as well as social, and each member pledged himself to engage actively in

---

[26] *Plaindealer*, Oct. 31, 1890; *Freedmen's Progress*, p. 138; Ulysses W. Boykin, *A Handbook on the Detroit Negro* (Detroit, 1943), p. 107. The charter membership of Wolverine Lodge of the Elks can be found in Turner and Moses, *Colored Detroit 1924*, pp. 10, 57.

politics. The club exerted great political power in Detroit for a time, but it was disbanded in the depression year of 1894. Three years later, the Iroquois Club emerged to replace it. With its membership drawn from the elite, the club became sufficiently influential to gain a listing among the city's clubs in the *Detroit City Directory 1903*. The club's quarters were on St. Antoine, where it held exclusive receptions, with an orchestra "screened from view" providing background music. Like the Sumner Club, its members were politically active. The Pingree Light Artillery, an integrated volunteer company organized in 1898 just prior to the United States' entry into the war against Spain, was formed in the rooms of the Iroquois Club.[27]

The literary societies and social clubs were similar to the men's clubs, though smaller in membership and less concerned with formal structure. Their major function was social and the members regularly entertained each other with parties, dinners, and dances. These organizations were the lineal descendants of the literary and benevolent societies of the Jacksonian era, but in their post–Civil War reincarnation they were almost purely of a social nature.

Information survives on only a small number of the late nineteenth-century Negro societies, all of them in the elite category. Among the earliest was the Oak and Ivy Club, formed in 1881 at the home of City Councilman S. C. Watson. The organizers, nearly all of whom were college graduates, included Watson (Oberlin College, University of Michigan), David Watson (Michigan), Meta E. Pelham (Alma College, Columbia University), O. C. Wood (Oberlin), and Ida Wilson and Alfred Wilson, whose father had been president of the Humane Mechanic Society of Philadelphia during the 1830s and 1840s. In the following fifteen years additional elite clubs were organized, all with overlapping memberships. Among them were the Meylkdi Literary Society, the West Side Pedro Club, the Klondike Club, the Home Social Club, the Detroit Study Club, and the Dumas Literary Society. The members—or if it were a women's club, their fathers or husbands—tended to hold professional or white-collar jobs, to belong

---

[27] *The Sumner Club* (Detroit, n.d.), pamphlet in "Detroit Negro Societies," E & M file, Burton Historical Collection; *Detroit Tribune*, Dec. 25, 1894, p. 5; *Detroit City Directory 1903*, p. 104; *Detroit Sunday News-Tribune*, Apr. 24, 1898, p. 21.

to St. Matthew's, and to be at least high-school graduates, with probably a majority having attended a college or professional school. Many were related through marriage. Nearly all were relatively well-to-do financially, and they participated actively in politics. Collectively, they were referred to as the colored "150" or the "cultured colored '40' [families]." In 1892 the Meylkdi Literary Society's officers were barber shop owner William H. Langston, tailor Benjamin Lambert, letter carrier Frank Shewcraft, and dentist William E. Johnson. The officers of the Detroit Social Club that year were organ manufacturer and future state legislator Joseph Dickinson, William H. Anderson, engineer Fred Pelham, and stenographer Charles Webb. Members included the Levi Johnsons, Albert Hills, George A. Barriers, William Langstons, William W. Fergusons, and school teachers Flossie Cole, Lulu Gregory, and Azalia Smith, as well as other unmarried men and women of the Cole, Harper, Hill, Mirault, Pelham, Watson, and Webb families. Their dances were catered, and attended by an orchestra.[28]

Some of the clubs had serious intellectual goals—the Detroit Study Club, founded by Mrs. Robert Pelham, Jr., at first studied "the lives of English and American poets"—but most had less lofty aspirations. The Pastime Social Club was dedicated to card playing, probably whist, and the Detroit Social Club was devoted to entertainment. Meetings were mostly social in character rather than intellectual, and entire families rather than individuals were generally invited to the various functions.[29]

The women's clubs, by and large, seemed to be of a more serious nature than were the literary societies, and they managed to combine exclusiveness with good works. The Society of Willing Workers was the most self-consciously elite benevolent organization among black

[28] *Detroit Post & Tribune*, Nov. 7, 1881, p. 2; *Plaindealer*, Mar. 11, 1892, May 8, 1891, Dec. 4, 1891, Jan. 1, 1892, Jan. 8, 1892; *Detroit Sunday News-Tribune*, Oct. 24, 1897, p. 24, Nov. 14, 1897, p. 3, Jan. 30, 1898, p. 12, Apr. 3, 1898, p. 16; *Detroit Evening News*, Nov. 25, 1903, p. 1; *Detroit News-Tribune*, Apr. 27, 1902, p. 7; Elizabeth Lindsay Davis (comp.), *Lifting as They Climb: 1933. National Association of Colored Women* (n.p., n.d.), p. 331.

[29] W. E. B. DuBois, *Efforts for Social Betterment Among Negro Americans* (Atlanta, 1909), p. 105; *Detroit Sunday News-Tribune*, Nov. 14, 1897, p. 3; *Plaindealer*, May 8, 1891; *Detroit News-Tribune*, Apr. 27, 1902, p. 7.

women in Detroit. Organized in 1887 and still functioning effectively more than a half-century later, Willing Workers limited its membership to fifty women. Among the charter members had been Mrs. William H. Anderson, Mrs. William W. Ferguson, Mrs. Walter Stowers, Mrs. George Barrier, and Mrs. Robert Pelham, Sr. Their monthly and annual dues and the money they raised through bazaars was used to aid individuals temporarily out of work because of sickness or accident. They also aided what they patronizingly called the "very poor," dutifully recording in their ledgers the reports of members on the families that they had helped. W. E. B. DuBois reported in 1909 that the Detroit Willing Workers regularly supported four black people in addition to giving aid to an occasional "worthy" white person.[30]

Other benevolent activities of black elite women were similar to the activities of the upper-class progressive white women. Like many white women, black women were slowly becoming aware of the environment around them and the changes occurring in society.[31] They responded, as had the increasingly socially aware pulpit, by stressing good character and good works and by banding together to help those who wanted to help themselves. They established such organizations as the Phillis Wheatley Home for Aged Colored Ladies, founded in 1897, and the Labor of Love Circle established in 1907 and dedicated to charity work among the inmates of the home. While women were the prime movers in establishing the home, the trustees were all men: James H. Cole, Sr., D. Augustus Straker, Frank May, Dr. Albert H. Johnson, contractor William Ellis, and Dr. James Ames. Although the Phillis Wheatley Association functioned as an elite Detroit society, the project was important to many of Michigan's black communities. DuBois had noted in 1909 that "the most characteristic Negro charity is the Home for Old People," and accordingly Michigan blacks made the Phillis Wheatley Home their major philanthropic recipient. With the help of societies such as the

[30] "Willing Workers," in "Miscellaneous," NHRSM; *Plaindealer*, Dec. 5, 1890, Jan. 30, 1891; DuBois, *Efforts for Social Betterment*, p. 45.

[31] For a summary of Negro benevolence and welfare work at the national level see Isabel Burns Lindsay, "Some Contributions of Negroes to Welfare Services, 1865–1900," *Journal of Negro Education*, XXV (Winter, 1956), 15–24.

Ann Arbor Women's Club, the association secured in 1901 an eleven-room house on Elizabeth Street in Detroit. At the same time the Detroit Study Club joined the white Detroit Federation of Clubs in 1900, and broadened its work to include child welfare and philanthropy, and the sponsoring of a junior civic league.[32]

Around the turn of the century new kinds of women's clubs began to appear in black Detroit. The old societies tended to be exclusive and without any national affiliation. Though interlocked with each other and with St. Matthew's, they did not identify with any larger movement; it was friendship among members that served as the ultimate attraction. The new clubs were more active within the black community, and less exclusive. Though somewhat patronizing in their rejection of lower- and working-class mores, they seemed more genuinely concerned with the plight of the poor and the urban newcomer and they were dedicated to elevating the masses. They sought to foster race pride, stressing "moral uplift"; their motto was "Lifting as we climb."[33]

The organization of the Michigan State Federation of Colored Women's Clubs would mark the rise in the black community of the new middle-class club woman. The old upper class had been more self-centered; most of their clubs had stressed entertainment and personal uplift and development. They tended to stand apart from the black community and were oriented toward white organizations. They acted as if social involvement in the Negro community would jeopardize their favorable position; indeed, they fostered the legend that anti-Negro prejudice in Detroit arose out of an inevitable white reaction to the growth of a black criminal element in the 1880s that was drawn to the city by the construction of some race tracks. The new middle class, however, seemed more black-oriented. Their roots within the community were deep, and they committed themselves to

[32] *Detroit Journal*, Dec. 25, 1897, p. 8; Turner and Moses, *Colored Detroit 1924*, pp. 35, 39; *Freedmen's Progress*, pp. 141–143; *Detroit Sunday News-Tribune*, Jan. 8, 1898, p. 13; DuBois, *Efforts for Social Betterment*, pp. 59, 65, 76.

[33] *Detroit Sunday News-Tribune*, May 8, 1898, halftone supplement, p. 2; Mary Taylor Blauvelt, "The Race Problem as Discussed by Negro Women," *American Journal of Sociology*, VI (March, 1911), 665, 668, 672. For the women's clubs in Detroit see Davis, *Lifting as They Climb*, pp. 316–323. Blauvelt's article deals with the Michigan State Federation of Colored Women's Clubs.

uplifting their community rather than disengaging from it. Although they shared some of the old elite's patronizing attitudes toward the poor and failed at times to understand or sympathize with the life styles of the lower class, they appeared more genuinely interested in all blacks than the old elite had been, and they sought to help all who were in need. Unlike the old elite, they recognized that society imposed a common destiny on all Negroes and that the improvement of their own lives was linked with the advancement of the whole black community.

The clubs of the new middle class were intended to improve the race—spiritually, morally, and physically. Some, like the Detroit branch of the national Lydian Association, were beneficiary as well as benevolent societies, designed to uplift their working- and middle-class members as well as the race in general. The new middle-class clubs also showed a greater interest in the fate of the urban newcomer. In April 1906, a Refugee and Rescue Home was formed to protect decent girls and to reform fallen women by teaching homemaking arts—millinery, dressmaking, and embroidery. In 1909 the Christian Industrial Club, an uplift club, would be organized to provide a home for working Afro-American girls. Two years later the Detroit Women's Council would be initiated to aid strangers arriving in the city. Clubs of a similar nature would be promoted by the statewide Federation of Colored Women's Clubs, affiliated with the national association.[34]

Black women in Detroit were less active in the temperance movement of the late nineteenth century than their sisters in outstate communities. Although church workers Lucy Thurman of Jackson and Frances Preston of Detroit both served the National Women's Christian Temperance Union (WCTU) as superintendents of colored women, the movement in Detroit was small. In the nineteenth century, black women in Detroit had belonged to an integrated WCTU chapter, and Mrs. Preston had served as a delegate from the Central Detroit WCTU to the 1886 state convention. In 1913, however, the Preston Union—an all black WCTU chapter—would be formed in

[34] *Freedmen's Progress*, pp. 141–142; DuBois, *Efforts for Social Betterment*, p. 102.

Detroit, and it fought not only to ban liquor but also to close Detroit's "red light" district, and it held a woman's suffrage program in the Phillis Wheatley Home.[35]

Three distinct networks of social interaction are evident in the pattern of club, lodge, and church membership: at the top was the elite, whether the old upper class or part of the new middle class; next was the middle group, the middling classes composed of the small middle class and the larger working class; and finally, there was the lower class. Within each stratum, individuals tended to be not only members of the same voluntary associations but also to have a good deal in common when it came to occupation, wealth, education, place of residence, family background, life styles, and future expectations.[36]

[35] Mrs. N. F. Mossell, *The Work of the Afro-American Woman* (Philadelphia, 1908), p. 178; *Minutes of the Tenth Annual Meeting of the National W.C.T.U. 1883*, p. xxiii; *Thirty-sixth Annual Report of the Michigan State W.C.T.U. 1913*, p. 123. From Xeroxed pages of WCTU reports in possession of Larry Engelmann. Both Preston and Thurman served as president of the Michigan Federation of Colored Women's Clubs. *Freedmen's Progress*, p. 72.

[36] "Classes" as used in this study are not the same as occupational groups. Although I agree with Everett C. Hughes's dictum that "a man's work is as good a clue as any to the course of his life, and to his social being and identity," it is not the only factor in determining class. Life styles and life chances, the basis of Max Weber's "class situation," mean the individual's "typical chance for a supply of goods, external living conditions, and personal life experiences." They connote the probabilities of achieving a particular life style. Individuals within the same social class should have similar life chances. They should also have a consciousness of their roles, a point stressed most articulately by Richard Centers. Everett C. Hughes, *Men and Their Work* (Glencoe, Ill., 1958), p. 7; Max Weber, "Class, Status and Party," in Reinhold Bendix and Seymour M. Lipset (eds.), *Class, Status and Power* (Glencoe, Ill., 1953), p. 64; Richard Centers, *The Psychology of Social Classes: A Study of Class Consciousness* (Princeton, N.J., 1949).

Although the terms elite, middling and lower classes have been imposed upon the strata, the groups themselves were not separated by artificially chosen dividing lines. I did not impose categorizations on the data; instead "class" clusterings emerged from matrices of occupation, wealth, residence, church membership, social and political club participation, education, kinship, and social interaction. The clusters were few in number and had discrete boundaries and characteristics. Because the quantity of information available on each individual varied directly with the person's class—the higher the class, the more data available—assumptions and generalizations at the higher level are the most accurate and the generalizations become less accurate at the bottom rungs of the class ladder.

Most of the black upper class in nineteenth-century Detroit were in either professional, white-collar, or entrepreneurial occupations. The physicians, dentists, and attorneys had mostly white practices, and the managers and clerks worked for white businesses or were in government service. At any time, more than half of the male members of this class were college graduates; of the *Detroit News-Tribune* list of fifty-one members of the "cultured colored '40,' " at least twenty-six are known to have held college degrees. Although most of the degrees were received from Michigan schools, Negro colleges such as Howard, Straight, and Wilberforce were represented as well as universities and colleges such as Oberlin and Harvard. Michigan college graduates included William H. Anderson, William W. Ferguson, Dr. Albert H. Johnson, Dr. William E. Johnson, Fred Pelham, dentist Dr. Sylvester Smith, Walter H. Stowers, druggist David Watson, and attorney Robert J. Willis. Among those with degrees from Negro colleges were Dr. James W. Ames from Straight University, Robert C. Barnes from Wilberforce University, and D. Augustus Straker from Howard University. S. C. Watson and Obadiah Wood had attended Oberlin while Dr. H. Peyton Johnson had attended Harvard— as would his first cousins through marriage, dentist Frederick Barrier, son of Delia Pelham and George A. Barrier, and accountant, later Detroit comptroller, Alfred M. Pelham, son of Laura and Benjamin Pelham. Those without college degrees were generally older men and women from an earlier generation, but most of them had graduated from high school at a time when high school degrees were uncommon.

The elite were not only well educated themselves but were able to provide for the education and careers of their sons and daughters. In nearly every instance, the sons of the upper class attended college and then took either professional or white-collar jobs. Dr. Levi Johnson's sons, for instance, followed him into medicine; Dr. Joseph Ferguson's sons became professionals, one a surgeon, the other a lawyer; George Crissup's son became a lawyer; Daniel Cole, Jr., attained a law degree as did James H. Cole, Jr., and Henry Thompson's son; Dr. Chester Ames followed his father into medicine, and the Roxborough sons followed their father into law. All of Toussaint and Crummel Lambert's children attended college, and of the twenty-three offspring (including spouses) of the Pelham brothers and sisters, at least sixteen were college graduates. On the other hand, few blacks outside of the upper class in Detroit managed to attend high school, and none is known to have attended college.[37]

Life style was as important as occupation and education in distinguishing the elite.[38] Membership in St. Matthew's, in the Iroquois and Sumner Clubs, as well as in select study and social clubs set them apart from the rest of the black community. The men held jobs that permitted them to arrange their schedules to their own convenience, and they had time for politics, culture, and a formal social season lasting from the first of September until Lent. They prided themselves on avoiding the popular public dances at the dancing academies, and they limited their public appearances to the events sponsored by their own clubs. Most of the social affairs consisted of dinners and teas, and they entertained in a high, elaborate style, as evidenced by the "Pink Luncheon" given by Mrs. Thaddeus Warsaw, Sr., in honor of Mrs. Robert A. Pelham, Jr. Mrs. Warsaw offered a ten-course menu of appetizer, soup, fish, meat entree, chicken, vegetable, cheese, fruit, cake, and coffee. Pink roses, of course, dominated the settings. After the social season, many of the elite escaped the heat of the city by going north; the Pelhams, Fergusons, and Barrier families, for instance, summered on Bois Blanc Island. Vacations were frequent and most of the elite traveled extensively, whether in conjunction with

[37] The ability to educate their sons and to provide the nonprofessionals with white-collar political jobs was crucial in checking the downward mobility of the sons of the upper class. Although the fathers could not, in most instances, pass businesses on to their heirs, they could ensure them political jobs. Of the *News-Tribune's* list of black society in 1902, at least 63 percent of the men were known to have held government positions. This group included virtually all of the younger men.

[38] Most of the works dealing with aspects of late nineteenth-century black classes have focused on the elite and their life styles. For Boston see Adelaide Cromwell Hill, "The Negro Upper Class in Boston—Its Development and Present Social Structure," Ph.D. dissertation, Radcliffe College, 1952, and Dorothy West's novel, *The Living Is Easy* (Boston, 1947); and for Cleveland see Helen M. Chesnutt's biography of her father, *Charles Waddell Chesnutt: Pioneer of the Color Line* (Chapel Hill, N.C., 1952). Almost all writings on black Chicago have dealt with the "colored 400" there, and Frederic H. Robb, *The Negro in Chicago 1779–1929* (Chicago, 1929) is a good contemporary source.

conventions or just for a holiday. A few, like Dr. and Mrs. Levi Johnson, made the grand tour of Europe.[39]

Music was an important part of the upper-class life, and the elite included accomplished amateur musicians as well as recognized professionals. Susie Smith, daughter of AME Bishop C. S. Smith of Detroit, taught piano and harmony at the Michigan Conservatory of Music. During the week of celebration in Washington accompanying President Theodore Roosevelt's inauguration in 1905, Miss Smith gave a benefit recital, and received praise for her "masterful skill" and "perfect technique." Mrs. Molly E. Lambert, a graduate of a Canadian college, achieved a wide reputation as an authoress. She had been a special correspondent for the *Plaindealer* and the *Monitor*, and later edited the literary section of *Ringwood's Afro-American Journal of Fashion*. She also contributed both poetry and prose to the *New National Era* and the *AME Church Review*, and she made *St. Matthew's Lyceum Journal* an outlet for the works of Detroit's black elite.[40]

The pattern that most separated the upper class was their social interaction with whites on a regular and equal basis. Many of the elite had enjoyed a common educational experience with white political and economic leaders at the Detroit High School, the Detroit College of Law, the Detroit College of Medicine, or the University of Michigan in Ann Arbor. Alumni and professional associations offered them and their wives a continued contact with the white community that was denied to those of the classes below. Most important, politics provided the black elite with a wedge into the white world. Although occasionally middle- and working-class blacks stood for office, especially for the position of Wayne County coroner, the overwhelming majority of black candidates for political office were drawn from the highest class. Active in politics and elected to the city's governing councils, the state legislature, the judiciary, and the Republican party's conventions and committees, they easily gained

---

[39] *Plaindealer*, Apr. 28, 1893, July 24, 1891, July 8, 1892.

[40] Mary Church Terrell, "The Social Functions During Inauguration Week," *Voice of the Negro*, II (April, 1905), 240–241; M. A. Majors, *Noted Negro Women—Their Triumphs and Activities* (Chicago, 1893), p. 335; Mossell, *The Work of the Afro-American Woman*, pp. 15, 78.

membership in Detroit's Republican political-social clubs. The Michigan Club, the leading Republican men's club in Detroit, enrolled William Lambert, Robert Pelham, Sr., Robert Pelham, Jr., Benjamin Pelham, Walter Stowers, D. A. Straker, William Ferguson, Daniel Cole, and Albert Hill on its membership list. They were active members, serving on some of the club's committees, and they and their wives attended social activities of the Michigan. Some of these men also belonged to the Young Men's Republican League, of which Walter Stowers was treasurer. In the 1890s the city's reform clubs included upper-class blacks: the Detroit Reform Club, the Civic Federation, and the women's Twentieth Century Club all accepted a few elite blacks.[41]

When the two-hundredth anniversary of Detroit was celebrated in 1901, at least five black leaders served on official committees. Even some openly segregationist organizations such as the YMCA found openings for a few of the black elite. At the same time that most of Detroit's craft and factory jobs were closed to blacks, some Afro-Americans organized and participated with whites in small-venture projects such as the Smoke Preventative Company and the Detroit Window Ventilator Company. At one time Dr. Levi Johnson's partner in a pharmacy had been a white man, and Granville Purvis, pharmacist and one-time clerk for Dr. S. C. Watson, was a stockholder and director of the Detroit River Savings Bank. Many of the black professionals with an upper-class clientele, such as physicians Benjamin Clark and Levi H. Johnson, had primarily white practices, and some like Watson, Johnson, and William Ferguson were sufficiently prominent for their biographies to appear in widely distributed manuals advertising the business and industries of Detroit. It was only rarely indicated in these brochures and in the city directories, newspapers, and other printed materials that the upper-class blacks were "colored," whereas all other blacks had the designation "(col'd)" permanently affixed to their names. It is no surprise, there-

[41] *Announcements* of the Detroit College of Law in Burton Historical Collection; Michigan Law School *Yearbooks*; *Detroit Tribune*, Mar. 1, 1876, p. 4; membership and banquet lists of the Michigan Club in the Michigan Historical Collections; *Detroit Tribune*, Feb. 4, 1887, p. 4, Jan. 20, 1888, p. 4, Apr. 5, 1877, p. 4, Aug. 4, 1887, p. 4, Jan. 5, 1895, p. 5, June 8, 1895, p. 5; *Who's Who of the Colored Race 1915*, p. 6.

fore, that the *Plaindealer*, reflecting the view of upper-class blacks, editorially commented in 1892 that "prejudice in the North is now almost entirely confined, that is in its obnoxious features, to the lower and more ignorant classes."[42]

Unfortunately for Negroes below the elite level, it was almost impossible to escape the caste system by rising into the upper class. First of all, the caste system prevented anyone below the upper class from gaining access to opportunities for mobility. None of the black professionals or white-collar workers in Detroit is known to have come from a lower- or middle-class family in Detroit; indeed, not a single black high school graduate in nineteenth-century Detroit is known to have come from a family outside of the elite. There was mobility among the lower, working, and middle classes but, except through marriage and only rarely in that way, it was next to impossible for a black to move up into the elite class. Second, insofar as access to the top was not checked by the caste system, it was blocked by the upper class themselves. Although the elite lessened in numbers because of small family size, childless couples, and unmarried offspring, as well as by the out-migration of ambitious men and women to more westerly cities or to Washington, D.C., they refused to admit other local blacks into their ranks. They married within their class and in essence drew themselves into a circle, labeled by others the *"crème de la crème"* (possibly a pun on their light skin color) or "old Detroiter," and rejected all those Detroit Negroes who were outside.

Conscious of their status outside of the black caste, the upper class looked down upon those of lesser social standing and in the process earned the enmity of many Negroes. The elite generally agreed with white Detroiters "that the southern Negro is more criminal by nature

[42] *The Bi-Centenary of the Founding of Detroit, 1701–1901* (Detroit, 1902), pp. 297, 299, 300, 302; John Dancy, *Sand Against the Wind* (Detroit, 1966), p. 103; *Plaindealer*, Sept. 18, 1891, Feb. 5, 1892; Owens and Jackson, "Report on Negroes," p. 328; *Plaindealer*, Jan. 2, 1891, June 26, 1891; *Detroit Illustrated* (Detroit, 1891), p. 144; *Plaindealer*, Dec. 2, 1892. It is interesting to note that the elite had their own boat club, the Oriental Boat Club, with Dr. Joseph Ferguson as captain, and that in the 1880s the Detroit newspapers' New Years' Day calling lists included nearly a dozen black families. *Detroit Tribune*, Sept. 17, 1875, p. 4; *Detroit Post & Tribune*, Jan. 1, 1881, p. 3; *Detroit Post*, Dec. 31, 1884, p. 3, Jan. 1, 1885, p. 6.

than his northern brother," and they chose to disassociate themselves from the masses of the race. E. Azalia Smith Hackley, a member of an old Detroit family who had been a school teacher in Detroit for ten years before marrying Edwin Hackley and moving to Denver, and who had switched from the Second Baptist Church of her mother to St. Matthew's, must have drawn her view of black social life from her years in Detroit. She advised teen-age girls that the best people "go to church if only for example's sake." She cautioned that "the display of wealth is never original—only vulgar," and considered it "pathetic to watch the social efforts—'climbing'—of people with only money 'sans' brains and originality." "The race," Madame Hackley declared, "needs more quality in Emotion and less quantity."[43]

Above all else, Detroit's upper-class blacks were interested in preserving their own high status and prestige in the community. Although they waged their battle against discrimination with great intensity, they took care not to jeopardize their marginal position above the black caste. Addressing a black audience in 1873, Dr. Joseph Ferguson argued that, although he favored civil-rights legislation, he was opposed to social legislation. It was up to "the colored man himself," Ferguson said, "to get social position." "Nobody," he claimed, "wanted social equality." Two years later, at a meeting commemorating the passage of the 1875 Civil Rights Act, Dr. S. C. Watson moved "that we discountenance the overzealous action of some of the colored citizens, in testing the Civil Rights bill, but when necessity compels it, we shall demand a full recognition of our rights."[44]

Negro leaders were sensitive to black customs that would foster a division between themselves and whites. None of Detroit's leading black citizens would participate in the 1871 commemoration of the Fifteenth Amendment, and a few years later a black meeting approved a resolution recommending the discontinuance of celebrating

[43] Forrester B. Washington, "The Detroit Newcomers' Greeting," *Survey*, July 14, 1917, p. 335; E. Azalia Hackley, *The Colored Girl Beautiful* (Kansas City, Mo., 1916), pp. 89, 93, 126. The newcomers and others below the upper class retaliated against the elite by calling them snobbish and "cold and distant." Forrester B. Washington, "The Negro in Detroit: A Survey of the Conditions of a Negro Group in a Northern Industrial Center during the War Prosperity Period," 1920, typewritten, pp. 117–119, in Detroit Public Library.

[44] *Detroit Tribune*, Nov. 25, 1873, p. 4, Mar. 31, 1875, p. 4.

"all days that are only celebrated by them [blacks], as the tendency is to perpetuate caste feeling, and that in the future, they recognize only the national days of the country." Upper-class blacks rejected suggestions that they form black professional societies—D. A. Straker said that a Colored National Bar Association would "plant a barrier more firmly than now exists between us and our white brethren"—and organizations such as the Negro Business League failed to gain adherents in pre–World War I Detroit.[45]

Negro leaders also sought to escape from the white stereotype of the Negro. White Negrophobia hung like an albatross around the necks of all Negroes, and leading blacks in particular urgently felt the need to relieve the burden. It was for this reason that they sought to substitute the word "Afro-American" for "Negro." "The word 'Negro' as commonly used in America and as scientifically applied means everything low and degraded," argued the *Plaindealer*, which initiated the campaign for a new designation in Detroit in the 1880s. "Afro-American," with its ethnic implications and its categorization of Negroes as simply another hyphenated American group, would, it was hoped, release blacks from the stigma of caste.[46]

By World War I some members of the new middle class would completely displace the upper class as the elite group within the black community.[47] This was the result of a number of factors. First,

[45] Ibid., Mar. 16, 1871, p. 4, Mar. 25, 1871, p. 4, Mar. 31, 1875, p. 4; *Plaindealer*, Aug. 14, 1891.

[46] *Plaindealer*, Apr. 11, 1890.

[47] The concept of the new middle class is most commonly associated with the work of E. Franklin Frazier. I am, as are many others, indebted to his wide range of research and thought in this area. See his *Black Bourgeoisie: The Rise of a New Middle Class* (New York, 1957), and "The Negro Middle Class and Desegregation," *Social Problems*, IV (April, 1957), 291–301. As early as 1913, Robert E. Park, Frazier's mentor at the University of Chicago, had noticed the new black middle class as he distinguished between the descendants of pre–Civil War free families and the recent growth of "a vigorous and pushing middle class." Dealing almost exclusively with the South, Park concluded that the middle class "has served to fill the distance which formerly existed between the masses of the race at the bottom and the small class of educated Negroes at the top." "Negro Home Life and Standards of Living," *Annals*, XLIX (September, 1913), 147–148. For the most valuable and suggestive overall discussion of the Negro middle class see August Meier, *Negro Thought in America, 1880–1915* (Ann Arbor, 1963), pp. 139–157; for the best study of the new middle class in a single city see Allan Spear, *Black Chicago*, pp. 71–89.

the migrants who came into Detroit after 1900, whether well educated or not, primarily would identify with the ambitious, business-oriented middle class. The goals and life styles of the integration-minded old upper class were not totally forsaken, but black newcomers considered them irrelevant; the new middle class showed more interest in status and success within the black community than in prestige among and interaction with whites. Second, the old upper class rapidly diminished in number. Some of the families produced no male heirs, and many daughters left to marry upper-class blacks in other cities. Some progeny—attorneys, physicians, and teachers—left Detroit for greener pastures in newer, more westerly cities. Still others found that their civil service or patronage careers took them out of Detroit. The remaining members of the dwindling upper class would either withdraw from the black community altogether or make accommodation with the new middle class. A shift in white attitudes accompanied the rise of the black-oriented middle class. As the national Republican party's commitment to Negro equality diminished, and as the race issue lessened in importance as the mood of the North shifted to reconciliation with the South, politically initiated channels of upper-class black-white contacts slowly dried up. The urban reform movement that overlapped the progressive period would further undermine the position of upper-class blacks outside of the black caste. As old-line stalwart Republicans and practitioners of patronage politics, upper-class black politicians would be left on the fringes of the new, reform politics—a shift that coincided with the Republican disinterest in black voters. Long-time black leaders thus lost legitimacy as liaisons with the white community, and Negro leadership and power became dependent on internal structures within the black community. As nearly all of the old upper-class families disappeared, power would shift to a group within the new middle class, and those few old families that remained white-oriented vanished from sight and became anachronisms, unable to adjust to the new black community. Thus by World War I some of the new middle class had become a new elite.

At first, most of the new middle class were of southern birth. They were among the first trickle of migrants from the South into Detroit, and their interest lay primarily in earning a living. Their first successes changed the appearance of St. Antoine, Beaubien, and Hastings streets as the small retail stores of the new black businessmen became visible. For the first time, black Detroit would have a business district, and it would include everything from hotels to cigar stands. As the Negro population became increasingly concentrated in the St. Antoine district, and as the total black population grew, more and more men within the black leadership became oriented toward black patronage, whether political or economic.[48]

There is only a meager amount of information available about the middle and working classes. The members of the middle class, a step above the working class, included skilled artisans—bakers, coopers, masons, plasterers, and the like—lunchroom owners, cigar-store keepers, and similar petty entrepreneurs. The working class consisted of regularly employed laborers with steady jobs. All were handicapped by the stigma of caste in competing with Detroit's ethnic population for the better-paying, higher-status occupations opening in the expanding economy of the industrializing city of the late nineteenth century. They lived in an almost totally segregated world. Like the whitewasher whom a *Detroit News* reporter interviewed in 1891, the middling class managed to retain self-respect by looking down upon the immigrants who were able to pass them by: "Many wite men in the business? No, dere's no wite men. Dere's some Polacks, but dey ain't wite men, you know. Ha! ha! ha!"[49]

Aside from their churches and the fraternal and beneficiary societies, little is known about the organizations of the middling and lower classes. There were a few social agencies, such as the Douglass Institute at Columbia and St. Antoine, which would be established to provide a culturally and morally uplifting environment and to lure the working men away from the cafes (taverns) and billiard rooms. Opened in 1911 by the black elite and white philanthropists, the reading, lecture, and bathing rooms of the Douglass center failed to attract

[48] The appearance of the *Michigan Manual of Freedmen's Progress*, compiled by Francis H. Warren in 1915, represented the ascendancy of the new middle class. Success is measured in material acquisitions, and the book is filled with dozens of pictures of houses and has a list of "Negro Home and Property Owners" in the state. Cultural and literary achievements find only an incidental listing.

[49] Clipping [*Detroit News*], May 24, 1891, in Burton Scrapbook, III, 137.

the men of the working class. The informal cliques of the working and lower classes probably were the counterpart of the formal fraternal lodges of the "better classes." The ritual of the regular patronage at Booker's saloon, or later at those of Doston or Lucker, could hardly have been different from the meetings at Masonic Hall. In all likelihood the sailors at Charlie Butler's, the gamblers and pimps at Ed Booker's, and the longshoremen at any of the waterfront saloons experienced the same spirit of fraternity and sense of belonging and community that attorneys and physicians felt at the Sumner or Iroquois. After 1900 the number of respectable Negro taverns would increase sharply, and the working class was attracted to places like the Ellwood Cafe and J. B. Hutchins's. The men shared a camaraderie of similar occupations, like social standing, and common future expectations. Furthermore, the slang and jargon of the saloon could be expected to exclude the outsider as much as did the blackball of the men's club or the ritual of the lodges.[50]

Most of the middling classes appeared to be unconsciously torn between a desire to emulate the assimilationism of the elite or to live within a black world. Probably this group provided the largest market for hair straighteners and skin whiteners; no doubt they sought to copy the American preference for light skin color. There is strong evidence, on the other hand, to show that they also rejected the upper-class preference for integration. More than once they were successful in raising the issue of black orientation in a political campaign, charging the selected candidate with not having sufficient ties with the black community. In 1884 councilman Samuel C. Watson sought appointment as city tax assessor, but he was thwarted when a black group opposed him; the strongest argument against him was that he "was a regular attendant at a white man's church, and that the only time he associated with Negroes was on election day." Most dramatically, in 1872 the middling-class blacks rejected school integration, petitioning the board of education to assign a black teacher to instruct their offspring and asking "that their children may not be confined to an education from text books alone, but that they may be trained . . . in such deportment and principles as may best fit them

[50] *Detroit Leader*, Dec. 23, 1910, supplement.

for usefulness in the natural positions that they may be called upon to fill in life."[51]

Little is known about the bottom stratum of the black community, the lower class. The larger part of the lower class, possibly numbering one-third of the total black population of Detroit, were unskilled workingmen, mostly day laborers, dock workers, and servants. They received low wages, experienced frequent unemployment, and their associational activities, nearly exclusively of an informal nature, left them with shallow roots in the community. Most of them had been born outside of Detroit, but they had lived in the city long enough to establish a reputable existence, and a consciousness that Detroit was their home. Whether in the notorious Potomac and Heights districts near the river or in the Kentucky district north of Gratiot, the lower-class blacks lived in the worst housing in Detroit—in the frame tenements and propped-up sheds that were constructed amid the heaps of refuse and stagnant pools of flooded sanitary vaults in the alleys of the city. In essence, they lived within a subculture of poverty.[52]

---

[51] *Detroit Sunday News-Tribune*, Apr. 24, 1898, p. 15, May 1, 1898, halftone supplement; *Detroit Post*, Dec. 23, 1884, p. 5; *Detroit Tribune*, Nov. 12, 1872, p. 4.

[52] As Oscar Lewis has noted, "The most likely candidates for the culture of poverty are the people who come from the lower strata of a rapidly changing society and are already partially alienated from it." Often it originates among migrants. Many of the following characteristics which Lewis ascribes to the subculture clearly describe the black lower class of nineteenth-century Detroit:

"Lack of effective participation and integration...in the major institutions of the larger society."

"Low wages and chronic unemployment and underemployment lead to low income, lack of property ownership, absence of savings, absence of food reserves in the home, and a chronic shortage of cash."

They "produce very little wealth and receive very little in return. They have a low level of literacy and education."

They "are aware of middle-class values; they talk about them and even claim some of them as their own, but on the whole they do not live by them."

In "the local community, we find poor housing conditions, crowding, gregariousness, and, above all, a minimum of organization beyond the level of the nuclear and extended family."

"On the family level...the absence of childhood as a specially prolonged and protected stage, and disorganization of the traditional meaning of family."

And "on the level of the individual...strong feelings of marginality, of helplessness, of dependence, and of inferiority." *A Study of Slum Culture: Backgrounds for "La Vida"* (New York, 1968), pp. 4–21.

The annual reports of the Detroit Board of Poor Commissioners reveal the high degree of economic insecurity and the tenuous respectability of the lower class. In 1900, 120 black families (370 persons), nearly 6 percent of the city's black population, received aid from the commission. Most of the heads-of-families on aid were women: 57 percent of the black workers receiving help had been laundresses and 30 percent had been day laborers. Most of the lower class were employed on a daily basis and they were without the security that a steady job or savings could provide. Sickness or infirmity impoverished 47 percent of the black families on the commission's rolls; 21 percent sought aid because they had been widowed; 13 percent because of old age; and 9 percent because of unemployment.[53]

Booker T. Washington publicly argued that the northern black lower-class workers were victims of their own failure to acquire a trade and that they were insufficiently thrifty or industrious. Washington disregarded the factors of caste and prejudice, and, as a general rule, he had little sympathy for the consumption patterns of poor people who, in brief periods of steady employment, sought to share in the material wealth they saw around them and thus frequently fell victim to the shopkeeper willing to sell cheap goods at high prices and exorbitant rates of interest. On one of his trips to Detroit, Washington visited with a Mr. Brown, a day laborer, and used this worker's circumstances to illustrate the lack of direction and poverty of men without trades. Brown supported his family of six by odd jobs, sometimes furnished by the city. He never earned a sufficient wage to accumulate savings, and in an emergency or period of unemployment he had to turn to the Poor Commission for aid, an almost biennial embarrassment. On a visit to the Browns' apartment, Washington found the uncarpeted rooms nearly empty except for a "handsome bedroom suite and a very pretty baby carriage." The furnishings, bought "on

[53] *Annual Report of the Board of Poor Commissioners 1900* (Detroit, 1900), pp. 35–36, 38–39. The effect of black poverty occasionally could be seen in the school system. In 1857, for instance, an unidentified observer told a *Free Press* reporter "that there were at least one hundred and fifty colored children in the city who did not go to school *because* they had not shoes and clothes to wear." *Detroit Daily Free Press*, Dec. 18, 1857, p. 1.

contract" from a Gratiot Avenue furniture dealer for forty-one dollars, were probably not worth the price, and Washington pointed out that a simpler set and carriage could have been purchased for fourteen dollars and not on contract.[54]

The lowest black stratum were the "disreputable poor," men and women who, even during periods of prosperity and high employment, remained out of work or were only irregularly employed. This group, whose presence largely escaped both the city directory publisher and the federal census enumerator, contained the socially immobile descendants of old black families, the disabled and infirm, the alcoholics and the narcotics addicts, and the urban newcomers. Although recent arrivals were generally the largest numerical component of this group, Detroit-born Negroes were well represented among the disreputable class. The channels to respectable poverty—whether education, apprenticeship, or steady employment—remained closed to many blacks as poverty and caste discrimination and prejudice erected both visible and concealed barriers.[55]

The disreputable poor were paupers, and many were marginal criminals—men and women who committed criminal acts out of desperation. For them, crime offered neither a trade nor a means of earning a living but rather constituted a path to survival. From the earliest days of Detroit, merchants and homeowners had been plagued by the petty thefts of unemployed, often transient, blacks. The black poor who turned to thievery commonly stole food, clothing, or mon-

---

[54] *Detroit Sunday News-Tribune*, Jan. 26, 1896, p. 2.

[55] David Matza, "The Disreputable Poor," in Neil J. Smelser and Seymour Martin Lipset (eds.), *Social Structure and Mobility in Economic Development* (Chicago, 1966), pp. 311–326. The size of this class, which is difficult to estimate because few of them were recorded in the census, might have been as great as 15 percent of all blacks before 1900. In 1900, 6.5 percent of the city's black population received aid from the Board of Poor Commissioners, more than three times the city average. *Report of the Board of Poor Commissioners 1900*, p. 35. In a larger sense, social stratification may be seen not only as the rank order of life styles and life chances but also as the ability to survive. As one moves up the class ladder the chances of survival increase. The highest classes have more live births and more of their children reach their teens. But more important, they literally survive as human entities. They are people who fit, who have a place within a larger human community. Few lower-class blacks were able to survive in this fashion; too many were dregs, the bottom of society—men without roots, without a past, without a future.

ey; increasingly during the nineteenth century other blacks were their victims. The disreputable poor often found that the only employment available to them drew them within the criminal sphere. A 1913 report on prostitution by the state office of woman factory inspectors found the "larger percentage of girls in disorderly houses coming from domestic, hotel and restaurant service." They were young, unskilled, and often only seasonally employed, and in 65 percent of the cases investigated they reported nonsupport or desertion by their husbands as the immediate cause for their entering prostitution. More important, many black laborers and musicians could find employment only in disorderly houses, many of which hired exclusively black service staffs. Charles Smith (white), for example, ran a lodging house on Congress East, a front for a disreputable house. A visitor reported that the staff of prostitutes was integrated but the remaining employees, from the bouncer at the entrance to the organist singing about the farmer's daughter Kate, were all black. Similarly, numbers or policy—a form of lottery traditionally associated with the black community—was controlled by whites whose headquarters were in Covington, Kentucky, but blacks filled the perilous position of runner or collector, and the runners were the ones most frequently arrested.[56]

Not all of Detroit's black criminals were poor or disreputable. There flourished within the black district on the near east side a subculture of crime—black men and women engaged in satisfying the large demand, black and white, for illicit sex, illegal liquor, and unlawful gambling. A significant number of Negroes, possibly 10 percent of the adult working black population, earned a living as entrepreneurs or employees in the city's illegal saloon, gambling, and prostitution industries.[57]

[56] "Report of Special Investigations as to Relation of Occupation to Immorality," *Annual Report of the Department of Labor of Michigan 1913*, pp. 29–31, 42; *Detroit Post & Tribune*, Apr. 23, 1882, p. 4, July 3, 1882, p. 8; *Detroit Tribune*, Feb. 28, 1886, p. 3, Dec. 5, 1888, p. 5; *People* v. *Elliott*, 74 Michigan 264 (1889).

[57] A small number of blacks, taking advantage of Detroit's proximity to Canada, were involved in the smuggling of such items as kid gloves and cigars. *Detroit Advertiser & Tribune*, Jan. 30, 1869, p. 1, Mar. 19, 1869, p. 1; *Detroit Post & Tribune*, Feb. 28, 1881, p. 4.

Although many entrepreneurs met the fate of Slaughter, Peg Welch and Company (described earlier), a few had long careers, paying only infrequent fines as tokens to the occasional reform crusades that swept Detroit. In the late nineteenth century the "Heights," the major crime area, appeared to some as "one succession of colored dens," and the zone remained a red-light district until the police closed it down because of the housing shortage during World War I. Although the police tolerated nearly all of the illegal saloons, dance halls, and disorderly houses in the Heights, and permitted white-owned dens to operate elsewhere in the city, they regularly raided and shut down black-owned houses outside of the Heights or the Potomac Quarter. When blacks began settling in Kentucky in the 1860s, recreational facilities followed them, but the police were intent on restricting black entrepreneurial crime to south of Gratiot Avenue, and they used whatever force was necessary to confine illegal black activities to the traditional areas. In August 1866 the police raided a Negro dance hall on Indiana Street between St. Antoine and Hastings, arrested twenty-five black men and women, and fatally wounded George Douglas as he sought to escape. In the ensuing years the police closed down the illegal saloons, dance halls, and disorderly houses in Kentucky as fast as they discovered them.[58]

Saloon ownership was never a dishonorable profession among blacks in Detroit, not even during periods of prohibition. Whereas reformers condemned bars as dens of iniquity and rookeries harboring drunks, prostitutes, gamblers and thieves, working men accepted saloons as their clubs—places where they could find employment, quench their thirst, read a newspaper, obtain a line of credit, meet their friends, or engage in friendly games of poker, checkers, billiards, or dice. Single men had no other meeting places, and even married men probably sought a haven in the saloon away from their small, crowded apartments. The newspapers generally associated saloon gambling with thieves and concealed razors, but the black community

[58] *Detroit Post*, May 5, 1885, p. 5; *Detroit Advertiser & Tribune*, Aug. 24, 1886, p. 1; *Detroit Tribune*, Aug. 6, 1869, p. 3, Sept. 4, 1869, p. 3, Nov. 24, 1869, p. 3. As late as the 1930s, white prostitutes could be found walking black districts, but no black prostitutes worked outside of Negro areas. Lenn S. Taylor, "Prostitution in Detroit," typewritten report to the Earhart Foundation, n.d., in University of Michigan Library.

tended to be more sympathetic. "The majority were inclined to be tolerant of it," John Dancy observed, "even if they did not indulge in it themselves." Blocked from other professions, some black men of exceptional ability and little education or capital achieved financial success and brief respectability as entrepreneurs in the Heights or Potomac.[59]

Only a handful of black saloon and gambling-house owners succeeded in acquiring respectability within the black community. William Doston and Ed Booker were the most successful of these black entrepreneurs. Senior proprietor of a legal saloon, Doston found gambling more lucrative than selling beer, and he had turned his quarters at Macomb and Brush streets into a "notorious resort renowned for its crap games and white clientele." Doston retained respectability nonetheless—he had married into a well-respected family (the Richards) and he was an officer of the Sumner Club—and he remained an active churchgoer. Politically ambitious, Doston was an active Republican and gained appointment as a deputy sheriff in the 1890s. He died in 1896 at age thirty on the floor of his gambling-saloon, shot by a bartender after a dispute.[60]

Edward Booker, on the other hand, lived too long; after a career spanning nearly forty years, he achieved political power and community position without the respectability that Doston had secured, but he died alone and penniless. Booker, a dedicated worker, sought material possessions above all else. Thrifty and ambitious, he saved the profits from his first saloon to buy the building and land on the southwest corner of Monroe and Beaubien, and he turned his new location into the most notorious and toughest den in Detroit. He rented the upstairs apartments to "vile men and women," and ran betting, crap, faro, poker, and stud games in the saloon below. Booker's place was the scene of quarrels, fights, stabbings, and killings, but

---

[59] Raymond Calkins, *Substitutes for the Saloon* (Boston, 1901), pp. 9, 11, 13, 19; John C. Dancy, *Sand Against the Wind* (Detroit, 1966), p. 114.

[60] *Plaindealer*, Feb. 13, 1891; *Detroit Tribune*, Dec. 28, 1895, p. 1. Doston was not the only black deputy sheriff to fall dead on a saloon floor after a dispute. Hugh Moffat Carter, a former deputy sheriff and son of the wealthy realtor J. D. Carter, was murdered in Park's saloon on St. Antoine Street in 1908, following a gambling dispute. Clipping, *Detroit Journal*, Nov. 7, 1908, in Burton Scrapbook, XXX, 141.

Booker continued to expand his operations, extending his brick building back to the alley and adding additional gambling tables upstairs. He entered new fields, acquiring a fast racing horse, a bulldog, a gaming rooster, and Dace, a twelve-pound fighting tomcat. Wealth and success brought him other rewards, and at the crest of his career he gained election to committees at black community meetings and served in Republican political conventions. In the end, however, Booker had little. His wife had divorced him in 1887, no longer able to reconcile her Methodism with his gambling. By the 1890s his wealth, estimated at more than $30,000 in 1887, had been dissipated, and with it went the status and political power that he had achieved. He died in 1898, impoverished, his building long since mortgaged after his gambling trade had been lost to Doston's and Lucker's saloons. No mourners walked in his funeral, not even his fellow Knights Templar, and his possessions were not worth claiming: "his dog and pet chicken, a piano with three broken keys, a wheezy old organ, some carpet and a few chairs." [61]

More typically, Charlie Butler failed to gain the small portion of political success achieved by Doston and Booker. At various times owner of disorderly houses and saloons, sometimes in partnership with white men, Butler unsuccessfully sought political influence and power. Crime in black Detroit rarely led to respectability or political and community influence, and when it did, as Doston and Booker showed, it was short-lived. [62]

[61] *Detroit Tribune*, Mar. 17, 1876, p. 4, Mar. 25, 1876, p. 4; *Detroit Post & Tribune*, Sept. 25, 1883, p. 5, June 11, 1884, p. 5; *Detroit Post*, Oct. 7, 1884, p. 5; *Detroit Tribune*, Apr. 23, 1888, p. 6, Oct. 8, 1887, p. 4; *Detroit Sunday News-Tribune*, Sept. 18, 1898, halftone supplement, p. 2.

[62] *Detroit Post & Tribune*, Nov. 30, 1880, p. 4; *Detroit Post*, Sept. 24, 1885, p. 5, Oct. 8, 1885, p. 5.

CHAPTER VI

Politics

THE DETROIT BLACK COMMUNITY had been deeply involved in politics even before Michigan black men were enfranchised. The pre–Civil War abolitionist political campaigns, the suffrage fights, and the lobbying efforts for equal rights had left Negroes with a tradition of political participation. The rapid rise of the Republican party in Michigan—within a few months it grew from a political caucus under the Jackson oaks into an organization powerful enough to sweep the November 1854 state elections—served to increase black interest and involvement. The Michigan party and its leaders officially committed themselves to the welfare of black citizens, and the organization of a colored Civil War regiment stood high among their achievements. After the war, party leaders regularly attended black celebrations, and they welcomed black men into their ranks.[1]

Encouraged by the Republican party's stand for Negro rights, both in Lansing and Washington, Detroit blacks entered politics and pressed for enfranchisement. The campaign for constitutional revision, which achieved success only with the ratification of the Fifteenth Amendment, was supplemented by court suits, and in 1866 Negroes with racially mixed ancestry won the right to vote (*People v*

[1] Floyd Benjamin Streeter, *Political Parties in Michigan 1837–1860* (Lansing, 1918), pp. 197–198.

175

William Dean). Although most blacks remained disfranchised until the fall of 1870, early patronage rewards indicate that some had been politically active before then. In 1863 Richard Bush began his twenty-seven-year tenure as a bailiff in federal courts, the first of many Detroit Negroes who would spend nearly their entire working lives in the public service. In March 1869, W. G. Winn, a barber in John D. Richards's shop, won a clerkship in the Freedmen's Bureau, and four months later Richards secured for himself an appointment as customs' inspector.[2]

Aided by other black leaders in Detroit, Richards helped to identify the black community with the Republican party. Born in Fredericksburg, Virginia, and educated in Washington, D.C., Richards came to Detroit in 1851 and quickly rose to prominence in the black community. During the Civil War he served as a sutler of the 102nd United States Colored Infantry, and he built a reputation among black and white in the city "as a man of more than ordinary intelligence and culture" and as the most eloquent black orator in Detroit. Frequently mentioned as a candidate for Congress in the 1870s, and elected Wayne County coroner in 1880, Richards worked with William Lambert, Dr. Joseph Ferguson, and others to organize and sponsor many of the public meetings of the Detroit black community, and to make certain that the platform would be shared with Detroit's leading Republicans. Often a featured Negro orator at celebrations and meetings of the black community, Richards helped turn the affairs into Republican rallies. On March 31, 1870, for instance, Detroit Negroes held an informal assembly to commemorate President Grant's endorsement of the Fifteenth Amendment and to plan a more formal celebration. With Lambert in the chair and Richards dominating the proceedings, it readily became apparent that the celebration would be a Republican party event: marchers would carry banners with the portraits of prominent Republicans and the inscription, "The Republican Party Made Us Free."[3]

Although much of the loyalty of Detroit blacks to the Republican

[2] *Detroit Tribune*, Oct. 21, 1868, p. 3, Oct. 27, 1868, p. 3; *Detroit Free Press*, Oct. 23, 1895, p. 5; *Detroit Tribune*, Mar. 18, 1869, p. 1, July 26, 1869, p. 1.

[3] *Detroit Post & Tribune*, Apr. 14, 1882, p. 2; *Detroit Advertiser & Tribune*, Jan. 3, 1867, p. 3, Aug. 2, 1867, p. 1; *Detroit Tribune*, Apr. 1, 1870, p. 1.

party was based on the party's identification with Negro interests in the 1850s and 1860s and its support of Afro-American rights in the 1870s, the black leadership itself played an active role in support of the party within the black community. Black politicos such as Richards, Lambert, and Dr. Samuel C. Watson were motivated not only by a concern for the welfare of the black community but also by a desire for personal gain. In the end, these men and their close circle —all of whom were members of the black elite—would reap the greatest benefits from the black community's stalwart Republicanism. Political participation provided them with an entree into the white community, and they were responsible for making integration the primary articulated goal of black political activity during a period when employment, education, and housing should have been more essential issues for most Detroit blacks. The elite profited most directly by monopolizing nearly all of the patronage that flowed to the black community; little of it filtered down to the lower classes as it did in Detroit's white ethnic communities. It is likely that the black community as a whole would have benefitted more by acquiring the greatest possible number of jobs rather than by securing a significant number of the high-prestige city and county clerkships. The very low-paid black service worker and the frequently out-of-work day laborer and dock worker would have gained greatly if they could have left the private sector for the high pay and security of the municipal payroll. More important, large-scale city employment of Afro-Americans could have offered an occupational channel for escape from the caste system. Unfortunately, black leaders in seeking patronage never pressed beyond tokenism, except at the white-collar job level.

Public office became a prerogative of Detroit's upper-class blacks, and a political appointment might comprise a son's most important inheritance or a daughter's dowry. For many of these men, while political office served to reinforce their community standing, it also represented simply a more leisurely work style than private employment would have offered, since jobs of comparable prestige, security, and remuneration were available to them in the private sector. For a smaller number of families, however, political patronage represented an opportunity to break the downward mobility of less able, less well-educated elite kin. For this group, public office offered higher wages, more security, and greater status and prestige than any occupation in the private sector. Thus while the caste system prevented anyone below the upper class from gaining access to mechanisms for upward mobility, the elite were able to use their political influence to halt any downward mobility. Unwittingly, the mass of the black community concurred in this policy by permitting the upper class to set the goals of the entire political community.

The Republican hold on the black vote was cemented in 1870, the first year of general Negro enfranchisement. In June 1870, blacks founded their first political club, the Lincoln Sixth Ward Republican Club. A few months later, blacks in the adjoining ward organized the Seventh Ward Colored Republican Club. Nearly all of the community's prominent men joined the clubs and held office in them. In late nineteenth-century Detroit, ethnic political clubs were the cornerstone of party organization, and the immigrant nationality groups as well as Afro-Americans participated in politics through ethnic societies. In the campaign in 1870, black leaders rallied the community to the Republican standard as they reminded their listeners of the Negrophobia of the old Democracy. White Republicans recalled the "Democratic riot of 1863, in which a mob of Democrats hunted down and murdered the friends and relatives of the very colored men whose votes they now unblushingly seek." In the fall, George DeBaptiste was elected a delegate to the local senatorial convention, setting a precedent that would result in the sending of black delegates on a regular basis to city, county, and state Republican conventions over the next four decades.[4]

In the ensuing decades the Republican party would recognize the demands made by the black leadership. The party sponsored civil

4 *Detroit Tribune*, June 25, 1870, p. 3, Sept. 15, 1870, p. 1, Sept. 17, 1870, p. 3, Sept. 29, 1870, p. 1, Oct. 14, 1870, p. 1, Oct. 19, 1870, p. 1. When Thomas P. Tuite took over the chairmanship of the Detroit Republican City Committee in the campaign of 1888, he found the party weak and without an organization in some wards. The electoral successes of the 1880s had convinced Tuite that the organization had been strong; what he failed to realize was that the ethnic political clubs had provided the Republicans with a structure and organization in most wards. Thomas P. Tuite to Senator James MacMillan, September 28, 1892, MacMillan Papers, Burton Historical Collection, Detroit Public Library.

rights bills, struck down the miscegenation law, supported black aspirants for white-collar patronage, and regularly nominated blacks to office. The patronage list in late nineteenth-century black Detroit was a long one, and many important leaders spent nearly all their entire careers on the public payroll. Beginning in the 1870s, at least one Afro-American served as a deputy sheriff in each administration. At the same time blacks such as John C. Ferguson, who was putting himself through medical school, served as postal clerks while others, such as Toussaint L'Ouverture Lambert, served as mail carriers. Other blacks were attracted to clerkships and inspectorships in the customs house. Detroit Afro-Americans frequently received appointments to such other positions as city hall janitor, city physician, and deputy county clerk. The governor's notary lists always included black men, and even their wives were occasionally rewarded with the honorary position of public school examiner.[5]

Michigan's senators in Washington paid special attention to their black constituency. The relatively long list of federal jobholders from Detroit, both in the city and in the District of Columbia, attests to the concern of Senators Zachariah Chandler, Thomas Palmer, James Mac-Millan, and others. MacMillan and his staff, in particular, vigorously processed and supported patronage and pension applications from black Detroiters. He was acquainted with the black political leaders in Detroit, and worked closely with D. A. Straker and Robert A. Pelham, Jr.[6]

Not only did blacks secure a considerable amount of patronage; they were often elected to public office. Except for a printing error, Dr. Samuel C. Watson would have been the first Detroit black victor in an election. In November 1875, Watson ran as a Republican for one of the five at-large seats on the board of estimates, the city's

[5] *New National Era and Citizen*, Sept. 11, 1873, p. 1; *Manual of the Common Council...Detroit 1873* (Detroit, 1873), pp. 21–23; *Detroit Tribune*, July 26, 1869, p. 1, Feb. 22, 1871, p. 4, Apr. 19, 1871, p. 4, May 8, 1873, p. 4, Apr. 30, 1874, p. 1, June 23, 1874, p. 4, June 21, 1875, p. 1; *Detroit Post & Tribune*, Apr. 7, 1880, p. 4, May 18, 1880, p. 4, Oct. 23, 1882, p. 2.

[6] George M. Black to W. R. Bates, June 16, 1890, Charles A. Lincoln to James MacMillan, June 19, 1890, George M. Black to W. R. Bates, March 19, 1892, James MacMillan to George M. Black, June 4, 1894, Walter Y. Clarke to James MacMillan, June 5, 1894, MacMillan Papers, Burton Historical Collection.

upper house, but he lost by eighty-seven votes because 701 votes had been cast for Samuel G. Watson instead of Samuel C. Watson. Since the political parties supplied their own ballots, charges were made that Watson had been "cut" by a rival Republican faction. The following spring, M. I. Miles, the Democrat who had been elected, resigned to permit Watson to occupy his "rightful" place, and thus Watson was the first black to hold an elective office. Democrat John Wilson, a barber, became the first elected black officeholder when, in the fall of 1876, he was elected, in a Democratic sweep, as one of the two Wayne County coroners.[7]

In retrospect, the precedent of black candidates running for office in every election had been set in 1874 when barber Thomas D. Owens appeared as the Democratic nominee for county coroner while Dr. Watson ran on the Republican ticket for the state legislature. Both men lost. In 1875, as mentioned above, Watson sought a seat on the board of estimates, and the following year, while Wilson was elected coroner, Watson again lost for the state legislature and William Lambert unsuccessfully headed the Republican city ticket as the candidate for the remainder of Watson's term on the board of estimates. In 1877 Lambert again lost for the board of estimates, but three years later Obadiah C. Wood rode into office in a Republican sweep. That same November John D. Richards was elected county coroner. Watson finally won an election in 1881, when he gained a seat on the city council.[8]

Two factors in particular aided blacks in securing nominations for office. First, the decade of the 1870s initiated an era of close elections, and both major parties—probably overestimating the number of black voters—competed for the Negro vote. Second, the convention system, in which party caucuses chose delegates to nominating conventions, aided minority representation on political slates. Party conventions, not the electorate directly, selected the standard-bearers, and party leaders and the conventions themselves recognized the wisdom of

[7] William J. Simmons, *Men of Mark, Eminent, Progressive and Rising* (Cleveland, 1887), p. 864; *Detroit Tribune*, Nov. 3, 1875, p. 2, Nov. 6, 1875, p. 1, Mar. 7, 1876, p. 4, Nov. 24, 1876, p. 4.

[8] *Detroit Tribune*, Nov. 12, 1874, p. 4, Mar. 7, 1876, p. 4, Nov. 7, 1876, p. 4, Nov. 18, 1876, p. 4; *Detroit Post & Tribune*, Oct. 29, 1877, p. 4, Nov. 10, 1880, p. 4, Nov. 9, 1881, p. 2.

appealing to as many interest groups as possible by nominating minority group representatives for office. Blacks could thus gain nomination on a "balanced ticket" without first having to submit themselves to the party electorate. The significance of this can be seen in the track record of black candidates in the general election; they lost elections more often than they won, and they generally ran last in their party. In 1876, when John Wilson was elected coroner, he trailed his Democrat running mate in twenty-one of twenty-three election districts in Detroit. That same year, Watson improved his record in running for state legislature; he finished ninth among ten candidates whereas two years previously he had run last. In the Republican sweep of 1880, John D. Richards trailed his running mate, though both were elected coroners, and the following year, when Watson won a city council seat, he received the narrowest winning margin of all the candidates. In 1882 both black coroner candidates running on separate party tickets lost as their running mates were elected. In 1884 Republican Walter Y. Clarke finished last for coroner, and Republican Stephen Long would follow his example in 1886 and 1888. In Detroit, blacks were obviously hurting the ticket since the Republicans were electing their white coroner candidate. In the 1890s matters improved slightly; though the black Republican candidates for the legislature were successful, they consistently finished closer to the bottom than the top of the ticket.[9]

Nonetheless, the Democratic party, in spite of its vociferous opposition to Negro suffrage and its previous record of Negrophobia, welcomed the newly enfranchised electors in the 1870s. A Republican organ found it "strange, yet not an unusual sight, to see Democratic politicians about our city hob-nobbing with colored voters now-a-days." Nearly all of the black leaders, however, were committed to the Republican party, and the Democrats were unable to build a substantial base in the black community. Indeed, the credibility of the

[9] *Detroit Tribune*, Nov. 12, 1874, p. 4, Nov. 4, 1876, p. 4, Nov. 18, 1876, p. 4; *Detroit Post & Tribune*, Nov. 10, 1880, p. 4, Nov. 9, 1881, p. 2, Nov. 18, 1884, p. 5; *Detroit Tribune*, Nov. 4, 1886, p. 4, Nov. 7, 1888, p. 6; *Michigan Manual 1895–1896*, p. 388; *Michigan Manual 1897–1898*, p. 497. Blacks across the river in Windsor, Ontario, had better electoral success. When J. L. Dunn was re-elected an alderman in 1888, he led the reform ticket. *Detroit Tribune*, Jan. 3, 1888, p. 2.

party's new position must have been weak, especially in view of its tacit support of those opposing school integration in Detroit.[10]

In spite of their failure to enlist black support, in spite of their stand on school integration, and in spite of the large reservoir of Negrophobia among its members, the Democrats continued to woo Afro-Americans. When Republican Thomas D. Owens, a barber, lost the janitorship of the city hall in 1872, the Democrats welcomed him into their ranks, and a number of colored Greeleyites followed him into the party. Two years later Owens secured one of the two Democratic nominations for Wayne County coroner, and when he lost, the party rewarded him with an appointment as a deputy sheriff. The Democrats viewed Owens's candidacy for the coroner's post as "an opportunity . . . to test the sincerity of those blatant dema-gogues of the opposition who have always been prating about the good they *intended* to do the colored people, but never commence doing." Owens ran last of the four candidates, but the Democrats could con-sole themselves with the knowledge that Dr. Samuel C. Watson on the Republican ticket had run last of the ten candidates seeking election to the state legislature. The Democrats seemed to have benefitted little from Owens's candidacy, and the following year they were unable to capitalize on a Republican split. In 1875, a number of Republicans, black and white, supported the Democratic mayoralty candidate when he declared himself, under the banner of law and order, for the clos-ing of business on Sunday. But after the election of the Democratic nominee, the Republican insurgents returned to their own party.[11]

The year 1876 represented the high point of the Negro-Democratic rapprochement in nineteenth-century Michigan. The Democrats seemed to have demonstrated their abandonment of Negrophobia when M. I. Miles resigned in favor of Dr. Watson, after Watson had lost because of the printing error. Later that year, John Wilson, a

[10] *Detroit Tribune*, Sept. 3, 1870, p. 3, Oct. 11, 1870, p. 1. George French, delegate to the 1870 Democratic city convention and founder of the unsuccessful Zion Baptist Church, was the most prominent black attracted to the Demo-cratic party.

[11] *Detroit Tribune*, July 29, 1872, p. 4, Aug. 15, 1872, p. 4, Nov. 5, 1874, p. 3, Nov. 13, 1874, p. 1; clipping, *Detroit Free Press* [November, 1874], in James A. Randall Scrapbook, I, 266, Burton Historical Collection, Detroit Public Library; *Detroit Tribune*, Oct. 30, 1875, p. 4, Nov. 1, 1875, p. 1.

barber, was elected a Democratic county coroner. His election came at a time when the Democrats were making a major effort to lure Negroes into the party by working with the Colored Independent Club of Detroit, an organization dominated by the few black Democratic leaders and their nearly four dozen followers. Thomas Owens's name appeared prominently at all meetings, and it is possible that the Democrats thought that the organization of the club and the election of Wilson meant the winning over of the black voter.[12]

The next few years presented the Michigan Democrats with a golden opportunity to enroll Negro voters. At the national level, Negro disaffection with the Republican party was at a high point as a result of the compromise of 1877 and, later, President Chester Arthur's courting of Negrophobic white independents in the South. The ignored black leaders of the South—John Bruce, John R. Lynch, P. B. S. Pinchback, and D. Augustus Straker—accused the Republicans of abandoning the Negro. Straker, then dean of law at Allen University in Columbia, South Carolina, attacked the party in an open letter to the New York *Age*.[13] In Michigan and Detroit, the Democratic party by then publicly supported Negro rights, and it sought to match the Republican party in accepting blacks within its party councils, in nominating blacks to elective office, and in providing them with patronage.

The Democratic party was incapable of breaking the Republican hold on the black vote. Although national Republican policies left many black leaders disaffected, few actually changed their political allegiance. Men like Straker, no matter how bitterly they criticized Republican policies, never turned to the Democrats. More important, black Republicans were capable of discrediting any Negro who left the fold. The *Detroit Free Press* charged that colored men supporting presidential candidate Samuel Tilden in 1876 "are every day made the victims of the most intolerable persecution from the bigoted Republican partisans of their own race." Colored Democrats were

[12] *Detroit Free Press*, Aug. 29, 1876, p. 1, Sept. 24, 1876, p. 1, Sept. 27, 1876, p. 1, Nov. 1, 1876, p. 1.

[13] August Meier, "The Negro and the Democratic Party, 1875–1915," *Phylon*, XVII (Second Quarter, 1956), 175; Vincent P. DeSantis, "Negro Dissatisfaction with Republican Policy in the South, 1882–1884," *Journal of Negro History*, XXXVI (April, 1951), 148, 151–152, 154.

often insulted, and they were made unwelcome at black community meetings. When Dr. Watson defected to the Democrats in the late 1880s, after he had found his own political future blocked by competing Negro Republicans and after he had awakened to the advantages of playing one party against the other, community leaders appealed to Frederick Douglass to counter Watson's prestige. Douglass assured Straker that Watson's appeal on behalf of the Democratic party was treasonous to the interests of the colored race. Watson, who showed "not the slightest evidence of colored blood" and who was criticized for his white ways, was a leader without a following, and he failed to create an exodus from the Republican party.[14]

The Democratic appeal to the blacks was weakened by the party's inability to suppress caste feeling within its ranks. Even the election of Coroner Wilson in 1876 turned into a liability when he charged, soon after being sworn in, that the police department was discriminating against him "on account of his color." Coroners were paid for each body viewed, for each subpoena served, and for each witness sworn, as well as receiving a mileage allowance. The police gave the white coroner all of the available work so that Wilson's office yielded him virtually no income. The Democrats also could not compete with the Republicans in offering blacks patronage. Since the Republicans controlled Lansing as well as Washington for most of the period, the small number of municipal white-collar jobs the Democrats could provide were dwarfed by those available on the state and federal payrolls.[15]

In spite of the Republican hold on black political allegiance, other parties continued, with a mistaken optimism, to woo the black electorate. In the last quarter of the nineteenth century black candidates ran on Democratic, Prohibition, Labor, and Greenback slates. In particular the parties ran black men for office whenever the Republicans appeared to be vulnerable, as in 1898, when the Democrats nominated attorney William C. Swain for circuit court commissioner two

[14] *Detroit Free Press*, Oct. 24, 1876, p. 1; *Detroit Tribune*, Aug. 16, 1876, p. 4, Aug. 19, 1876, p. 4; Frederick Douglass to D. A. Straker, Aug. 2, 1888, Frederick Douglass Papers, Reel 1, microfilm, Library of Congress, Washington, D.C.; *Detroit Evening Journal*, Dec. 25, 1885, p. 1.

[15] *Detroit Tribune*, Mar. 5, 1877, p. 4; Silas Farmer, *The History of Detroit and Michigan* (Detroit, 1884), p. 58.

years after Straker had been denied the Republican nomination for a third term. The false hope of success in capturing the black vote usually rested on the defection from the Republicans of a prominent black leader. In 1878 a Greenback party leader deluded himself into believing that his party would capture 80 percent of Michigan's black vote after the Greenbackers had enlisted the support of William A. Sweeney, a newspaper editor and occasional Detroiter. Unfortunately for the Greenbackers, Sweeney was an itinerant Republican insurgent; he had supported the Liberal Republicans in 1872 and the Greenbackers in 1878, and he would support a nonpartisan movement in Philadelphia in 1882 and an anti-machine, anti-Republican campaign in Indiana in 1897. Similarly in 1886, a Detroit Knights of Labor official predicted that "the colored vote will be cast this year for the entire labor ticket."[16]

The Republicans and Detroit blacks remained united, and in the 1880s many of the older black leaders began to transfer their political positions to younger men, and sons and sons-in-law replaced their fathers at political conventions and in public office. The change in generations, however, did not produce a significant difference in political outlook as the generational difference in life style was small, and the level of group consciousness was high. The passing of position directly from father to son reflected, to a great degree, the importance of the family in the life of the upper class. Strong blood ties as well as the small size of the elite group—no more than forty families at any time during the nineteenth century—necessitated the involvement of even young children in the activities of the class and helped make the family, rather than the individual, the unit of elite life. The result was that the children of the upper class began to assume their role among the elite long before adolescence; by the time they were in their twenties they had long since served a social and political apprenticeship and were ready to assume a position at the top of the community.[17]

[16] *Detroit Evening News*, Oct. 23, 1898, p. 1; A. M. McNeil to Charles Franklin Bates, November 2, 1878, Bates Papers, Michigan Historical Collections, University of Michigan; Frank Lincoln Mather (ed.), *Who's Who of the Colored Race 1915* (Chicago, 1915), p. 257; *Detroit Tribune*, Oct. 27, 1886, p. 5.

[17] The Detroit *Plaindealer* rarely noted the participation of children in the activities of the upper class, but when the *News-Tribune* examined the life of

Robert A. Pelham, Sr., head of a leading black elite family, was deeply involved in politics and he passed this interest on to his off-spring. A brick mason in Petersburg, Virginia, Pelham left the South in 1859, bringing his family first to Columbus, Ohio, then to Philadelphia, and finally, around 1862, to Detroit, where he became a plasterer, mason, and independent contractor. Along with his eldest son, Joseph, who became a school superintendent in Hannibal, Missouri, Pelham became active in the black community, serving as a committeeman and officer of many organizations, including a trusteeship at Bethel AME. The senior Pelham frequently held elective office in black political organizations, and in 1872 he served as a delegate to a Republican congressional convention. A year later he represented Detroit at the state Republican convention and he remained a staunch party man until his death, often serving as a delegate at nominating conventions and occasionally as a member of a ward committee. Pelham belonged to the mostly white Michigan Club, and the family was among the few blacks listed in the New Year's Day calling lists that appeared in the daily newspapers. His oldest children graduated from high school and his youngest ones attended college. It is likely that he used his political influence to obtain prized positions on the Republican *Detroit Post* for his sons Robert, Jr., and Benjamin.[18]

Robert A. Pelham, Sr., taught his sons, and anyone else who would listen, that the Afro-American must participate in politics and must enter the primaries, the caucuses, and the campaigns as well as the election booth. His sons took these views to heart and, as soon as they reached voting age, joined the Republican party and remained Republicans throughout their lives. Robert A. Pelham, Jr., assumed the political leadership of the family in 1882 when he was twenty-three years old. In that year he served at his first Republican nominating meeting, and it is probable that the senior Pelham withdrew in favor of his son. Although he still remained active in politics, the elder

the "colored '40'," it was a pattern that was conspicuous. *Detroit News-Tribune*, Apr. 27, 1902, p. 7.

[18] *Detroit Tribune*, Jan. 29, 1870, p. 1, Jan. 9, 1871, p. 2, July 26, 1872, p. 1, Aug. 8, 1872, p. 4, Feb. 22, 1873, p. 4, Sept. 24, 1874, p. 4; *Detroit Post & Tribune*, June 23, 1880, p. 4, Oct. 29, 1880, p. 4.

Pelham never served at another convention once his son became an active politician.[19]

Robert A. Pelham, Jr., succeeded to political prominence after the death of John D. Richards in 1882, and for much of the remainder of the century he was the leading black politician in Detroit. His younger brother Benjamin remembered him as "the spark-plug of the party." A strikingly handsome man, Pelham was a sought-after bachelor until he married pianist Gabrielle Lewis in 1893. Like all of the Pelhams, he had light skin color and deep-set eyes with dark eyebrows. As a young man he had a mustache, possibly to deemphasize his political precociousness, and in later years, as his mustache whitened and his closely cropped hair grayed at the temples, he looked quite distinguished. Born in Virginia in 1859, shortly before his family migrated northward, Pelham had attended the Detroit public schools —at first a segregated one—and he began to work for the *Detroit Post* while still in grade school. After graduation from high school in 1877, he joined the newspaper on a full-time basis, and from 1884 to 1891 he and his brother Benjamin distributed the *Post* and its successors as independent contractors. From 1883 to 1891, Robert Pelham was also the major force behind the *Plaindealer*, and he left the Afro-American weekly only when a federal appointment took him out of Detroit.[20]

Robert Pelham, Jr., used his family ties, his involvement in local politics, and his editorship of the *Plaindealer* to achieve prominence in Afro-American affairs—local, state and national. Following his father's path, he played a leading role in organizing and running the political societies of black Detroit. He attended state colored conventions, and in 1884 he represented Detroit at the National Colored Men's Convention in Pittsburgh. In 1888 he served as temporary

[19] *Detroit Post & Tribune*, Sept. 5, 1882, p. 2, Sept. 26, 1882, p. 2, Feb. 18, 1881, p. 4, Sept. 14, 1882, p. 2.

[20] Benjamin Pelham quoted in Aris A. Mallas, Jr., Rea McCain, and Margaret K. Hedden, *Forty Years in Politics: The Story of Benjamin Pelham* (Detroit, 1957), p. 11; Frances H. Warren (comp.), *Michigan Manual of Freedmen's Progress* (Detroit, 1915), p. 91 (hereafter cited as *Freedmen's Progress*). Pelham's first venture into publishing, with his younger brother Benjamin, had been the *Venture* (1879), a short-lived amateur newspaper.

chairman of the Michigan colored convention. He was among the race leaders responsible for the creation of the first long-lived national Negro protest organization, the Afro-American League, in 1889, and he made the *Plaindealer* its Michigan organ. During the election campaigns of the 1880s he could be found organizing black political clubs to further both the interests of the black community and those of the Republican party.[21]

At the same time that Robert Pelham, Jr., was active in black community politics he also served as an important figure in the Republican organization. A founder of the political-social Michigan Club in 1884, Pelham also belonged to the overwhelmingly white Young Men's League and represented it at the National League of Republican Clubs. As the managing editor of the *Plaindealer*, Pelham achieved national recognition, and in 1888 he attended the Republican convention in Chicago with D. Augustus Straker and Walter Stowers. Straker ran the Michigan headquarters at the Palmer House, while Pelham, Stowers, and W. Q. Atwood, a black convention delegate from Michigan, lobbied among black delegates for the nomination of Michigan favorite-son candidate, Gen. Russell A. Alger. In 1896 Pelham was proposed as a delegate to the Republican National Convention, but he declined in favor of Henry Haigh, a white leader in the Michigan Club and president of the Detroit McKinley Club. Instead, Pelham and his older brother Joseph served as the only two Afro-American sergeants-at-arms at the 1896 convention. Later that year Pelham served in the Afro-American bureau of the Republican National Committee.[22]

Like many other upper-class blacks, Robert Pelham, Jr., was well

[21] *Detroit Post & Tribune*, Mar. 26, 1884, p. 4, Apr. 30, 1884, p. 4; *Detroit Tribune*, Apr. 25, 1888, p. 3; *Plaindealer*, Oct. 18, 1889, Dec. 27, 1889; *Detroit Post*, Oct. 14, 1884, p. 5. Pelham became sufficiently prominent so that his portrait and biography appeared in Simmons, *Men of Mark*, pp. 1022–1026, and in I. Garland Penn, *The Afro-American Press and Its Editors* (Springfield, Mass., 1891), pp. 159, 162–163.

[22] *Detroit Sunday News-Tribune*, Apr. 10, 1898, p. 22; *Proceedings Third Annual Meeting of the Michigan Club...1888* (Detroit, 1889), p. 78; *Detroit Tribune*, Jan. 20, 1888, p. 4; Henry A. Haigh, *The Michigan Club 1884: The Alger Movement 1888* (n.p., n.d.), pp. 36–37; *Detroit Tribune*, June 13, 1888, p. 2; Indianapolis *Freeman*, Apr. 17, 1897. Pelham had been secretary of the McKinley Club in Detroit.

rewarded for his service to the party. In 1884 he was appointed a clerk in the office of the internal revenue collector of Detroit. Three years later he received a statehouse appointment as deputy oil inspector for Detroit; he served in this capacity until 1891, when he received his first federal position as special agent of the United States Land Office. Like most Republican appointees, Pelham was removed in 1893 following the inauguration of Grover Cleveland as president, and he was then designated an inspector of the Detroit Water Department. With the return of the Republicans to the White House in 1897, Pelham was widely promoted for high government position, and when, in 1898, he was named a special agent of the general land office by the secretary of the interior, the *Freeman* said that it "is without doubt one of the most meritous appointments made by the administration." In 1900 Pelham left Detroit to assume a clerkship in the census bureau in Washington, D.C.[23]

In the 1890s David Augustus Straker replaced Robert Pelham, Jr., as the political leader of black Detroit. Prior to settling in Detroit, Straker had earned a national reputation as an author, attorney, and politician, and the Detroit newspapers welcomed his arrival in August 1887. The *Detroit Tribune* greeted Straker with a feature story which referred to the South Carolina lawyer as perhaps "the most prominent colored man in the south." Though driven from the South in part by

[23] *Detroit Post & Tribune*, Aug. 15, 1884, p. 5; *Freedmen's Progress*, p. 91; *Freeman*, Apr. 17, 1897; June 11, 1898. Pelham's later career is as interesting as were his years in Detroit. After 1900 he still maintained his legal residency in Detroit but he never returned there. While working for the census bureau he received, in 1904, an LL.B. from Howard University. In 1905 he invented the first tabulating machines used in the census of manufactures, and in 1913 he invented a tallying machine used in the population division. He compiled the "morality" and "home ownership" sections of the monumental demographic volume of the census bureau, *Negro Population in the United States 1790–1915*, and he also contributed the demographic chapter in *Michigan Manual of Freedmen's Progress*. When Pelham retired in 1937, at age seventy-eight, he returned to newspaper work, heading a Negro news service and publishing and editing the *Washington Tribune*. He died in Washington in 1943.

Mrs. Pelham had earned a Bachelor of Music degree from Adrian College, and in the 1890s she served on the executive committee of the Michigan State Music Teacher's Association and belonged to the Detroit Twentieth Century Club. In Washington she served as director of music at Howard University (1905–1906) and later operated a school of music.

its Negrophobic atmosphere, Straker arrived in Detroit with letters of commendation and introduction from the chief and associate justices of the South Carolina Supreme Court, from the governor and lieutenant governor of the state, and from Senator Wade Hampton.[24]

Straker had been born in Bridgetown, Barbados, in 1842, and was sometimes referred to as the "black Irish lawyer" because of his British accent. After he had exhausted the public education available to him, Straker apprenticed as a tailor, but he disliked the work and instead prepared under private tutors to teach school. At age seventeen he was appointed principal of St. Mary's School, Bridgetown, and he later taught at another school there. In 1867, Bishop S. S. Smith of the Protestant Episcopal Church (PEC) recruited Straker and two other West Indians to teach freedmen in the United States. For Straker it meant forgoing an opportunity to study at Oxford University, but, as he reminisced seventeen years later, the United States offered nearly equal advantages and "I owed a duty to my race."[25]

From 1868 to 1870 Straker taught in a Louisville, Kentucky, school jointly sponsored by the PEC and the freedmen's bureau. At the same time he studied to become an Episcopalian clergyman, but refused to take the "orders" when he was not assured that "the proscription shown his race as a layman . . . [would not] be his lot as a clergyman." Instead he returned to his first love, the law, and entered the law department of Howard University, graduating with honors in June 1871. After graduation he held for a brief time an appointment in the normal and preparatory department of Howard, and in 1905 the university awarded him an honorary LL.D.[26]

While at Howard, Straker had served as a stenographer to Gen. O. O. Howard, head of the Freedmen's Bureau, and in late 1871 he began a four-year tenure as a clerk in the treasury department. Dur-

[24] *Detroit Tribune*, Aug. 6, 1887, p. 3. Biographical data on Straker in this and the following paragraphs have been drawn from *Detroit Free Press*, Aug. 31, 1885, p. 4; *Detroit Tribune*, Nov. 3, 1894, p. 5; and Simmons, *Men of Mark*, pp. 473–482.

[25] *Detroit Free Press*, Aug. 31, 1885, p. 4.

[26] Simmons, *Men of Mark*, p. 246; Walter Dyson, *Howard University: The Capstone of Negro Education* (Washington, 1941), p. 234. Straker also received an honorary degree from Selma University.

ing this time he worked in politics and frequently contributed essays to Frederick Douglass's *New National Era*. In 1875 he moved to Charleston, South Carolina, as inspector of customs at the port. Shortly afterward he resigned his post to practice law in Orangeburg, nearly seventy miles northwest of Charleston. In 1876 he was elected to the state general assembly, but the house ejected Straker from his seat on the grounds that "he was not a citizen," although Straker had offered his naturalization papers in evidence. He was reelected in 1878 and 1880, but again denied his seat. In the interim he formed a law partnership with R. B. Elliot, former speaker of the assembly and former attorney general of South Carolina, and T. McCants Stewart, later a prominent black Democrat in Brooklyn, New York, where he would serve on the city's board of education.[27]

In 1880 Straker gained appointment as a special inspector of customs and as a special agent of the treasury department. He served only two years, however, for in 1882 Straker became dean and professor of law of the newly organized law department of Allen University, an AME-supported school in Columbia, South Carolina. In 1884, while at Allen, he ran unsuccessfully for lieutenant governor. Although he was widely praised as an attorney and dean, he found both his income and civil rights declining, and in 1887 he moved to Detroit.[28]

Once Straker chose to leave the South it was understandable that he would select Detroit as his home. In 1871 he had married Annie Carey, the niece of John D. Richards, and he had been well received in his frequent visits to Detroit. He knew many of the city's prominent attorneys; in 1885 he addressed the Detroit Bar Association and returned under the auspices of some Detroit judges to give a well publicized lecture at Merrill Hall on "The New South." Finally, Detroit's reputation for fair treatment of black men attracted Straker. "I was

[27] *New National Era*, June 30, 1870, p. 1, Aug. 25, 1870, p. 1, Mar. 16, 1871, p. 3, Mar. 28, 1872, p. 1; Lawrence C. Bryant (ed.), *Negro Lawmakers in the South Carolina Legislature 1868–1902* (Orangeburg, S.C., 1967), p. 95.

[28] The first two graduating classes of the law department showed such high standards in examination before the state supreme court that Straker received a special commendation. George Brown Tindall, *South Carolina Negroes 1877–1900* (Columbia, S.C., 1952), p. 145.

impressed by the broad and liberal views entertained here toward the colored people," he told a reporter in 1887.[29]

Within a few months of his arrival in Detroit, Straker had become prominent in the city's politics. He joined the Michigan Club, and in November 1887 Straker attended a conference of Michigan Republican leaders. The following year Straker presided over the Michigan headquarters at the Republican National Convention in Chicago. In the remaining two decades of his life he remained an indefatigable Republican and race leader, pressuring whites to abandon caste feelings and urging blacks to organize and improve themselves. In Detroit he led the fight for municipal employment of blacks and against discrimination in unions, and served as the attorney in all local major civil rights cases. The Detroit Industrial and Financial Cooperative Association was organized in Straker's office in 1890, and he served as chairman of the 1890 convention of the Afro-American League as well as the organization's attorney. In 1895 he helped organize the National Federation of Colored Men, and served as its president. In representing black interests he was outspoken and direct; in 1892 he told an Afro-American League audience: "We indict the white race of American citizens for injustice towards us not only for the period of more than two hundred and fifty years, during which time we physically endured an inhuman bondage . . . but we complain that although we are no longer slaves, but freeman . . . we are oppressed and denied our rights."[30]

Straker built his reputation and career not only through politics but also by writing. After graduation from Howard he continued as a newspaper essayist, regularly contributing letters and essays to black

[29] *New National Era and Citizen*, Sept. 11, 1873, p. 1; *Detroit Free Press*, Sept. 1, 1885, p. 8; *Detroit Tribune*, Aug. 6, 1887, p. 3.

[30] *Detroit Tribune*, Nov. 1, 1887, p. 2, Nov. 26, 1887, p. 4, July 22, 1895, p. 5; *Plaindealer*, May 16, 1890, July 25, 1890, June 3, 1892; *Freeman*, Dec. 28, 1895. In 1915 Azalia Hackley, who had been raised in Detroit, listed Straker among the twenty-five greatest Negroes she had known. M. Marguerite Davenport, *Azalia: The Life of Madame E. Hackley* (Boston, 1947), p. 21. Straker, however, stood partly in the white community as well. He lived in a white neighborhood and belonged to a number of nearly all-white organizations. Besides belonging to the Michigan Club, he was a director of the Newsboys' Association and a member of the reform Detroit Civic Federation. *Plaindealer*, Feb. 26, 1892; *Detroit Tribune*, Jan. 30, 1895, p. 5.

weeklies. Later he frequently wrote for the *AME Church Review*, the *Freeman*, and the *Colored American Magazine*. After 1901 he would publish and edit his own weekly, the *Detroit Advocate*. Most important, he authored six books—a biography of Toussaint L'Ouverture, a memoir of a pilgrimage to the West Indies, two tracts on economic and political conditions in the South, and two legal treatises —and numerous pamphlets.[31]

Themes of race pride and militancy permeated nearly all of Straker's writings. In his biography of Toussaint L'Ouverture, Straker sought only to serve "the just pride of the negro race." Let the Negro "learn to love and praise the greatest man in the negro race that ever lived," he urged. "In song and in prose let us keep fresh his deeds of courage and his bravery, so that by reading the same the negro's soul may be inspired, and that he may emulate his virtues."[32]

In both prose and politics, Straker trod a path that wandered between the activism of W. E. B. DuBois and the accommodation of Booker T. Washington. His own experiences in the South, as well as his studies of that section, led him to caution against blacks' confronting southern segregationists, while his experiences in the North as a member of the elite led him to feel secure enough to militate against discrimination in municipal employment and against civil rights violations. Until his death (in 1908) he advocated two separate paths to achieve black equality; in a 1900 speech before the Woman's State Federation of Colored Clubs, for example, he advocated "Ladies, Agitate! Agitate!! Agitate!!!" yet at the same time advised that as long as blacks are disfranchised, "Let the colored voters in the South let State politics alone."[33]

[31] D. Augustus Straker, *Reflections on the Life and Times of Toussaint L'Ouverture, the Negro Haytien* . . . (Columbia, S.C., 1886); idem, *A Trip to the Windward Islands, or Then and Now* (Detroit, 1896); idem, *The New South Investigated* (Detroit, 1888); idem, *Negro Suffrage in the South* (Detroit, 1906); idem, *Circuit Court and Commissioner's Guide: Law and Practice, State of Michigan* (Detroit, 1897); idem, *Compendium of Practice* (Detroit, 1899).

[32] Straker, *Toussaint L'Ouverture*, preface.

[33] Straker, "Manhood and Womanhood Development," *Colored American Magazine*, II (1901), 313. August Meier has noted Straker's moderate path, and indicated that "Washington's critics considered Straker one of their number." His criticism of Washington, however, was firm but tempered, as in 1901 when he wrote: "God has raised us up an Educator than whom along

Straker's reward for his energetic political and race activities was nomination and election to the highest elective office held by a Detroit black man before the Second World War. Although he was frustrated in his desire to gain a major federal appointment as either a judge or a consul, Straker was twice elected a Wayne County circuit court commissioner (1892, 1894), the equivalent of a judge. When in 1908 he died of pneumonia after a short illness, both black and white Detroiters mourned him, and the Detroit Bar Association held a memorial meeting to honor the late black Irish lawyer.[34]

Benjamin Pelham, like his older brother Robert, spent nearly all of his life on the government payroll. A co-editor of the *Plaindealer* and a partner in Pelham Brothers, Benjamin followed his father and brothers into politics. Like his older brother, he held his first patronage job as a member of the staff of the Detroit Internal Revenue Collector, James H. Stone. Turned out of office by the Democratic administration in the early 1890s, Pelham entered the county treasurer's office as a junior clerk, and he remained on the Wayne County payroll for nearly fifty years.[35]

The sons-in-law of Robert Pelham, Sr., benefitted as much from politics as did Robert and Benjamin Pelham. George A. Barrier of Lockport, New York, married the oldest Pelham daughter, Delia, and the newlyweds settled in Detroit, where Barrier opened a barber shop. Shortly afterward Barrier followed his in-laws into politics, and by the late 1880s he was being elected annually to the Third

the lines of practical achievement no greater has appeared than Mr. Booker T. Washington; but we need a leader and a defender of our civil rights...." Meier, *Negro Thought in America 1880–1915* (Ann Arbor, 1963), p. 242; *Detroit Advocate*, Mar. 23, 1901, p. 2.

[34] *Detroit Journal*, Feb. 14, 1908, p. 3; *Detroit Free Press*, Feb. 15, 1908, p. 5. In 1891 when Straker sought appointment to the federal bench, the Detroit Bar Association had endorsed him, and both Republicans and Democrats supported his candidacy. *Plaindealer*, Apr. 10, 1891, Sept. 11, 1891, Sept. 25, 1891.

[35] Mallas et al., *Benjamin Pelham*, pp. 35, 38, 40. Like his brother Robert, Benjamin Pelham was among the few nineteenth-century politicians who adapted to the bureaucratization of government. Although a believer in the spoils system he nevertheless became the complete bureaucrat, and after about a decade of county service he severed nearly all of his political ties. Among the positions he held were those of county accountant, clerk to the board of supervisors, and clerk to the board of auditors. By the time he retired he was recognized as performing the functions of a county manager.

Ward Republican Committee. At the same time Barrier abandoned barbering for a patronage position with the board of public works. He remained on the public payroll the rest of his life, serving as a sidewalk inspector and head of the sidewalk department for the board and as permit clerk for its successor organization, the department of public works. Emma, the youngest Pelham daughter, married William W. Ferguson, the son and brother of Detroit physicians. Proprietor of the Ferguson Printing Company and later an attorney and realtor, Ferguson was an active Republican and in 1892 he was elected the first black legislator in Michigan's history. He held many political offices in Detroit, and he used his political and social connections as a base for his real-estate agency.[36]

Walter H. Stowers and William H. Anderson served with the Pelham brothers on the staff of the *Plaindealer*. Like the Pelhams, Stowers spent most of his working life in political positions. Born in Kentucky in 1859 and brought to Detroit soon after, Stowers later graduated from the Detroit College of Law, co-founded the *Plaindealer*, and followed the lead of the Pelhams into politics. He served in the late 1880s as a Wayne County deputy sheriff and simultaneously held the office of treasurer of the Young Men's Republican League. He served a four-year tenure as a clerk in the assessor's office in the 1890s and then was appointed deputy county clerk, serving until 1905. During World War I, after a long absence from politics, he would serve on a local draft board. In 1922 he would be elected a Wayne County supervisor, and would serve until his death in 1932.[37]

William H. Anderson, a co-editor with Stowers and co-author with him of the novel *Appointed*, joined his fellow editors in politics, although the lure of public office never tempted him away from his position as bookkeeper with Newcomb-Endicott, a large Detroit department store. His years with the *Plaindealer*, his role in the Republican party, his leadership in black organizations, and his ties with the Pelhams all added to his political influence, and no doubt he aided

[36] *Detroit Tribune*, Oct. 30, 1886, p. 4, Nov. 3, 1887, p. 4; *Plaindealer*, Apr. 7, 1893, Nov. 3, 1894; Mallas et al., *Benjamin Pelham*, p. 85; *Freeman*, May 9, 1896. Ferguson's father, Dr. Joseph Ferguson, also held a patronage position in Detroit, serving four terms as a city physician.

[37] *Detroit News*, Aug. 28, 1932, p. 12; *Detroit Tribune*, Dec. 31, 1886, p. 4, Feb. 4, 1887, p. 4.

his brother John in acquiring patronage positions. John B. Anderson had a long career as a customs officer and also served, at one time or another, as one of the few black streetcar conductors, a census enumerator, clerk and assistant bookkeeper of the school board, and a clerk in the city auditor's office. Similarly, Walter H. Stowers's brother Joseph was the first Afro-American appointed to the metropolitan police force.[38]

The foundation of black achievements in politics rested on the ability of the black community to remain united and thus exploit the parties' competition for ethnic and interest-group support, the social ties of the black elite with the city's upper-class politicos, and the Republican party's traditional commitment to Negroes. Until the 1880s, Michigan Republican leaders had been drawn from the ranks of former abolitionists or Civil War officers, and the dominant party leaders in the late nineteenth century—Zachariah Chandler and James MacMillan—worked closely with black politicians. A founder of the Republican party and Michigan senator for nineteen years, Chandler had been an avid abolitionist and, later, a Radical Republican. In 1879 MacMillan, who served as senator from Michigan from 1889 until his death in 1903, replaced Chandler as chairman of the Republican State Central Committee. Though of a younger generation, MacMillan reaffirmed the party's commitment to Negroes. Not only did he work closely with black leaders in Detroit, some of whom were the sons of Chandler's black allies, but he also, in part, built his Republican alliance on the integrated Michigan Department of the Grand Army of the Republic, the Union soldiers' veteran organization. Not until the 1890s, when Hazen S. Pingree and the Republican progressives entered state politics, would the Republican party break its ties with the old abolitionist tradition and bury its appeal as the party that saved the Union and freed the slaves.[39]

[38] *Detroit Sunday News-Tribune*, Nov. 7, 1897, p. 24; Fred Hart Williams and Hoyt Fuller, "Anderson Brothers," in "Detroit Heritage," typewritten, Fred Hart Williams Papers, Burton Historical Collection, Detroit Public Library; *Plaindealer*, June 27, 1890, Apr. 24, 1891, July 11, 1890; *Freedmen's Progress*, p. 86.

[39] For information and background on Michigan governors and senators see Henry M. Utley and Byron M. Cutcheon, *Michigan as a Province, Territory, and State* ... (4 vols.; New York, 1906), V, passim; for Chandler see Sister Mary Karl George, *Zachariah Chandler, A Political Biography* (East Lansing, 1969);

Black politicos recognized the significance of unity in maintaining their position within the Republican party, and black leaders and newspapers called upon Afro-Americans to organize and unite. In the 1870s they rallied the community into a cohesive group by recounting the confederate and Democratic outrages against black men. In the 1880s the civil rights issue and political patronage helped weld the diverse factions within black Detroit. The outcome of black unity and political organization and pressure could easily be measured in the 1870s and 1880s: the large number of patronage appointments and party nominations attested to their success.[40]

An even more striking achievement of black organization was the selection of two black delegates-at-large from Michigan to the Republican National Conventions of the 1880s. In 1884, a month before the Republican state convention, a colored men's convention, the first Afro-American convention in the state since the Civil War period, convened in Battle Creek. The assembly condemned the striking down of the federal civil rights act, criticized the attitude of the Bourbon Democracy in the South, and, most important, petitioned the state Republican party to send a black delegate to Chicago, the site of the national convention. As a result the Republicans selected Dr. S. C. Watson as a delegate-at-large to Chicago. Four years later the scenario was repeated. In the month before the state Republican convention, an Afro-American convention was convened at Jackson. With Robert A. Pelham, Jr., presiding, the assembly recommended that the Republicans elect the black Saginaw lumber merchant, W. Q. Atwood, as a delegate to the Chicago convention. A month later, at the Republican convention, Atwood was selected as a delegate-at-large.[41]

---

for MacMillan see David J. Rothman, *Politics and Power: The United States Senate 1869–1901* (New York, 1967), passim, and Stephen Sarasohn and Vera H. Sarasohn, *Political Party Patterns in Michigan* (Detroit, 1957), p. 10.

[40] *Plaindealer*, Sept. 27, 1889, Oct. 18, 1889; *Detroit Tribune*, Aug. 16, 1876, p. 4, Aug. 19, 1876, p. 4, Oct. 3, 1876, p. 4, Oct. 5, 1876, p. 1; *Detroit Post & Tribune*, Oct. 28, 1880, p. 4.

[41] *Detroit Post & Tribune*, Mar. 24, 1884, p. 2, Mar. 26, 1884, p. 4, Apr. 25, 1884, p. 4; *Detroit Tribune*, Apr. 25, 1888, p. 3, May 9, 1888, p. 1. An opponent of Atwood—H. J. Lewis of East Saginaw—charged that the 1888 Afro-American convention had only one purpose: to put forward W. Q. Atwood as a delegate to the National Republican Convention. *Detroit Tribune*, Apr. 30, 1888, p. 3.

If organization and unity enabled blacks to capitalize on the Republican commitment to the black community, then dissent and conflict undermined the influence of the Detroit black community. Negro leaders were aware of this and they tried to build permanent political institutions, but without success. In 1874 a plan was put forth to turn the Detroit Political Union, a black organization, into a permanent and representative body by having it receive elected delegates from each ward. Conflict among factions was too great, however, and the club appears not to have lasted beyond the elections. Five years later, at a memorial meeting for William Lloyd Garrison at Bethel AME with Robert A. Pelham, Sr., presiding, Dr. S. C. Watson proposed the election, by wards, of a standing committee to call public meetings and act on behalf of the community. It was the first attempt to create a nonpolitical communitywide representative association since the 1840s, but it died at the proposal stage. Increasingly in the 1880s dissident groups hurt black candidates. In 1882 when Albert Hill was nominated for the state legislature, his black opposition outpetitioned his supporters two to one. The issue became extremely controversial, and Walter Stowers stated that Hill's opponents "conscientiously believe him a man unfit to represent them." The *Detroit Post & Tribune* editorially deplored the split among the colored Republicans and advised black men not to give ammunition to the Democrats and to cast their votes for the Republicans. Hill lost the election, and two years later Dr. Watson was denied an appointment as city assessor, because of black opposition.[42]

The 1890s was the decade of the greatest black electoral successes before World War I. It was a period dominated by the reform administrations of Republican Hazen S. Pingree, mayor of Detroit from 1889 to 1897 and governor of Michigan from 1897 to 1901. In 1889, in the first of his four successful mayoralty campaigns, Pingree achieved his victory by attacking the corrupt political "ring" that had dominated municipal government and by breaking the traditional Democratic hold on some of the city's German- and Polish-Americans. Black leaders and the *Plaindealer* supported the entire

[42] *Detroit Tribune*, Apr. 30, 1874, p. 1; *Detroit Post & Tribune*, June 3, 1879, p. 4, Oct. 16, 1882, p. 2, Oct. 18, 1882, p. 2, Oct. 19, 1882, p. 2, Nov. 6, 1884, p. 10, Dec. 23, 1884, p. 5, Dec. 24, 1884, p. 4, Jan. 24, 1885, p. 5.

Republican ticket as they had in the past. Most of the elite blacks identified with the reformers in Detroit, and they allied themselves with the "best people" in attacking the corruption of municipal government and in calling for such civic improvements as cheaper rapid transportation. In other cities the election of reform business-men such as Pingree (a shoe manufacturer) would lead to the tempo-rary elimination of ethnic influences at city hall, as bureaucracies began to replace patronage appointments and electoral changes de-stroyed the convention system. In Detroit, Pingree appealed to the German-Americans and the largely neglected Polish-Americans and he promised to consider their interests if he was elected. As the prin-cipal minority within the Republican party, blacks were outraged, fearing that their influence would diminish; the *Plaindealer* charged that appeals to ethnic groups were "un-American and a great evil." Within weeks of Pingree's inauguration the Afro-Americans' worst fears seemed to have been realized.[43]

In his first administration Mayor Pingree slighted black leaders while he rewarded the Polish- and German-Americans. At the be-ginning of Pingree's term, the *Plaindealer* decried "the neglect and apathy on the part of the Republican party" toward blacks. Attorney Robert C. Barnes, then of Straker and Barnes, charged that blacks were "used for the sole purpose of promoting the interests of his white brother." "When it comes to the nominations," Barnes con-tended, "he is pushed aside and told that his duty ends at the polls . . . [while] he sees the German, the Pole, the Irishman and Frenchman nominated and elected as a recognition of their political influence." "No wonder the Negro is dissatisfied with his party," Barnes con-cluded. Negro discontent was pacified when a black policeman was appointed in April 1890, but black resentment was manifested again when the policeman was abruptly dismissed from the police force without cause. In August the *Plaindealer* accused Pingree of recog-nizing "every nationality but the Afro-American," and by Thanksgiv-ing black leaders were indignant that Pingree's only Negro appointee filled the office of chimney sweep. Nearly a year later, in June 1891,

---

[43] Melvin G. Holli, *Reform in Detroit: Hazen S. Pingree and Urban Politics* (New York, 1969), pp. 18–21; *Plaindealer*, Nov. 1, 1889, Nov. 15, 1889, Mar. 14, 1890.

the Afro-American weekly repeated the charges for the last time; as the fall municipal elections drew near, the black community's relationship with the mayor sweetened, and the *Plaindealer* endorsed him for reelection.[44]

Black leaders greeted the second-term mayor with an enthusiasm not seen during his first two years in office, as Pingree now included blacks as a favored ethnic group. In August 1892 the *Plaindealer* announced that more blacks held government clerkships than ever before. A month later the weekly declared that although Afro-Americans should hold more responsible jobs, they were politically well off. In the November 1892 elections, William W. Ferguson received the Republican convention nomination for the legislature, and D. Augustus Straker was designated a circuit court commissioner candidate. Both men won election, thus giving Michigan its first black legislator and judge. Two years later the two men won again. Although Straker was defeated for reelection in 1896 as an independent after he had been denied renomination on the Republican ticket, Pingreeite Joseph H. Dickinson was elected the same year to the first of his two consecutive terms in the state legislature. Dr. James W. Ames succeeded Dickinson in Lansing, gaining election in 1900 for the 1901–1902 term. He was the last Detroit black man elected to political office before the First World War.[45]

There is no doubt that the regular election of black men to public office in Michigan in the 1890s reflected the Republican sweeps of the decade. Other Negroes had been defeated for legislative posts in Democratic years in the 1870s and 1880s, but the pendulum now swung in the opposite direction. When Straker and Ferguson were elected in 1892 the newly chosen state lower house consisted of ninety-nine Republicans and one Democrat, and the state senate had thirty-two Republicans and no Democrats. Moreover, an increasing

44 *Plaindealer*, Mar. 17, 1890; undated address by Robert C. Barnes in "Robert Barnes," in file "Negro," Historical Records Survey of Michigan, Michigan Historical Collections, University of Michigan (hereafter cited as NHRSM); *Plaindealer*, Apr. 18, 1890, July 11, 1890, Aug. 8, 1890, Nov. 21, 1890, June 5, 1891, Oct. 30, 1891.

45 *Plaindealer*, Aug. 26, 1892, Sept. 2, 1892, Nov. 3, 1894, Nov. 8, 1894; *Detroit Tribune*, Oct. 18, 1896, p. 10, Oct. 21, 1896, p. 1; Detroit *State Affairs*, I (Nov. 2, 1900), 10–11.

number of nominations were going to black men. The *Plaindealer* had urged the black community to follow the example of the city's ethnic groups by organizing and by learning "the value of agitation." Goaded by the Afro-American weekly, the state's Negroes organized statewide black civil rights groups which effectively enabled them to exploit the Republican party's ties with the black community. The associations included the Michigan Protective League, the Afro-American League, and the Michigan Equal Rights League. Detroit black leaders also played a significant role in the national Afro-American League movement and were the primary force behind the creation of the National Federation of Colored Men in December 1895. These organizations met regularly and influenced the Republican party to give a greater share of political appointments and nominations to blacks.[46]

Black leaders reciprocated Pingree's responsiveness to their organizational pressure by becoming rabid Pingreeites. Robert Barnes thus became a staunch supporter of Pingree and spoke on his behalf. Paul Laurence Dunbar, the black Ohio poet, penned the multiverse "Vote for Pingree and Vote for Bread" on a trip to Detroit in the 1890s:

> Come comrades, hear the record fair
> That clings about the present mayor—
> The man who gives us gas galore,
> For two-thirds what we paid before;
> Who takes out pavements rough and old
> And makes them worthy to behold.
> What patchers used to get from you,
> You pay to have your streets made new,
> For Pingree's at the city's head,
> We'll vote for him and vote for bread.[47]

[46] *Plaindealer*, Nov. 8, 1894, July 10, 1891, Mar. 14, 1890, May 16, 1890, Mar. 17, 1893; *Freeman*, Dec. 14, 1895, Dec. 28, 1895, Jan. 18, 1896; "Memorial of the National Association of Colored Men," U.S. Congress, Senate, *Documents*, 54 Cong., 1 Sess., No. 61.

[47] Barnes's speeches in "Robert Barnes," NHRSM; Dunbar poem in "R. T. Shewcraft," NHRSM. In 1898 an advertisement by Governor Pingree supporting local convention delegates endorsed three black men plus Representative Joseph Dickinson for the legislature. *Detroit Evening News*, Oct. 19, 1898, p. 7, Oct. 22, 1898, p. 1.

Paradoxically, those blacks who supported Pingree would sow un-intentionally the seeds of their own elimination from elective office. Pingree headed the anti-MacMillan faction, and he and his allies would remake the Republican party, turning the party away from the rhetoric and concerns generated by the Civil War and Reconstruc-tion, focusing instead on reforming and restructuring American society. Pingree buried the banner long carried by the Republican abolitionists and Civil War generals and replaced it with one herald-ing efficiency and promising a better life for the immigrant poor. The result was that Republican sympathy and attention shifted from a traditional concern for black Americans toward a paternalistic in-terest in ethnic groups. Not only did the reform politics of Pingree focus attention away from conditions and problems of black life but also substantive progressive reforms unintentionally made Negroes their major victim. Pingree initiated a "good government" assault to eliminate the positions or reduce the pay of city inspectors, city hall janitors, and municipal clerks—the very jobs that blacks filled on the city payroll. More important, Pingree's administrations marked the rise of the Michigan movement for electoral changes, the success of which would lead to the elimination of black candidates. The 1890s were a period of electoral reform in the United States, and Michigan enacted statutes providing for party primaries for some offices in cities and in Wayne County, for printed government-supplied ballots, and for a fixed primary day. Although delegates to party conventions had to face primaries following 1893, Pingree was still not satisfied. The movement for direct primaries was really an anti-convention crusade; the reformers were convinced that conventions were an effective instrument for the subversion of democracy and for domination by sinister forces. Pingree felt personally aggrieved as well, since he be-lieved that he had twice been denied the Republican nomination for governor because the MacMillan alliance had rigged the caucuses and conventions against him and his supporters. In his first annual message as governor to the state legislature in 1897 Pingree called for the abolition of party conventions, and the call was repeated in 1899 and 1901 as he charged that conventions were boss-dominated and corrupt.[48]

[48] Holli, *Reform in Detroit*, p. 29; Charles E. Merriam and Louise Overacker,

The change from a convention to a primary system served to block Negroes from elective office.[49] The conventions had not been deliberative bodies, and they tended to approve the party committees' choices. With blacks represented at every level, and logrolling and a balanced ticket important means and ends, blacks were ensured representation on the ticket. With the primary system, however, the horse-trading and slate balancing of conventions were eliminated and majority rule prevailed. Voters who might cast their vote for any Republican, even a black one, against a Democrat in the general election were not obligated to support black candidates in the primaries. Although party leaders sometimes endorsed Negro candidates, black men met defeat in the primaries. Comprising less than 2 percent of the total city population, Detroit Negroes had little hope of nominating a black man themselves. The primaries made it possible for caste feelings to predominate in elections in Detroit.

Detroit's first experiment with primaries on a large scale took place in 1902. The legislative slate, with eleven positions to be filled, attracted the most attention from politicians and reformers, and five slates of Republican candidates were endorsed by various Republican factions. Attorney Charles A. Roxborough received the backing of the Russell A. Alger slate and that of the saloonkeepers. Attorney Robert J. Willis was supported by the park board, but neither the Municipal League nor the school board endorsed a black man for the state legislature. The Municipal League, however, did endorse D. A. Straker for justice of the peace in a race in which few endorsements were made. Nonetheless, not a single black man was nominated; the introduction of the primaries in Detroit eliminated the black man from office. It is almost certain that, except for the primaries, Roxborough would have been elected to the legislature. Roxborough served as a deputy oil inspector under Governor Chase S. Osborn, and when Osborn sought to recapture the statehouse in 1914, Rox-

---

Primary Elections (Chicago, 1928), pp. 27, 28, 32; George N. Fuller (ed.), *Messages of the Governors of Michigan*, (4 vols.; Lansing, 1926–1928), IV, 2, 28, 142, 244.

[49] William M. Tuttle, Jr., and August Meier have suggested that this might have been one intent of the direct primary reforms. See Tuttle's insightful "Racism in the Progressive Era: An Essay Review," *Wisconsin Magazine of History*, LIII (Spring, 1970), 228.

borough ran the Osborn Colored Republican Club in Detroit. After 1902 men like Roxborough could not hope to win office until blacks comprised a voting majority within a legislative district.[50]

Cleavages within the black community further compounded the effects of the electoral changes. In 1896 the Republican county convention ignored the numerous Afro-American aspirants for office and denied Circuit Court Commissioner Straker's bid for a third term largely because the blacks could not build a consensus and place the interests of the black community above individual concerns. The Douglass Frontier League met to reconcile the conflicting groups, but the assembly was tumultuous and the effort to achieve harmony failed. This was not the only time black men, in effect, denied Straker a nomination; a few years later he declined to accept a nomination for office because it had been offered by white leaders but was opposed by black men. Even the 1900 nomination of Dr. James Ames, the last black man elected to office until the 1920s, was achieved only after bitter competition among a number of Negroes.[51]

Blocked from office by electoral reforms and hindered from attaining appointive office by civil-service reforms, black men began to turn to the Democratic party. With black political organizations factionalized and unstable, and with new issues—monopoly and municipal reform—replacing the Republican party's concern for black citizens, a number of Afro-Americans, closely identified with the interests of the new middle class, sought to build a new political base within the old opposition. In the early years of the twentieth century Thomas Cole, son of James H. Cole, would switch from the Republicans to the Democrats. Francis Warren, editor of the *Detroit Informer* after 1904, "braved the criticism of his people" and joined the Democratic party "with the hope of securing more favor from that organization for the colored people and of stifling the opposition of such

[50] Clippings, *Detroit Journal*, October–December 1902, in Russell Alger Scrapbook, "Politics, Detroit Papers, 1902–3," Clements Library, University of Michigan; John T. Owens to M. F. Hadrick, October 11, 1912, Charles A. Roxborough to Chase S. Osborn, October 7, 1914, Roxborough circular, October 8, 1914, in Osborn Papers, Michigan Historical Collections, University of Michigan.

[51] *Detroit Tribune*, Oct. 18, 1896, p. 12, Oct. 27, 1896, p. 5; *Freeman*, Dec. 5, 1896; *Detroit Advocate*, May 4, 1901, p. 2; *State Affairs*, I (Nov. 12, 1900), 10.

men as Tillman, Vardaman, et al." A member of the executive committee of the National Independent Political Club, Warren never
would be able to build an organization among the largely apolitical
new middle class.[52]

Thus the turn of the century was a changing of the old guard in
the black community; the position of the black elite was eroded both
from within and without. As the old elite diminished in numbers
within the black community they were drawn into the caste, and

[52] Clipping in "J. W. Ames" NHRSM. As an entrepreneur, Warren was
second only to George DeBaptiste in black Detroit before World War I. Born
in Sarnia, Ontario, Warren as a youth had wanted to study medicine, and lived
with a Dr. Thomas in Reading, Michigan. He was forced to return home,
however, to help support his family, and he worked in various Michigan and
Canadian towns as a plasterer, then a painter, a waiter, and a pullman porter. In
the 1880s he opened a barbershop in northern Michigan and his success enabled
him, in 1894, to open a laundry and a restaurant on Mackinac Island, and he
expanded later to St. Ignace. In the late 1890s he became a well-known advocate of Henry George's single-tax, and contributed essays on social and
economic questions to midwestern black weeklies. In 1899, at age thirty-five,
he sold his businesses and came to Detroit to enter the Detroit College of Law.
After graduation, and admission to the bar in 1903, he served nearly two years
as a clerk in the Wayne County treasurer's office, and then bought and ran the
Detroit Informer. In the meantime he had become interested in the colonization
movement of Bishop Henry Turner, and Warren became a leading advocate of emigration to Liberia. He saw the Liberian experiment as an opportunity not only to provide a haven for southern blacks but also as a chance
to bring the light of civilization to Africa, and to institute an economy based on
George's single-tax ideas. Warren served as president of the Liberian Development Association, and he sought to exploit Liberia "whether Liberia wants us or
not." He himself chose not to emigrate, and he remained an important black
businessman and lawyer in Detroit. While editor of the *Informer* he was president of the Michigan Co-Operative League, and after selling the newspaper in
1912 to devote more time to his law practice, he served as secretary of the Wolst-
Rees Silver Mining Company, as president of the Michigan Life and Accident
Association, and as attorney for the Detroit branch of the National Association
for the Advancement of Colored People. In 1914 Democratic Governor Wood-
bridge N. Ferris appointed Warren to the Freedmen's Progress Commission, a
committee charged with commemorating the 1915 Lincoln Jubilee, and Warren
became editor of the *Michigan Manual of Freedmen's Progress. Freedmen's
Progress*, pp. 6, 33; *Who's Who of the Colored Race 1915*, pp. 276–277; Edwin
S. Redkey, *Black Exodus* (New Haven, 1969), pp. 279–281; Walter F. Walker,
"News About Liberia and Africa Generally," *Alexander's Magazine*, V (Nov.
15, 1907), 17; Francis H. Warren, "The Upbuilding of Liberia, West Africa,"
Alexander's Magazine, III (Feb. 15, 1907), 183–185; Warren, "Does Liberia Want
Us, Or Do We Want Liberia," *Alexander's Magazine*, V (Mar. 15, 1908), 148–150.

would be replaced in status and power by blacks from the new middle class. At the same time, their base of political power outside the community was undermined by the progressive reforms of the era and the passing of the traditional groups within the Republican party who had been concerned with Negroes. By 1900, for the first time, the foundation of black politics was the black community itself, and political involvement and success would have to await the increase of the ghetto population in the 1920s.

Epilogue

I

DURING THE YEARS 1910 to 1920 Detroit's black population increased sevenfold, to 40,000. During the 1920s southern migrants continued to flow into the industrial city, and Detroit's black community numbered 120,000 in 1930.

The increase in population wrought great changes in the black community. Detroit's "black bottom" became literally a city within a city; the variety and breadth of life and institutions within the black community could match that of Detroit itself. In a larger sense, however, nothing had changed. The caste system was not a creation of the migrants, for it had been inherited from the nineteenth-century city. Proscription and segregation remained, as did the wooden rooming houses and alley sheds and the jobs at the bottom of the economic scale. Little of black Detroit after 1915 was new; no other group had changed so little in more than a century.

II

In walking the streets and byways of the modern black Detroit community, there are few physical artifacts to be noted that recall the old near east side. Black Detroit today ranges from the suburbs to the

207

inner city, from luxurious homes to wretched slums. The old district has been buried beneath the sterile asphalt and institutional brick supplied by highway and housing programs. Whatever physical ties existed between 1870 and 1970 fell long ago beneath the wrecking ball and bulldozer.

The similarities of style and life, however, are more abundant. There is—as this study notes for Detroit, and as Allan Spear noted for Chicago and Gilbert Osofsky for New York—a tragic sameness in the lives of black people today and in the past. In spite of all the changes in American society—the weakened proscription, the increased affluence, the improved education—so much of the quality of black life dependent upon the rest of society remains disturbingly inferior to that of white people. Even more dismal, the same cries of militancy and protest have been repeated in generation after generation, with only token response, so that voices must be uplifted again and again. In the final analysis, the structure—economic, social, and political—that proscribes black life has remained too much the same.[1]

Fundamentally, proscription—caste-like discrimination and prejudice—determined the direction of nineteenth-century Detroit black life. Those within the caste could find no relief; it touched every aspect of their lives, and the legal assaults on caste failed to significantly alter social custom. It is this structuring and rigidity of black-white relations that most suggests caste, and it is probable that similar patterns existed in cities throughout the North. Unfortunately, few studies have dealt with this critical period in the formation and growth of black communities, and none has examined, in detail, the social structure over time.

The life style of the elite has been dealt with extensively, indicating not only their importance in urban politics in the late nineteenth century but also reflecting their own articulation of their life style. Joy Jackson has noticed "a small tight-knit, mainly French-speaking Negro elite" in New Orleans; Adelaide Cromwell Hill has written of the brown Brahmins of Boston; Helen Chesnutt has told the story

[1] Allan H. Spear, *Black Chicago: The Making of a Negro Ghetto, 1890–1920* (Chicago, 1967); Gilbert Osofsky, "The Enduring Ghetto," *Journal of American History*, LV (September, 1968), 243.

of her father and the Cleveland elite; and Frederic H. Robb has recorded the story of Chicago's "400" of black society. The role of the elite outside of the caste can easily be seen in their own testimony; many black leaders bore witness that personally they had never experienced discrimination. Fannie Richards, who taught both in the segregated colored schools and the gerrymandered integrated schools of Detroit, said upon her retirement in 1915, "I never felt the least discrimination against me." D. A. Straker claimed that "the highly cultured, talented and white American of good birth and training never practices discrimination or prejudice on account of color, or race." In essence, they were brown Americans who were widely accepted as white by middle- and upper-class whites.[2]

In spite of the eventual disappearance of the old elite around the turn of the century, their persistence throughout the nineteenth century is an example of a resilient and resourceful class. Though the elite excluded Detroit blacks below the upper class from moving into their tightly knit group, they survived by absorbing new families from outside Detroit. While recruits might come from different social origins outside of the city, the elite would convert them to the values and ways of the black upper class.

The elite as a separate and distinct group apart from the rest of the black community disappeared around the turn of the century, to be replaced by the more black-oriented, business-minded, new elite. Unlike that of Chicago, Philadelphia, and New York, the development of a new black middle class and a black business community in Detroit preceded the great population increase that would help organize blacks into a viable, self-contained community. As August Meier and Allan Spear have noted, it was the distinctive ideology of

[2] Joy J. Jackson, *New Orleans in the Gilded Age: Politics and Urban Progress 1880–1896* (Baton Rouge, La., 1969), p. 19; Adelaide Cromwell Hill, "The Negro Upper Class in Boston—Its Development and Present Social Structure," unpublished Ph.D. dissertation, Radcliffe College, 1952; Helen M. Chesnutt, *Charles Waddell Chesnutt: Pioneer of the Color Line* (Chapel Hill, N. C., 1952); Frederic H. Robb, *The Negro in Chicago 1779–1929* (Chicago, 1929); clipping, *Detroit News-Tribune*, June 20, 1915, in C. M. Burton Scrapbook, LXXII, 20, Burton Historical Collection, Detroit Public Library; D. Augustus Straker, *A Trip to the Windward Islands, or Then and Now* (Detroit, 1896), p. 42.

race pride, group solidarity, and self-dependence that set the new middle class apart from the old elite. Though they had, as E. Franklin Frazier has pointed out, a vested interest in segregation, in the end, it was the force of proscription and discrimination that tied them completely to the black community. Without the elite's entree to the white world or their political power, those in the new middle class found themselves, whatever they might wish, bound to the black community.[3]

The remaining classes within the black community—the bulk of the caste—knew no other world than that of the caste. Their world was sharply limited, and escape was impossible. What was most ironic, however, was that they suffered all the evils of segregation, yet were never able to exploit some of the advantages to be gained from separatism. The caste followed the lead of the elite, a class that identified with the native-born white groups and rejected the ethnocentrism of the immigrant groups. Fatally, they stressed individualism and self-help, thus failing to unite, save in politics, in the interest of all blacks. They shared the native-born rejection of cooperation and community—ethnocentric self-defense—that so much characterized the tightly knit immigrant groups.

From the earliest days, Afro-American communities were anything but communal. In their excellent study of black community building before the Civil War, William and Jane Pease caught the spirit of black community life that describes Detroit and probably all other black societies in the nineteenth century: "If they partook of any specific social, economic, and political philosophy, it was the philosophy of the American Middle Class. Far from aiming at an Utopian communal society, the Negro communities were dedicated to training their inhabitants in the virtues of self-reliance, individualism, and independence."[4]

[3] August Meier, *Negro Thought in America, 1880–1915* (Ann Arbor, Mich., 1963); Allan H. Spear, *Black Chicago: The Making of a Negro Ghetto, 1890–1920* (Chicago, 1967); E. Franklin Frazier, "Human, All Too Human: The Negro's Vested Interest in Desegregation," in G. Franklin Edwards (ed.), *E. Franklin Frazier on Race Relations* (Chicago, 1968).

[4] William Pease and Jane Pease, *Black Utopia: Negro Communal Experiments in America* (Madison, Wis., 1963), p. 18.

III

In the nineteenth century prejudice and discrimination remained well entrenched. The structure of black-white relations had remained essentially the same since the Civil War; whatever progress seemed to be achieved did little to alter the basic system. Only some of the etiquette of caste had changed. What made it appear increasingly harsh was the great industrialism which the United States underwent and the successes of ethnic groups in sharing in the greater prosperity. Thus the gulf between black and white increased; while all else progressed, blacks remained the same. By 1900 blacks were less in the mainstream of American life than they had been in the previous four decades. With politics, their last important link with the white community, cut off by reform, blacks were left even more isolated.

Thus, finally, what was most tragic about the relative sameness of black life both before and after the ghetto was the black faith in view of caste, the black optimism in the face of proscription, and the black accommodation in the light of rejection. Blacks shared deeply in the American dream of individualism, hard work, and success, yet the American dream shared little with them. It shared neither its warmth nor its bounty, neither its confidence nor its freedom. If it shared anything at all, it showed blacks its ability to isolate, to impoverish, and to enslave. That blacks survived—and they did—and that they built their twentieth-century ghettos on the foundation of their nineteenth-century communities—and they did—is all the more remarkable.

APPENDIX A

A Note on "Caste"

HISTORIANS HAVE BEEN HESITANT to fit American black-white relations within a systematic format. They especially have been shy of using the word "caste." Two recent, well-received studies of northern black urban communities—Allan Spear's *Black Chicago*, and Gilbert Osofsky's *Harlem: The Making of a Ghetto*—illustrate this point, and the resulting dilemma. Under the chapter heading "Jim Crow's Triumph," Spear wrote that blacks suffered "systematic proscription," but did not describe the system. Furthermore, he concluded that "by 1915, Negroes had become a special group in the social structure of pre-war Chicago," and that this group "could not be classified as merely another of Chicago's many ethnic groups." But he goes no further; without the concept "caste," he cannot convey the essence of this "systematic proscription." Similarly Osofsky's *Harlem* failed to describe the structure of black-white social interaction. In lieu of analyzing the framework of relations among blacks and whites, the two authors have catalogued manifestations of caste. In the final analysis, Spear and Osofsky, in otherwise excellent studies, have failed to convey the essential meaning or systematic nature of the subordinate status of Negroes in a northern urban environment.[1]

The use of caste as a framework for describing the American black-white relationship is not new. The concept owes much to the work

[1] Allan H. Spear, *Black Chicago: The Making of a Negro Ghetto, 1890–1920* (Chicago, 1967), p. 49; Gilbert Osofsky, *Harlem: The Making of a Ghetto* (New York, 1966).

213

of W. Lloyd Warner and the series of socio-anthropological studies that he advised and sponsored in the late 1930s. Warner greatly influenced John Dollard's *Caste and Class in a Southern Town*, and he wrote methodological notes in *Deep South*, by Allison Davis, Burleigh Gardner, and Mary Gardner, and in *Black Metropolis*, by St. Clair Drake and Horace R. Cayton. In the late 1930s both Hortense Powdermaker, in her study of a southern town—*After Freedom*—and Buell G. Gallagher, in his report on American colleges—*American Caste and the Negro College*—came to use caste analysis independently of Warner. The monumental Carnegie study, *An American Dilemma*, of which Gunnar Myrdal was the senior author, also used the concept of caste to convey the peculiar American relationship between black and white. More recently, St. Clair Drake, G. Franklin Edwards, and Lee Rainwater have used this framework in separate articles in Talcott Parsons and Kenneth B. Clark (eds.), *The Negro American*, while sociologists Edward W. Pohlman, Gerald D. Berreman, and Reinhard Bendix have argued, on theoretical grounds, for the application of caste analysis to American black-white relations.[2]

Although the Warner school has continued to use caste analysis in studying American black-white relations, other social scientists have generally neglected the use of a caste model. Oscar Handlin had used an ethnic model, depicting blacks as one among many competing ethnic groups in a generally fluid and mobile society. More recently Glazer and Moynihan, in *Beyond the Melting Pot*, have taken the

[2] Dollard, *Caste and Class in a Southern Town* (New Haven, 1937); Davis, Gardner and Gardner, *Deep South* (Chicago, 1941); Drake and Cayton, *Black Metropolis* (New York, 1945); Powdermaker, *After Freedom* (New York, 1939); Gallagher, *American Caste and the Negro College* (New York, 1938); Gunnar Myrdal et al., *An American Dilemma* (New York, 1944); Parsons and Clark (eds.), *The Negro American* (Boston, 1966); Pohlman, "Evidences of Disparity Between the Hindu Practice of Caste and the Ideal Type," *American Sociological Review*, XVI (June, 1951), 375–379; Gerald D. Berreman, "Caste in India and the United States," *American Journal of Sociology*, LXVI (September, 1960), 120–127; Bendix, "Comparative Sociological Studies," *Transactions of the Fifth World Congress of Sociology* (Louvain, Belgium, 1964), pp. 21–30.

For Warner's writings on caste see his "American Caste and Class," *American Journal of Sociology*, XLII (September, 1936), 234–237; (with Allison Davis), "A Comparative Study of American Caste," in Edgar T. Thompson (ed.), *Race Relations and the Race Problem* (Durham, N.C., 1939), pp. 224–235; "Introduction," in Davis, Gardner, and Gardner, *Deep South*, pp. 3–14; "A Methodological Note," in Drake and Cayton, *Black Metropolis*, pp. 769–782; and "Social Class and Color Caste in America," in *American Life: Dream and Reality* (Chicago, 1962), pp. 68–101.

same course. Most historians and sociologists, however, have fallen back on narrative descriptions of discrimination and segregation, as did Spear and Osofsky.[3]

Oliver Cromwell Cox has mounted the most sustained attack on caste analysis. Cox maintained that "caste" was inapplicable to any society other than that of India. In his 1948 book, *Caste, Class and Race*—a Marxist analysis of class and race relationships—Cox contended, as had Marx, that the history of western society was the history of class struggle. Caste could not exist in the West, Cox argued, because the black-white relationship "is part and parcel of this class struggle, because it developed within the capitalist system as one of its fundamental traits."[4]

"Much of this debate, in retrospect," the sociologist Herbert M. Blalock, Jr., recently noted, "seems to be largely semantic." In effect, as Edward Pohlman had noted in 1952, the critics of the caste model such as Cox have described the phenomena of a caste system, even if they choose to call it racism, race relations, or whatever.[5]

The terms "racism" and "race relations" are inadequate in describing the structure of American black-white relations. Racism refers to an emotional set rather than to the social structure of a community. Race relations, on the other hand, covers a wide spectrum of human interaction without conveying any concept of the essential attitudes or structure of the actions involved. The term "caste," however, connotes a specific and widely understood image of human relationships and human interactions. More important, it denotes specific characteristics of the structure and behavior of a society or a community. In pointing out that caste was both a rigid system of social stratification and one of socio-cultural pluralism, Gerald D. Berreman in the *International Encyclopedia of the Social Sciences* defined caste as a system of social stratification that "can be said to occur when a society is composed of birth-ascribed, hierarchically ordered, and culturally distinct groups (castes)." Applied to nineteenth-century Detroit, caste signifies a divided and differentiated community. It indicates

[3] Handlin, *Boston's Immigrants* (Cambridge, Mass., 1941); Nathan Glazer and Daniel P. Moynihan, *Beyond the Melting Pot* (Cambridge, Mass., 1963). Handlin has since modified his ethnic approach in *The American People in the Twentieth Century* (Boston, 1963).

[4] Cox, *Caste, Class and Race* (reprinted New York, 1959), pp. 154, xxx.

[5] Blalock, *Toward a Theory of Minority-Group Relations* (New York, 1967), p. 63n; Pohlman, "Semantic Aspects of the Controversy Over Negro-White Caste in the United States," *Social Forces*, XXX (May, 1952), 416.

immobility, endogamy, and social isolation in a community separated into black and white.[6]

The use of the concept of caste, or similar comparative terms when appropriate, is of particular utility to historians. As Reinhard Bendix has argued, the study of caste and caste-like situations in all societies not only sheds light on the unique qualities of the Indian system but also reveals the characteristic ways in which men have provided solutions for problems within many societies. Berreman has stressed the same point: "It should be possible to derive further insight, not only into caste in India, but into a widespread type of relations between groups—insight which is obscured if we insist upon treating Indian caste as entirely unique."[7]

The hesitancy of historians to develop utilitarian cross-cultural and socio-historical concepts, as well as methods, has led to a vast literature in black and urban history which has obscured comparative information. The fine studies of black communities by Spear, Osofsky, and their predecessors as well as the thorough city biographies by Pierce, Still, McKelvy, Fogelson, Green, and others has led us no closer to understanding American black or urban life as opposed to the unique qualities of each city. While this study is limited to only one city, the use of the structural concept "caste" is meant to provide a framework to be tested and compared in other studies.[8]

[6] Berreman, "The Concept of Caste," in *International Encyclopedia of the Social Sciences* (New York, 1968), II, 333, 334.

[7] Bendix, "Comparative Sociological Studies," p. 28; Berreman, "Caste in India and the United States," pp. 126–127.

[8] Spear, *Black Chicago*; Osofsky, *Harlem: The Making of a Ghetto*; Bessie L. Pierce, *A History of Chicago* (3 vols.; New York, 1937–1957); Bayrd Still, *Milwaukee: The History of a City* (Madison, Wis., 1948); Blake McKelvey, *Rochester* (4 vols.; Cambridge, Mass., and Rochester, N.Y., 1945–1961); Robert M. Fogelson, *The Fragmented Metropolis: Los Angeles, 1850–1930* (Cambridge, Mass., 1967); Constance M. Green, *Washington* (2 vols.; Princeton, N.J., 1962–1963).

APPENDIX B

Detroit Occupational Structure 1870-1910

T A B L E 10 *Occupational Structure, Males, Detroit 1870*

	White	Percent	Black	Percent
Professional	5,008	23.9	19	2.9
Skilled	9,002	43.0	67	10.2
Semiskilled	1,600	7.7	102	15.5
Unskilled	4,662	22.3	184	28.0
Service	643	3.1	285	43.4
		100.0		100.0

SOURCE: 1870 manuscript census; *Ninth Census 1870*, I, 785.

Professional: Drugstore clerk, hotel clerk, physician, attorney, nurse, restaurant owner, minister, grocer, letter carrier, customs inspector, caterer, boarding house owner, farmer, and musician.

Skilled: Printer, clothes cleaner and repairer, blacksmith, shoemaker, carpenter, cooper, baker, mason, butcher, tanner, photographer, stone cutter, tailor, tobacco factory worker, confectionary factory worker, horse trainer.

Semiskilled: Railroad conductor, hack driver, coach driver, drayman, teamster, plasterer, sailor, whitewasher, paperhanger, boat deckhand, janitor, fireman on boat, livery worker, hostler, peddler, huckster, painter, mill engineer, tobacco shop worker, store worker.

Unskilled: Laborer.

Service: Steward, coachman, barber, servant, porter, cook, waiter, bell boy, sleeping-car conductor, hairdresser, cabin boy, launderer, saloonkeeper.

TABLE 11   *Occupational Structure,*
Black Males, Detroit 1880

	Blacks	Percent
Professional	47	5.7
Skilled	95	11.5
Semiskilled	107	12.9
Unskilled	162	19.6
Service	417	50.3
		100.0

SOURCE: 1880 manuscript census.

Professional: Restaurant keeper, peddler, minister, gardener, farmer, tailor, caterer, livery-stable keeper, fish seller, grocer, clerk, drug clerk, store clerk, office clerk, bookkeeper, school teacher, laundry keeper, postal clerk, stenographer, secondhand dealer, printer, poster wholesaler, hotel keeper, wood dealer, deputy U.S. Marshal, letter carrier, doctor, lawyer, customs inspector.

Skilled: Carpenter, plasterer, cooper, blacksmith, musician, painter, brick layer, baker, engraver, wood sawyer, moulderer, mason, railroad brakeman, butcher, ironer, organ worker, factory worker, brick maker, negative retoucher, shoemaker, harness maker.

Semiskilled: Sailor, teamster, whitewasher, dock hand, printshop worker, boat fireman, night watchman, tobacco-factory worker, wire-factory worker, engineer, fireman, iron worker, mill engineer, stone-foundry worker, wood-yard worker, shipping clerk, railroad employee, soda-water maker, mechanic, trainman.

Unskilled: Laborer, farm laborer (excluding farm laborer in prison).

Service: Waiter, barber, cook, servant, porter, janitor, hotel worker, hostler, newsboy, bellboy, bartender, barbershop worker, conductor, coachman, bathhouse worker, city-hall worker, errand boy, sexton, steward, expressman, yardman, jockey, bootblack.

TABLE 12   *Occupational Structure, Males, Detroit 1890*

	Native White	Percent	Foreign-born White	Percent	Colored*	Percent
Professional	9,532	39.0	5,770	19.0	61	5.1
Skilled	8,192	33.5	11,676	38.5	119	9.9
Semiskilled	3,621	14.8	3,476	11.5	176	14.6
Unskilled	2,052	8.4	8,228	27.1	277	23.0
Service	1,053	4.3	1,174	3.9	571	47.4
		100.0		100.0		100.0

* Colored: Negroes, Chinese, Japanese, civilized Indians.
SOURCE: *Eleventh Census 1890*, II, 664.
Professional: proprietary and clerical, gardener, clergyman, civil engineer, lawyer, physician, surgeon, agent, banker, merchant, peddler, manufacturer, commercial traveler, clerk, restaurant and saloon keeper, government official, policeman, fireman.
Skilled: Baker, blacksmith, boot and shoe maker, brass worker, brewer, butcher, cabinet maker, carpenter, harness maker, iron and steel worker, machinist, mason, stonefitter, painter, plasterer, plumber, printer, stove worker, tailor, tinner, tobacco and cigar worker, wood worker.
Semiskilled: Engineer, fireman, boatman, drayman, hackman, teamster, livery-stable worker, apprentice, bartender, street-railroad employee, street-railway employee.
Unskilled: Laborer.
Service: Barber, messenger, servant.

TABLE 13   *Occupational Structure, Males, Detroit 1900*

	Native White	Percent	Foreign-born White	Percent	Negro	Percent
Professional	16,873	37.9	8,260	20.2	120	8.3
Skilled	16,672	37.4	18,220	44.4	137	9.4
Semiskilled	5,872	13.2	4,421	10.8	148	10.2
Unskilled	3,314	7.4	8,568	20.9	329	22.7
Service	1,809	4.1	1,505	3.7	717	49.4
		100.0		100.0		100.0

SOURCE: *Twelfth Census 1900*, II, 544, 546.
Professional: Farmer, gardener, professional service, agent, banker, clerk, commercial traveler, foreman, livery-stable keeper, merchant, company officer, manufacturer, salesman, stenographer, nurse.
Skilled: Telegraph lineman, telegraph operator, undertaker, manufacturing and mechanical pursuits minus manufacturer.
Semiskilled: Soldier, watchman, boatman, drayman, hostler, huckster, messenger, packer, street-railway employee, steam railroad employee, lumberman.
Unskilled: Unspecified laborer, agricultural laborer.
Service: Porter, domestic and personal service minus soldier, watchman and nurse.

TABLE 14   *Occupational Structure, Males, Detroit 1910*

	Native White	Percent	Foreign-born White	Percent	Negro	Percent
Professional	21,056	33.9	10,403	18.2	157	9.9
Skilled	22,919	36.9	19,391	34.0	176	11.1
Semiskilled	11,821	19.0	6,766	11.9	183	11.6
Unskilled	4,056	6.5	18,054	31.6	282	17.8
Service	2,324	3.7	2,447	4.3	785	49.6
		100.0		100.0		100.0

SOURCE: *Thirteenth Census 1910*, IV, 553–554.

Professional: Draftsman, lawyer, musician, physician, clerk, bookkeeper, agent, trade (minus deliveryman and laborer), manufacturer and official, manager, superintendent, foreman, overseer.

Skilled: manufacturing and mechanical industries (minus apprentice, foreman, laborer n.o.s., manager, manufacturer, semiskilled operative), locomotive engineer, motorman.

Semiskilled: Apprentice, semiskilled operative, conductor, drayman, switchman, deliveryman, fireman, guard, policeman, soldier, messenger.

Unskilled: Laborer.

Service: Domestic and personal service.

TABLE 15   *Occupational Structure, Females, Detroit 1870*

	White	Percent	Black	Percent
Professional	255	.9	3	1.2
Manufacturing	1,327	4.6	—	—
Service	27,315	94.5	180	98.8
		100.0		100.0

SOURCE: 1870 manuscript census, *Ninth Census 1870*, I, 785.

Professional: Boarding-house keeper, government official, physician, teacher, trader, clerk.

Manufacturing: Skilled, semiskilled and factory work.

Service: Hairdresser, domestic servant, hotel employee, laundress, seamstress.

TABLE 16 *Occupational Structure, Black Females, Detroit 1880*

	Black	Percent
Professional	12	3.6
Manufacturing	4	1.7
Service	322	94.7
		100.0

SOURCE: 1880 manuscript census.
Professional: Teacher, nurse, fortune teller, public singer, restaurant keeper, hair-store keeper, prostitute.
Manufacturing: Milliner, ice-cream maker.
Service: Domestic servant, laundress, seamstress, hotel worker.

TABLE 17 *Occupational Structure, Females, Detroit 1890*

	Native White	Percent	Foreign-born White	Percent	Colored*	Percent
Professional	2,384	28.8	1,034	13.7	22	5.1
Manufacturing	3,339	40.4	2,420	32.0	60	14.0
Service	2,549	30.8	4,115	54.3	346	80.9
		100.0		100.0		100.0

* Colored: Negroes, Chinese, Japanese, and civilized Indians.
SOURCE: *Eleventh Census 1890*, II, 664.
Professional: Teacher, boarding-house keeper, nurse, bookkeeper, clerk, merchant, saleswoman, stenographer, telephone worker.
Manufacturing: Skilled and factory work.
Service: Housekeeper, laborer, laundress, servant.

TABLE 18 *Occupational Structure, Females, Detroit 1900*

	Native White	Percent	Foreign-born White	Percent	Negro	Percent
Professional	5,615	33.4	1,867	18.7	32	5.3
Manufacturing	6,395	38.1	3,497	34.9	75	12.4
Service	4,774	28.5	4,638	46.4	496	82.3
		100.0		100.0		100.0

SOURCE: *Twelfth Census 1900*, II, 548.
Professional: Agricultural pursuits, professional service, trade, and transportation.
Manufacturing: Manufacturing and mechanical pursuits.
Service: Domestic and personal service.

TABLE 19   *Occupational Structure, Females, Detroit 1910*

	Native White	Percent	Foreign-born White	Percent	Negro	Percent
Professional	12,435	45.8	3,389	27.0	40	4.6
Manufacturing	8,568	31.5	3,685	29.5	74	8.6
Service	6,165	22.7	5,441	43.5	749	86.8
		100.0		100.0		100.0

SOURCE: *Thirteenth Census 1910*, IV, 554–555.
Professional: Professional service, transportation, trade, clerical.
Manufacturing: Manufacturing and mechanical industries.
Service: Domestic and personal service.

A Note on Sources

NEITHER I NOR PERSONS connected with the Michigan Historical Collections of the University of Michigan were able to locate the manuscript collections of any nineteenth-century Detroit blacks. A few letters by Robert Banks, pre–Civil War merchant and community leader, are in the Gerrit Smith Papers at the Carnegie Library, Syracuse University. A black woman's certificate of freedom can be found in the John J. Bagley Papers at the Michigan Historical Collections. Also at the Collections are the Nathan Thomas Papers, relating to the Underground Railroad in Michigan; the Charles Adam Weissert Papers, containing some information on the early history of the Calvin settlement in Cass County; the papers of the Protestant Episcopal Church of Michigan, including a file on St. Matthew's Church; the Detroit Urban League Papers, containing a few items relating to the pre–World War I years; and the Chase S. Osborn Papers, which include a number of items relating to black involvement in politics.

The Burton Historical Collection of the Detroit Public Library contains two collections relating to the 1833 riot—the Marshall Chapin Papers and the John Mason Papers—and another dealing with the 1863 riot, the Samuel T. Douglass Papers. The ledger of "The Rector's Aid Society" of St. Matthew's Church, 1896–98, is also located at the Burton Historical Collection. The papers of Senator James MacMillan, in the same institution, shed light on the Republican party's concern for its black constituents.

The single most important manuscript collection for this study was the inventory of manuscripts, ledgers, speeches, and clipping collections relating to Negro life in Michigan that was prepared by the Michigan Historical Records Survey as part of the nationwide Inventory of American Negro Manuscripts. The inventory, prepared in cooperation with the Detroit black community, has been deposited in the Michigan Historical Collections. This survey attempted to locate and abstract all manuscripts in the state relating to Negroes, whether the papers were in public collections or in private hands, in order to chronicle the story of the Negro in Michigan. "History of the Negro in Michigan," the uncompleted narrative by the Historical Records Survey, can be found at both the Burton and Michigan Collections. The history, which deals almost exclusively with the slavery and abolitionist periods, is inaccurate and incomplete. The files of the survey itself, however, are most valuable, though they defy classification.

Among manuscript collections the enumerated schedules of the United States Census from 1830 to 1880 were second in value only to the Historical Records Survey materials. The schedules offer information on nearly every individual in the community, and they provided an important source of information for the chapter on class.

NEWSPAPERS

The most important source for the study of nineteenth-century black communities is the contemporary newspaper. For Detroit, only one long run of a black newspaper is extant—the weekly *Plaindealer* from 1889 to 1893. The Burton Historical Collection has a number of scattered issues of other Afro-American weeklies for the early twentieth century: the *Detroit Informer* (photostat), 1900; the *Detroit Advocate*, 1901; the *Detroit Leader*, 1910, 1914; and the *Detroit Contender*, 1920. Other black weeklies also carried Detroit news. Frederick Douglass's *North Star*, and its successors, were consulted for the 1840s and 1850s, and Henry Bibb's *Voice of the Fugitive*, published in Canada and available for 1851–52 in the rare book room of the General Library of the University of Michigan, contains information on Detroit of the 1850s. For the post–Civil War period, the weekly *New National Era and Citizen* (Washington), 1870–74, was helpful, as were weeklies from midwestern black communities: the *Freeman* (Indianapolis), which was consulted for the years 1892–1904, and the *Cleveland Gazette*, which was used for the period 1893–1901.

Surprisingly, the white newspapers of Detroit—the weeklies of the 1820s and 1830s and the dailies thereafter—proved to be a very valuable source. Too often neglected by historians, the white press throughout the nineteenth century regularly reported the political, religious, and social activities of the black community. Most newspapers identified Negroes with the word "(col'd)" after their names, although the elite were often not designated in this way. (In any event, with the use of the manuscript census schedules and the Detroit city directories as guides, I did not have to rely on the racial identifications of the newspapers.) Long runs of a number of newspapers were consulted: the weekly *Detroit Gazette*, 1817–29, of which photostatic copies can be found in the Michigan Historical Collections; the weekly and daily editions of the *Democratic Free Press*, 1829–53; the weekly abolitionist *Signal of Liberty*, 1841–48, in the Michigan Historical Collection; the weekly Baptist *Michigan Christian Herald*, 1840–46, in the Burton Historical Collection; and the daily *Detroit Tribune* and its successor newspapers, 1865–90, 1895–1902. As the leading Republican newspaper in Detroit, the *Tribune* reported the activities of the black community more extensively than did any other Detroit newspaper.

A number of clipping collections were also of great aid. The Burton scrapbooks at the Burton Historical Collection cover every aspect of Detroit life and are indispensable. Invaluable, too, is the Reading Room File of the collection, which contains a special file of the newspaper obituaries of Detroit blacks. Also at the Burton Collection are Friend Palmer's scrapbooks dealing with Detroit during the era of slavery and abolition, and James A. Randall's scrapbooks on the politics of the post–Civil War period.

MISCELLANEOUS UNPUBLISHED MATERIALS

There are a number of unpublished materials dealing with the Negro in Detroit. Steven Serlin, "The Negroes in Detroit in the 1880's and Early 1890's," senior honors thesis, University of Michigan, 1968, is the best among the lot. Unlike his predecessors, Serlin used the manuscript census for 1880, the annual city directories, and the *Plaindealer*. He was the first researcher to identify the area of nineteenth-century black settlement in Detroit. Other academic writers have been less successful. June Baber Woodson, "A Century With the Negroes of Detroit, 1830–1930," M.A. thesis, Wayne University, 1949, is a weak, general survey and is not worth consulting. J. Carleton Hayden's "Negroes in Detroit, 1890–1900," seminar paper, Wayne State University, 1962, in the Burton Historical Collection, is interesting in its discussion of politics, but like Woodson, Hayden generalizes from a few inadequate sources. Arthur Raymond Kooker, "The Anti-Slavery Movement in Michigan, 1796–1840," Ph.D. dissertation, University of Michigan, 1941, discusses the early period of slavery. More ambitious is Fred Hart Williams and Hoyt Fuller, "Detroit Heritage," a typewritten copy of which can be found in the Fred Hart Williams Papers, at the Burton Historical Collection. The text is a biographically organized history of Negroes in Detroit and it contains much valuable information, but it is unfootnoted.

More specific materials include Forrester B. Washington, "The Negro in Detroit: A Survey of the Conditions of a Negro Group in a Northern Industrial Center During the War Prosperity Period," a study prepared for the Associated Charities of Detroit, 1920, in the Detroit Public Library. A valuable source for the wartime period, it was the foundation for the 1926 Mayor's Inter-racial Committee report, *The Negro in Detroit*. Glen E. Carlson's survey for the 1926 study led to "The Negro in the Industries of Detroit," Ph.D. dissertation, University of Michigan, 1929, which has but scant information on the pre–World War I period. Henry Allen Bullock, "The Role of the Negro Church in the Negro Community of Detroit," sociology paper, University of Michigan, [1935], in the General Library of the University of Michigan, deals with fundamentalist churches. It contains data on the movement in Detroit, but Bullock failed to uncover the pre–World War I fundamentalist churches in Detroit. Of less value were Joseph E. MacMahon, "The Michigan Civil Rights Act of 1885," seminar paper, University of Michigan Law School, 1965—a legislative history of the act—and the altogether inaccurate William W. Stephenson, "The Colored Schools of Detroit," seminar paper, University of Michigan, 1959. Both are in the Michigan Historical Collections.

Other general studies dealing with nineteenth-century black history that were helpful include Howard H. Bell's history of the early Negro convention movement, militancy, colonization, and emigration: "A Survey of the Negro Convention Movement, 1830–1861," Ph.D. dissertation, Northwestern University, 1953; and Sidney H. Kessler's equally well-researched "The Negro in the Knights of Labor," M.A. thesis, Columbia University, 1950. Especially useful for background material was Leslie H. Fishel, Jr., "The North and the Negro, 1865–1900: A Study in Race Discrimination," 2 vols., Ph.D. dissertation, Harvard University, 1955.

A few unpublished studies were useful for an understanding of Detroit in general: Albert Mayer's "A Study of the Foreign-Born Population of Detroit, 1870–1950," mimeographed, 1951, in the Michigan Historical Collections, is a statistical history of the changing patterns of Detroit immigration; Gilbert Anderson, "A Study in Italian Residence Succession in Detroit, Michigan," 1935, in the Bureau of Government Library of the University of Michigan, deals with the Detroit Italian community; and Glen J. Taylor, "Prostitution in Detroit," [1930s], in the General Library of the University of Michigan, treats a neglected, primarily urban, institution.

CASTE AND CLASS

The use of caste as a framework for describing the American black-white relationship owes much to the work of W. Lloyd Warner, both his own writings and the series of socio-anthropological studies that he sponsored for which he served as an adviser in the late 1930s: W. Lloyd Warner, "American Caste and Class," *American Journal of Sociology*, XLII (September, 1936), 234–237; John Dollard, *Caste and Class in a Southern Town* (New Haven, 1937); Edgar T. Thompson (ed.), *Race Relations and the Race Problem* (Durham, N.C., 1939); Allison Davis, Burleigh B. Gardner and Mary R. Gardner, *Deep South* (Chicago, 1941); St. Clair Drake and Horace Cayton, *Black Metropolis* (New York, 1945); Allison Davis, "Caste, Economy, and Violence," *American Journal of Sociology*, LI (July, 1945), 7–15; and W. Lloyd Warner, *American Life: Dream and Reality* (Chicago, 1962).

Other studies that have applied a caste analysis to American society include Gunnar Myrdal, *An American Dilemma* (New York, 1944); Edward W. Pohlman, "Evidences of Disparity Between the Hindu Practice of Caste and the Ideal Type," *American Sociological Review*, XVI (June, 1951), 375–379; Talcott Parsons and Kenneth B. Clark (eds.), *The Negro American* (Boston, 1966); and Michael Banton, *Race Relations* (New York, 1968). In contrast, Oliver Cromwell Cox has led the attack against using caste as a framework for analysis. In *Caste, Class and Race* (New York, 1959), Cox maintained that "caste" was inapplicable to any society other than that of India and that the black-white relationship in the United States is a function of the class structure.

Charles S. Mangum, Jr., *The Legal Status of the Negro* (Chapel Hill, N.C., 1940), and Gilbert Thomas Stephenson, *Race Distinction in American Law* (New York, 1910), two studies of state legislation, deal with the legal framework of black-white relations. Less valuable is Franklin Johnson, *The Development of State Legislation Concerning the Free Negro* (New York, 1918). American attitudes toward proscription are dealt with more generally in Thomas F. Gossett, *Race: The History of an Idea in America* (Dallas, 1963); and John Higham, *Strangers in the Land* (New York, 1965).

The literature on class is enormous, but a few books were found to be especially helpful. Both Reinhold Bendix's and Seymour M. Lipset's *Class, Status and Power* (Glencoe, Ill., 1953), and Neil J. Smelser's and Seymour M. Lipset's *Social Structure and Mobility in Economic Development* (Chicago, 1966), contain much valuable literature on the subject. In addition I also found useful Richard Center's, *The Psychology of Social Classes: A Study of Class Consciousness* (Princeton, N.J., 1949), and Oscar Lewis's work on the subculture of poverty, *A Study of Slum Culture: Backgrounds for "La Vida"* (New York, 1968).

Allan H. Spear, *Black Chicago: The Making of a Negro Ghetto, 1890–1920* (Chicago, 1967); August Meier, "Negro Class Structure and Ideology in the Age of Booker T. Washington," *Phylon*, XXIII (Fall, 1962), 258–

266; August Meier, *Negro Thought in America, 1880–1915* (Ann Arbor, Mich., 1963), and E. Franklin Frazier, *Black Bourgeoisie: The Rise of a New Middle Class* (New York, 1957), are the most valuable works dealing with classes in the black community.

DETROIT

The finest general history of Detroit—although published nearly ninety years ago—is Silas Farmer, *The History of Detroit and Michigan* (Detroit, 1884). Well written and exhaustively researched, the volume is a compendium of nearly every aspect of Detroit municipal government and urban development up to the date of publication. The city's later growth can be traced in Leonard S. Wilson, "Functional Areas of Detroit, 1890–1933," *Michigan Academy of Science, Arts and Letters*, XXII (1937), 397–409. Other studies include Almon Ernest Parkins, *The Historical Geography of Detroit* (Lansing, 1918), an economic and geographic history of the city, and Clarence M. Burton, *History of Detroit 1780 to 1850 : Financial and Commercial* (Detroit, 1917), an economic history by the founder of the Burton Historical Collection. More personal and more anecdotal are Robert B. Ross and George B. Catlin, *Landmarks of Detroit: A History of the City* (Detroit, 1898), and George B. Catlin, *The Story of Detroit* (Detroit, 1923).

Although the variety and quality of data vary from census to census, the United States decennial census is the most important source of statistical information about Detroit. Not all data for Detroit in the nineteenth century were aggregated and published in the printed census volumes, and additional tables can be calculated from the schedules of the manuscript census. The federal census occasionally deals with qualitative as well as quantitative factors—as in 1880, when it offered a narrative ward by ward description of major American cities, including Detroit. Complementing the United States Census in the nineteenth century was the Michigan decennial census conducted in the fourth year of each decade. Probably less accurate, and definitely less ambitious in scope, than the federal government's surveys, the Michigan census nonetheless offers additional data. The Detroit city directories, which appeared occasionally in midcentury and annually by the close of the century, also contain much quantitative as well as qualitative information about Detroit.

Travelers' accounts and memoirs, and magazine articles by visitors to Detroit and urban reformers are another significant source of information on Detroit life. Travelers visiting both the United States and Canada often made Detroit their port of entry or re-entry after they had visited Niagara

Falls and the Ontario countryside, and their accounts reveal much of the ordinary life of the city. Among the more valuable works are James William Massie, *America: The Origin of Her Present Conflict; Her Prospect for the Slave, and Her Claim for Anti-Slavery Sympathy* (London, 1864); and those of two visitors of the 1870s—William Morris, *Letters Sent Home* (n.p., [1874]), and Charles Morley (ed. and trans.), *Portrait of America: Letters of Henry Sienkiewicz* (New York, 1959). Russell McLauchlin's memoir of Detroit around the turn of the century recounts the history of a street later occupied by the black elite: *Alfred Street* (Detroit, 1946).

Industrialization drew more attention to Detroit, and the city of the 1890s was described in J. W. Sullivan, "Detroit in the Van," *American Federationist*, II (December, 1895), 188–190. Hugo Ericksen caught the mood of the 1900s in "The New Detroit," *The World To-Day*, XI (July, 1906), 703–709. By 1911 Detroit's problems were large enough to capture the attention of reformers. In 1903 Robert W. DeForest and Lawrence Veiller had virtually omitted Detroit from their *The Tenement House Problem* (2 vols.; New York, 1903), but within a decade, housing and social conditions in Detroit became a widely discussed problem as evidenced in the following: Henry Oyen, "The Awakening of the Cities, III," *The World's Work*, XXII (August, 1911), 14725–14733, and "The Awakening of the Cities, V," *The World's Work*, XXII (October, 1911), 15000–15005; Myron E. Adams, "The Housing Awakening, XII: A City Awake—Detroit," *Survey*, XXVI (Aug. 5, 1911), 666–671; John Ihlder, "Booming Detroit," *Survey*, XXXVI (July 29, 1916), 449–450; Michigan Housing Commission, *Report* (Lansing, 1916); and Hume McPherson, "Aid for Home Builders," *Survey*, XLII (Aug. 16, 1919), 723–724. The first report of the Detroit Housing Commission, formed in the 1930s, recalled the World War I period: *First Annual Report of the Detroit Housing Commission* (Detroit, 1934).

In tracing the development of American industry in the late nineteenth century, Victor S. Clark, *History of Manufactures in the United States, 1860–1914* (Washington, 1928), dealt extensively with the growth of Detroit. Illustrated commercial directories of Detroit also serve to record the economic development of the city and provide biographical information on important businessmen. Examples are [Richard Edwards], *Industries of Michigan, City of Detroit* (New York, 1880), and *Detroit Illustrated* (Detroit, 1891). Extremely important in recording the growth of the city, in a social as well as an economic sense and in qualitative as well as quantitative terms, is Great Britain, *Parliamentary Papers* (Commons), "Cost of Living in American Towns: Report of an Enquiry by the Board of Trade," 1911. The result of a Board of Trade investigation of American cities, the report included Detroit among the cities surveyed, and, most important, it broke the city down into its component ethnic communities.

Although the columns of the nineteenth-century newspaper serve as a constant reminder of the ethnicity of the city, few historians have dealt with this factor, and there is no study of Detroit comparable to the studies of other cities, such as Oscar Handlin, *Boston's Immigrants* (Cambridge, Mass., 1941); the New York study of Nathan Glazer and Daniel Moynihan, *Beyond the Melting Pot* (Cambridge, Mass., 1963); Gerd Korman, *Industrialization, Immigrants and Americanizers: The View from Milwaukee 1866–1921* (Madison, Wis., 1967); or the Newburyport survey by W. Lloyd Warner and Leo Srole, *The Social Systems of American Ethnic Groups* (New Haven, Conn., 1945). Lois Rankin, "Detroit Nationality Groups," *Michigan History Magazine*, XXIII (Spring, 1939), 129–205, is the only comprehensive ethnic approach to Detroit history, and it reflects the inadequacy of research in the area. The only worthwhile study of a Detroit ethnic community is Sister Mary Remigia Napolska, "The Polish Immigrant in Detroit to 1914," *Annals of the Polish R.C. Union Archives and Museum*, X (1945–1946). Information on Detroit ethnic institutions can be found in Michigan Historical Records Survey, *Inventory of the Church and Synagogue Archives of Michigan: Jewish Bodies* (Detroit, 1940); Michigan Historical Records Survey, *Inventory of the Church Archives of Michigan: The Roman Catholic Church, Archdiocese of Detroit* (Detroit, 1941); and Robert A. Woods and Albert J. Kennedy (eds.), *Handbook of Settlements* (New York, 1911).

BLACK DETROIT

General Works

There have been only a small number of general works relating to the Negro in Detroit or Michigan. The *Michigan Manual of Freedmen's Progress* (Detroit, 1915), compiled by Francis H. Warren, attempted to recount the history of black men in the state by gathering, to the extent possible, all of the available information relating to Michigan Negroes. The resulting volume is a valuable compendium of biographical and institutional data of contemporary vintage, but without any historical perspective. A. L. Turner's and Earl Moses's directory of the Detroit black community, *Colored Detroit 1924* (Detroit, 1924), in the Burton Historical Collection, supplements the 1915 work; valuable for its contemporary information on individuals and organizations, it is essentially present-minded and provides little history of the community. Two years later the report of the Mayor's Inter-racial Committee appeared, *The Negro in Detroit* (Detroit, 1926). Issued in twelve parts and based on Forrester B.

Washington's unpublished survey of 1920, the report is the most thorough contemporary investigation of Detroit black life ever undertaken. Its historical scope was narrow, however, and it dealt only incidentally with the period prior to World War I.

In 1940, John C. Dancy, head of the Detroit Urban League, published "The Negro People in Michigan," *Michigan History Magazine*, XXIV (Spring, 1940), 221–240. Concentrating mostly on the slavery and abolitionist periods, Dancy probably relied heavily on the Historical Records Survey of Michigan manuscript, "History of the Negro in Michigan." A few years later, Ulysses W. Boykin issued *A Handbook on the Detroit Negro* (Detroit, 1943). For the nineteenth-century background he relied greatly on the *Michigan Manual of Freedmen's Progress*; his *Handbook* is most valuable for bringing the *Manual* up to date. The best statistical source is U.S. Bureau of the Census, *Negro Population 1790–1915* (Washington, 1917).

A number of other narrower studies deal directly with the Negro in Detroit and the great changes in the black community during the World War I period. Forrester B. Washington discussed these matters in "The Detroit Newcomers' Greeting," *Survey*, XXXVIII (July 14, 1917), 333–335, as well as in his larger unpublished study. George Edmund Haynes wrote extensively on the period; he dealt with both the migrants and their effect on the Detroit black community in "Negroes Move North: 1. Their Departure from the South," *Survey* XL (May 4, 1918), 115–122, and *Negro New-Comers in Detroit, Michigan: A Challenge to Christian Statesmanship. A Preliminary Study* (New York, 1918). A few years later John Marshall Ragland treated the same problems in "The Negro in Detroit," *Southern Workman*, LII (November, 1923), 533–540.

A number of biographical works have served as histories of the black community for one period or another. Aris A. Mallas, Jr., Rea McCain, and Margaret K. Hedden, *Forty Years in Politics: The Story of Benjamin Pelham* (Detroit, 1957), and John C. Dancy's autobiography, *Sand Against the Wind* (Detroit, 1966), provide much information on the black community as well as their subjects. In addition, the fugitive slave autobiography, *The History of William Webb, Composed By Himself* (Detroit, 1873), in the Burton Historical Collection; the biography of the voice teacher Azalia Hackley, by M. Marguerite Davenport, *Azalia: The Life of Madame E. Azalia Hackley* (Boston, 1947); and the story of the Virginia migrants in W. B. Hartgrove, "The Story of Maria Louise Moore and Fannie M. Richards," *Journal of Negro History*, I (January, 1916), 23–33, all yield much information on life in black Detroit.

Also of great value is the novel by Walter H. Stowers and William H. Anderson: Sanda, *Appointed: An American Novel* (Detroit, 1894), which deals in part with the Negro in late nineteenth-century Detroit.

Black Detroit Before 1870

Several items were consulted for their references to slavery in Michigan and its survival in face of the Northwest Ordinance's apparent bar on its existence. Many articles and documents in the multivolume *Pioneer and Historical Collections of Michigan* attest to the tenacity of the institution, and a number of cases relating to the legality of slavery can be found in William Wirt Blume (ed.), *Transactions of the Supreme Court of the Territory of Michigan 1805–1814* (2 vols., Ann Arbor, 1935). For a general discussion see David M. Katzman, "Black Slavery in Michigan," *Midcontinent American Studies Journal*, XI (Fall, 1970), 56–66.

Michigan and Detroit were important midwestern abolitionist centers. John E. Kephart has written about the *Signal of Liberty* and other abolitionist newspapers in "Antislavery Publishing in Michigan," in David Kaser (ed.), *Books in America's Past: Essays Honoring Rudolph H. Gjelsness* (Charlottesville, Va., 1966), pp. 220–235. Arthur Kooker's dissertation, "The Anti-Slavery Movement in Michigan," dealt with the abolitionism rooted in western New York and New England, and more recently Merton L. Dillon has discussed the Quaker element in the Michigan movement: "Elizabeth Chandler and the Spread of Antislavery Sentiment to Michigan," *Michigan History*, XXXIX (December, 1955), 481–494. Most writers have stressed the importance of the Underground Railroad in sending fugitives northward to Michigan or Canada. Wilbur H. Siebert, *The Underground Railroad from Slavery to Freedom* (New York, 1898), articulately set forth this traditional interpretation, and it has been most recently exemplified by Katherine DuPre Lumpkin, " 'The General Plan was Freedom:' A Negro Secret Order on the Underground Railroad," *Phylon*, XXVIII (Spring, 1967), 63–77. In reality, the primary and secondary sources for Michigan seem to confirm Larry Gara's myth-breaking *The Liberty Line: The Legend of the Underground Railroad* (Lexington, Ky., 1961). Laura S. Haviland's autobiography, *A Woman's Life-Work* (Cincinnati, 1882), lends no credence to the idea of a national organization. Harold B. Fields, "Free Negroes in Cass County Before the Civil War," *Michigan History*, XLIV (December, 1960), 375–383; John Hope Franklin, *The Free Negro in North Carolina, 1790–1865* (Chapel Hill, N.C., 1943); and Luther Porter Jackson, *Free Negro Labor and Property Holding in Virginia 1830–1860* (New York, 1942), all give information on the free status and migration of pre–Civil War Michigan blacks.

Contemporary white attitudes toward blacks are reflected in the debates of the constitutional conventions of the period: Harold M. Dorr (ed.), *The Michigan Constitutional Convention of 1835–1836: Debates and Proceedings* (Ann Arbor, 1940); *Report of the Proceedings and Debates in the Convention to Revise the Constitution of the State of Michigan 1850* (Lansing, 1850); and *Debates and Proceedings of the Constitutional Convention of the State of Michigan 1867* (2 vols.; Lansing, 1867). Emil Olbrich's *The Development of Sentiment on Negro Suffrage to 1860*, Bulletin of the University of Wisconsin, History Series, III, (1912), and Mary Joice Adams's *The History of Suffrage in Michigan*, Publications of the Michigan Political Science Association, III (March, 1898), trace white resistance to black enfranchisement. The results of these attitudes, mostly unfavorable to blacks, can be seen in the annual collections of *Michigan Legislative Documents*, Senate, House, and Joint; the published *Journals* of the Michigan House and Senate; the compiled statutes in *Laws of the Territory of Michigan* (4 vols.; Lansing, 1874); *The Compiled Laws of the State of Michigan* (2 vols.; Detroit, 1857); and the annual *Acts of the Legislature of the State of Michigan*.

Black responses to caste status are evident in a variety of publications. Robert Banks, *An Oration Delivered at a Celebration in Detroit on the Abolition of Slavery in the West Indies* (Detroit, 1839), in the Burton Historical Collection, represents the view of one black leader. Black conventions gave Negro leaders a platform for their abolitionist and reform views; many excerpts from their meetings are reprinted in Herbert Aptheker (ed.), *A Documentary History of the Negro People in the United States* (2 vols.; New York, 1963). *Minutes of the State Convention of the State of Michigan* (Detroit, 1843), published by the first state black convention, is available at both the Burton Historical Collection and Clements Library, and a microfilm copy of the 1865 State Equal Rights League meeting, *Proceedings of the Colored Men's Convention of the State of Michigan 1865* ... (Adrian, Mich., 1865), is in the author's possession.

The Chatham conventions represented a more militant response of some blacks to the existence of slavery. James Redpath, *The Public Life of Captain John Brown* (Boston, 1860), reprinted the provisional constitution, and the journal of the two conventions. Some of the testimony in the U.S. Congress, Senate, Select Committee on the Harper's Ferry Invasion, *Report, Journal and Testimony*, 36 Cong., 1 Sess. (Washington, 1860), also deals with the Chatham conventions. Other primary sources are reprinted in F. B. Sanborn, *The Life and Letters of John Brown* (Boston, 1885), and Richard J. Hinton, *John Brown and His Men* (New York, 1894).

The Civil War years are treated in Norman McRae, *Negroes in Michigan During the Civil War* (Lansing, 1966), a publication of the Michigan Civil War Centennial Observance Commission. It is best for its history of the state's black regiment, the First Michigan Colored Infantry Regiment (102nd U.S. Colored Infantry). *A Thrilling Narrative from the Lips of the Sufferers of the Late Detroit Riot, March 6, 1863* (reprinted Hattiesburg, Miss., 1945) includes eyewitness accounts of the riot as well as the long narrative poem, and two Michigan Civil War Centennial Observance Commission pamphlets deal with some of the riot's backgrounds: Albert A. Blum and Dan Georgakas, *Michigan Labor and the Civil War* (Lansing, 1964), and George S. May, *Michigan and the Civil War Years 1860–1866: A Chronicle* (Lansing, 1964). Similar conflicts in other cities are dealt with in Williston H. Lofton, "Northern Labor and the Negro during the Civil War," *Journal of Negro History*, XXXIV (July, 1949), 251–273, and Albion P. Man, Jr., "Labor Competition and the New York Draft Riots of 1863," *Journal of Negro History*, XXXVI (October, 1953), 375–405. More general, and concerned with white attitudes toward blacks, are Wood Gray, *The Hidden Civil War* (New York, 1942); Eugene Converse Murdock, *Patriotism Limited 1862–1865: The Civil War and the Bounty System* (n.p., 1967); V. Jacques Voegeli, *Free But Not Equal: The Midwest and the Negro During the Civil War* (Chicago, 1967); and Forest G. Wood, *Black Scare: The Racist Response to Emancipation and Reconstruction* (Berkeley, 1968).

In the 1860s much attention was focused on the question of integrated schools at both the local and national levels. The subject of school integration at the national level is discussed in Alfred H. Kelly, "The Congressional Controversy over School Segregation, 1867–1875," *American Historical Review*, LXIV (April, 1959), 537–563. The outlines of the Detroit and Michigan battles can be followed in Caroline W. Thrun, "School Segregation in Michigan," *Michigan History*, XXXVIII (March, 1954), 1–23, and the *Annual Reports of the Board of Education of the City of Detroit* (Detroit, 1842), in the Burton Historical Collection, which includes the rules of the colored school. Arthur B. Moehlman's *Public Education in Detroit* (Bloomington, Ill., 1925), is valuable for background information on the Detroit school system.

Additional information on the period is supplied in Martin Robison Delany, *The Condition, Elevation, Emigration and Destiny of the Colored People of the United States, Politically Considered* (Philadelphia, 1852) which includes an account of Delany's brief visit to Detroit. *The Journals of the Proceedings of the Common Council of the City of Detroit* for the period also deal with many black activities in the city. Leon Litwack, *North of Slavery, The Negro in the Free States, 1790–1860* (Chicago, 1961) provides an excellent overview for much of the era.

Biographical Material

A number of widely circulated directories contained biographies of Detroit blacks: William J. Simmons, *Men of Mark, Emminent, Progressive and Rising* (Cleveland, 1887); I. Garland Penn, *The Afro-American*

Press and Its Editors (Springfield, Mass., 1891); M. A. Majors, *Noted Negro Women–Their Triumphs and Activities* (Chicago, 1893); Mrs. N. F. Mossell, *The Work of the Afro-American Woman* (Philadelphia, 1908); Frank Lincoln Mather (ed.), *Who's Who of the Colored Race 1915* (Chicago, 1915); and Joseph J. Boris (ed.), *Who's Who in Colored America 1927* (New York, 1927).

Works by Detroit blacks were also valuable. Those not mentioned elsewhere include Robert W. Bagnall, "Two Decades of Negro Life," *New Republic*, LIX (Aug. 7, 1929), 304–306; Henry Bibb, *Narrative of the Life and Adventures of Henry Bibb, an American Slave* (New York, 1850); E. Azalia Hackley, *The Colored Girl Beautiful* (Kansas City, Mo., 1916); and the works of D. Augustus Straker: *Reflections on the Life and Times of Toussaint L'Ouverture, The Negro Haytien . . .* (Columbia, S.C., 1886), *The New South Investigated* (Detroit, 1888), *A Trip to the Windward Islands, or Then and Now* (Detroit, 1896), and *Negro Suffrage in the South* (Detroit, 1906).

Negro exclusion from both occupations and labor unions has been long recognized. W. E. Burghardt DuBois (ed.), *The Negro Artisan* (Atlanta, 1902), James Samuel Stemons, "The Industrial Color-Line in the North," *Century Magazine*, LX (July, 1900), 477–478, and U.S. Bureau of the Census, *Statistics of Women at Work* (Washington, 1907), reveal the caste line in the trades. A number of works are concerned with the relationship of labor unions and Negroes: John R. Commons (ed.), *Trade Unionism and Labor Problems* (reprinted New York, 1967); Gerald N. Grob, "Organized Labor and the Negro Worker, 1865–1890," *Labor History*, I (Spring, 1960), 164–176; Sterling D. Spero and Abram L. Harris, *The Black Worker* (reprinted New York, 1968); and F. E. Wolfe, *Admission to American Trade Unions* (Baltimore, 1912). James B. Kennedy's *Beneficiary Features of American Trade Unions* (Baltimore, 1908), serves as a catalog of benefits unobtainable by excluded blacks.

Profiles of occupations are important but are too often overlooked by the historian. Edith Abbott surveys the general position of the ordinary laborer in "The Wages of Unskilled Labor in the United States, 1850–1900," *Journal of Political Economy*, XIII (June, 1905), 321–367. One particular group of workers is treated broadly in Charles B. Barnes's pioneering study, *The Longshoreman* (New York, 1915); and one portion of this group–black dock workers–is dealt with in E. Franklin Frazier, "A Negro Industrialist Group," *Howard Review*, I (June, 1924), 196–232. Most important for an understanding of barbering during the period of this study are the various union monthlies: *The Barbers' Journal* (Cleveland, Ohio), 1901–1902; *The Journeyman Barber* (Los Angeles), 1905–1913; and *The Barbers' Journal* (New York City), 1908–1909. The history of the trade, as well as its development in America, is presented in M. J.

Vieira, *The Tonsorial Art Pamphlet, Origin of the Trade, the Business in America and Other Countries* (Indianapolis, 1877), in the New York Public Library. The *Annual Reports of the National Negro Business League 1900–1910*, have much information on the proprietorship of barbershops, and the *Biennial Report of the Michigan State Board of Examiners of Barbers 1913–1914* (Lansing, 1915), reveals the trend toward the licensing of barbers. *The Gillette Blade*, 1918–1919, the monthly magazine of the safety razor company, recounts the rise of the razor that was responsible for the decline of the barbershop.

Hotel and restaurant work is treated in "Condition of Bakers, Waiters and Miners," *Social Economist*, V (November, 1893), 282–286; Frances Donovan, *The Woman Who Waits* (Boston, 1920); and, indirectly, in Jefferson Williamson, *The American Hotel: An Anecdotal History* (New York, 1930). The *Freeman* (Indianapolis) also gave special attention to the trade.

The best studies of domestic service are Lucy Maynard Salmon, *Domestic Service* (New York, 1897), and Mary V. Robinson, *Domestic Workers and Their Employment Relations* (Washington, 1924). Nineteenth-century housewives' guides deal extensively with the service problem and assume the low status of domestics: Catherine E. Beecher, *A Treatise on Domestic Economy for the Use of Younger Ladies at Home and at School* (3rd ed., New York, 1845); Catherine E. Beecher and Harriet Beecher Stowe, *The American Woman's Home; or Principles of Domestic Service* (New York, 1869); and Marian Harland, *House and Home: A Complete Housewife's Guide* (Philadelphia, 1889).

The multivolume investigations of the United States Industrial Commission focused extensively on the working conditions of a variety of occupations: *Report of the Industrial Commission on the Relations and Conditions of Capital and Labor* (19 vols.; Washington, 1901). Testimony on dock work, waiting, domestic service, and factory work can be found in Commission on Industrial Relations, *Final Report and Testimony* (Washington, 1916).

For occupations in Michigan, the *Annual Reports of the Bureau of Labor and Industrial Statistics*, appearing first in 1885 and retitled the *Annual Reports of the Department of Labor of Michigan* in 1910, are indispensable. The bureau (later department) regularly investigated working conditions and wages in many of the state's industries and trades. Occasionally special reports appeared, such as the "Report on Negroes" in 1899, or the studies dealing with tenement houses, prostitution, and barbershops.

The inadequate security provided by some trades and the effect of the skewed occupational distribution of blacks can be seen in the *Annual Reports*, 1880–90, of the Detroit Association of Charities, and in the *Annual Reports of the Board of Poor Commissioners* (Detroit), 1900–1912.

Organizations

General information on black social organizations and societies can be found in Albert C. Stevens, *The Cyclopaedia of Fraternities* (2nd ed.; New York, 1907); W. E. B. DuBois, *Efforts for Social Betterment Among Negro Americans* (Atlanta, 1909); and Edward Nelson Palmer, "Negro Secret Societies," *Social Forces*, XXIII (December, 1944), 207–212. For Michigan, and Detroit in particular, the newspapers, city directories, and general studies of the Negro in the city all deal with the community's voluntary associations. In addition, Earl E. Nelson, "Sketches of Our Music History," *Michigan Challenge*, VIII (June, 1968), 34–35, 61–62, mentions early cultural organizations; W. H. Grimshaw, *Official History of Freemasonry Among the Colored People in North America* (New York, 1903), describes the growth of freemasonry in Michigan; W. P. Burrell and D. E. Johnson, Sr., *Twenty-five Years History of the Grand Fountain of the United Order of True Reformers 1881–1905* (Richmond, 1909), records the development of the order; Mary Taylor Blauvelt, "The Race Problem as Discussed by Negro Women," *American Journal of Sociology*, VI (March, 1911), 662–672, deals with the Michigan State Federation of Colored Women's Clubs; and the *Social Service Directory of Detroit 1917* [Detroit, 1917] gives information on black philanthropic organizations—the Urban League and Phyllis Wheatley Home. The manual of one elite black social club, *The Summer Club* (Detroit, n.d.), has survived; it can be found in "Detroit Negro Societies," E & M file, Burton Historical Collection.

A good general guide to religious bodies is Frank S. Mead, *Handbook of Denominations in the United States* (New York, 1956). E. Franklin Frazier's *The Negro Church in America* (New York, 1966), is a stimulating, perceptive analysis of black religious institutions. George F. Bragg's *History of the Afro-American Group of the Episcopal Church* (Baltimore, 1922), a chronicle of the church of the black elite, contains much information on St. Matthew's.

Four publications of the Historical Records Survey of Michigan deal in part with Detroit black churches: *Inventory of the Church Archives of Michigan: African Methodist Episcopal Church, Michigan Conference* (Detroit, 1940); *Inventory of the Church Archives of Michigan: Church of God Michigan Assemblies* (Detroit, 1841); *Inventory of the Church Archives of Michigan: Protestant Episcopal Church, Diocese of Michigan* (Detroit, 1940); and *Inventory of the Church Archives of Michigan: The Roman Catholic Church, Archdiocese of Detroit* (Detroit, 1941).

Specific information on churches and their officers can be obtained from the souvenir publications of the churches. Both *A Historical Sketch Published on the Occasion of the Eightieth Anniversary of Bethel A.M.E.*

Church, Detroit, Michigan, 1841–1921 [Detroit, 1921], and *One Hundred Years at Bethel* [Detroit, 1921], contain information on Bethel and Ebenezer AME churches. St. Matthew's is treated in *Joint Celebration of the 75th Anniversary of St. Matthew's Church . . .* [Detroit, 1924], and St. Matthew's Episcopal Church, *Centennial Celebration 1845–1946* [Detroit, 1946]. The annual *Journals of the Proceedings of the Convention of the Protestant Episcopal Church in the Diocese of Michigan*, 1850–1860, 1868–1910, reprint the reports of St. Matthew's, and *History and Directory of the Churches of Detroit* (Detroit, 1877), gives information on all the black churches and prints the membership lists of Bethel and Ebenezer AME churches.

Politics

Appleton's *American Annual Cyclopaedia*, 1866–1870, reported the response of Michigan's political parties to the issue of black enfranchisement. The general positions of the state's parties and their electoral battles in the post–Civil War period can be followed in Harriette M. Dilla, *The Politics of Michigan 1865–1878* (New York, 1912). The views of the Michigan governors are detailed in their annual messages, reprinted in George N. Fuller (ed.), *Messages of the Governors of Michigan* (4 vols.; Lansing, 1926–1928). The best work on Detroit politics is Melvin G. Holli, *Reform in Detroit: Hazen S. Pingree and Urban Politics* (New York, 1969), an excellent study on the rise of Hazen Pingree and reform in Detroit.

The alliance between the Republican party and Negroes can be seen in Philip S. Foner, *The Life and Writings of Frederick Douglass* (4 vols.; New York, 1952). Henry A. Haigh's memoir, *The Michigan Club 1884: The Alger Movement 1888* (n.p., n.d.), relates the deep involvement of Detroit blacks in the Republican party as do the miscellaneous materials of the Michigan Club, all in the Michigan Historical Collections. Afro-American holders of patronage and elective office are listed in the *Manuals of the Common Council . . . of the City of Detroit*, of which an incomplete series can be found at the Detroit Public Library; the *Michigan State Manuals*—the biennial "Redbooks"; and the *Bi-Centenary of the Founding of Detroit, 1701–1901* (Detroit, 1901).

The appeal of the Democratic party to Negroes is treated in August Meier, "The Negro and the Democratic Party, 1875–1915," *Phylon*, XVII (Second Quarter, 1956), 172–191, and Vincent P. DeSantis, "Negro Dissatisfaction with Republican Policy in the South, 1882–1884," *Journal of Negro History*, XXXVI (April, 1951), 148–159.

Index

Abbott, Edith, 106
Abolitionists: in Michigan, 33–34; endorsed by black convention, 39; political activity of, 196
Afric-American Philharmonic Association, 22
African-American Mysteries, 41
African Methodist Episcopal Chapel, 78
African Methodist Episcopal Church: as leading denomination, 136; and elite, 136; parsonages of, 143
"Afro-American," substituted for "Negro," 164
Afro-American League, 188, 192, 201
Alger, Russell A.: supported for president, 188; slate endorses Roxborough, 203
Allen University, 191
Alleys, 74–75
A. M. E. Church Review, 160, 193
American Federation of Labor, 125
American Protective Association, 122–123
Ames, Chester, 158
Ames, James W.: education of, 65, 158; as member, white church, 136; in fraternal societies, 148, 149, 151;

as trustee, Wheatley Home, 154; elected legislator, 200, 204
Amherstburg, Ont., 88 n
Anderson, John B., 196
Anderson, Mrs. William H., 154
Anderson, William H., 158; biographical sketch of, 100; as coauthor *Appointed*, 100, 106; as cofounder *Plaindealer*, 128; church, club affiliations of, 139, 153; political activity of, 195–196
Anglo-American immigrants, 59
Ann Arbor, Mich., 66
Ann Arbor Women's Club, 155
Anti-Catholicism, 123
Appointed: An American Novel ("Sanda"), 100, 106
Armenian immigrants, 78
Arthur, Chester A., 183
Attorneys, black, 128
Atwood, W. Q., 188, 197

Bagg, John H., 18; opposes integration, 35, 40
Bagnall, Robert W., 137, 139
Bailey, John, 36
Baldwin, Henry P., 4, 50
Banks, Robert, 13, 39; as clothing mer-

A Note on the Author

DAVID M. KATZMAN teaches Afro-American and urban history at the University of Kansas. In 1972–1973 he was a Research Fellow in Ethnic Studies at Harvard University and a National Endowment for the Humanities Afro-American Studies Fellow, and in 1971–1972 he was a Senior Research Fellow in Southern and Negro History at the Institute of Southern History, the Johns Hopkins University. Educated in New York City public schools from kindergarten at P.S. 46 through graduate school at Queens College, he also attended the University of Michigan, where he received his Ph.D. in history. He lives in Lawrence, Kansas, with his wife, Sharyn, and children, Andrea Rachel and Eric Michael.